I0878661

Panic Fiction

Panic Fiction

Women and Antebellum Economic Crisis

Mary Templin

The University of Alabama Press
Tuscaloosa

Copyright © 2014
The University of Alabama Press
Tuscaloosa, Alabama 35487-0380
All rights reserved
Manufactured in the United States of America

Typeface: Minion

Cover photograph: Copyright © Ken Cave | Dreamstime.com
Cover design: Mary Elizabeth Watson

∞
The paper on which this book is printed meets the minimum requirements of American National Standard for Information Sciences—Permanence of Paper for Printed Library Materials, ANSI Z39.48-1984.

Library of Congress Cataloging-in-Publication Data
Templin, Mary, 1959–
Panic fiction : women and antebellum economic crisis / Mary Templin.
pages cm
Includes bibliographical references and index.
ISBN 978-0-8173-1810-9 (hardback) — ISBN 978-0-8173-8719-8 (ebook)
1. American prose literature—Women authors—History and criticism. 2. Economics in literature. 3. Financial crises in literature. 4. American prose literature—19th century—History and criticism. 5. Women and literature—United States—History—19th century. 6. Popular culture—United States—History. 7. Literature and society—United States—History. 8. Financial crises—United States—History. I. Title.
PS374.E4T46 2014
810.9'9287—dc23

2013023599

For Mom and Dad, who showed me how to live well on "no money," and without whom this book would not exist.

And for my "pack": Doug, Alexi, and Kira.

Contents

Acknowledgments

This book would not have been possible without the help and encouragement of many people. My deepest thanks go to Dale Bauer, who guided this work early on at the University of Wisconsin-Madison. It was Dale who originally gave me the idea of investigating the Panic of 1837, and over the subsequent years her knowledge of current scholarship and her close reading of numerous drafts proved invaluable at every stage. I hope this book will make her proud. I am also grateful to Jeffrey Steele, whose class on American women writers introduced me to Caroline Kirkland and Catharine Sedgwick and thus started me on this path. His expertise and enthusiasm were critical to the project, and his model of scholarship has continued to inspire me.

Other early readers include Susan Bernstein and Sue Zaeske, whose probing questions helped me to define my argument; David Zimmerman, whose shared interest in panic led to many helpful suggestions; and Lisa Schreibersdorf and Shannon Smith, my faithful writing partners, who persuaded me to throw out half of what I wrote and always liked the parts in brackets the best.

As I began the work of revision for publication, a journey that has proven to be long but rewarding, I received crucial assistance from Jamie Barlowe at the University of Toledo, who helped me to identify and articulate the value of my work and to negotiate the revision and editorial processes.

I also owe many thanks to librarians, conference organizers, and editors who have assisted in numerous ways. Without the excellent librarians at Wisconsin and Toledo I would have had a much harder time locating examples of the panic fiction I discuss, as well as the nineteenth-century primary sources that helped me to understand their historical context. I am grateful to the Society for the Study of American Women Writers and the Program in Early American Economy and Society, in particular, for providing forums at which early versions of chapters were tried out and comments from audience members incorporated.

I am especially appreciative of Dan Waterman, my editor at the University of Alabama Press, who has shown incredible patience with the slow evolution of this project, and of the two readers he recruited, whose astute comments enabled me to make this a much better, more focused book. Many thanks also to Crissie E. Johnson, my managing editor, for seeing the manuscript through the final stages and making the process relatively painless.

Finally, I would like to thank family and friends who have been incredibly supportive. Paul Cantor and Yvonne Lopaur are among my biggest cheerleaders, always confident of my abilities and proud of my achievements. My circle of "sisters"—Jocelyn Blaufuss, Clara Chambers, Leslie Chambers, Diane Reamer-Evans, and Dorothy Shorter—are always there for me with encouragement and distraction. My colleagues in the Honors College at UT are the best I could ask for, making my work a real pleasure. I am particularly grateful to my parents, Lawrence and Orletta Templin, who instilled in me a love of literature at an early age, and my brother, John Templin, and sister, Sara Velasquez, all of whom have been regular sounding boards for ideas and sources of sympathy for my frustrations over many years now. More and more I realize just how lucky I have been in my "choice" of family. And last but definitely not least, I could not have done this without Douglas Swiatecki, whose daily support and love give meaning to my work and my life.

Some of the material in this book first appeared in a different arrangement in my essay "Panic Fiction: Women's Responses to Antebellum Economic Crisis," published by *Legacy: A Journal of American Women Writers* in 2004 (volume 1). Similarly, portions of chapters 2 and 3 first appeared in "'Dedicated to Works of Beneficence': Charity as Model for a Domesticated Economy in Antebellum Women's Panic Fiction," a chapter I contributed to Debra Bernardi's and Jill Bergman's book *Our Sisters' Keepers: Nineteenth-Century Benevolence Literature by American Women*, also published by the University of Alabama Press, which appears here by permission of the University of Alabama Press.

Introduction

Defining a Genre, Recovering Panic Fiction

In Caroline Kirkland's fictionalized memoir of life on the Michigan frontier, *A New Home, Who'll Follow?,* she regales her audience with many humorous stories about her attempts to set up housekeeping in primitive conditions—baking bread in the fireplace, trying to find room in a log cabin for her "delicate japanned tables" (73), and employing local girls to help with the chores. Dividing responsibilities along traditionally gendered lines, Kirkland largely confines her alter ego Mary Clavers's role to such domestic matters, while terming Mr. Clavers the "proprietor" of and sole investor in the newly acquired village they are there to develop (23). But her interest in (and knowledge of) the financial aspects of western settlement are evident throughout the narrative. At a wifely distance, Mary comments on the "immense sum" that the construction of houses, shops, and a sawmill are "sure to cost Mr. Clavers," but she subsequently signals her own involvement by supplying details of building sizes and dollar amounts (22). Similarly, it is Mr. Clavers who ventures out with a group of men to examine another possible townsite, while Mary remains in the Detroit boardinghouse, but afterward she comments satirically on the speculative hype with which the men are enticed—"Only one hundred shares at three hundred dollars each!"—noting that "the whole had been purchased for four hundred dollars, just a week before they reached Detroit" (53).

I first read Kirkland's work in a graduate class on American women writers and was fascinated by her incorporation of economic discourse into a domestic narrative, similar to the way, as a whole tradition of scholarship has revealed, different modes of political discourse are embedded in many early American novels, including sentimental and domestic genres.[1] Kirkland and her husband were caught up in the economic turbulence of the 1830s, moving to Michigan in 1835, near the height of a national economic boom, and then suffering through the Panic of 1837, which devastated many western communities. Her account of their experiences in *A New Home*, published just two years after the panic, documents much of the financial madness that marked that period, including land speculation and "wildcat" banking. In the amused and sometimes astonished voice of Mary Clavers, an outsider to Michigan and a supposed outsider to the masculine world of finance, Kirkland entertains her eastern readership with outrageous stories of financial naïveté and outright fraud on the frontier.

But her light tone masks some serious commentary, such as when the fraudulent fiasco of the Merchants' and Manufacturers' Bank of Tinkerville—its grand name a front and its specie reserves actually boxes of broken glass and nails covered with a few coins—moves her to comment on the "General Banking Law" (203). Comparing bankers to magicians, Kirkland, through the character of Clavers, ridicules and condemns the "necromantic power" that "allowed any dozen of men who could pledge real estate to a nominal amount, to assume the power of making money of rags . . . [and] whose powers were destined to transmute these acres of wood and meadow into splendid metropolitan residences" (204). In other words, she suggests, the law permitted anyone to charter a bank, print their own paper currency, and encourage fantasies of city and empire building on the plentiful credit thus created. Kirkland goes on to describe the largely unregulated banking practices of the 1830s in some detail and documents the effects they had on the surrounding Michigan communities.

I became curious to know whether Kirkland's familiarity with financial matters and her forthright discussion of them in her novel—at odds with nineteenth-century women's supposed remove from the marketplace—was an anomaly or whether other women had also used fiction to express economic views, so I went looking for economic discourse in the fiction of other female authors of that period. What I found astonished me. Between 1836 and 1840 alone—the period spanning the peak of the speculative boom of the 1830s to the beginnings of the depression that followed the Panic of 1837—women had written and published dozens, perhaps hundreds, of novels and stories that were even more centered on economic themes than Kirkland's novel, responding directly to the panic but within a domestic context. Narrative after narrative, with titles like *Failure Not Ruin*, *Two Roads to Wealth*, and *Rich Enough*, presented fictional scenarios of economic failure and its effects on the home. In nearly all of these stories, merchants and other businessmen failed financially—either as part of a general economic crisis or due to individual failings—forcing their families to cope with sudden loss. Interwoven with details of domestic downsizing ran distinct threads of economic thought on topics such as financial speculation, the use of paper money and instruments of credit, repayment of debt, consumerism, and modes of economic development.

Even aside from the inherent interest of these individual narratives—and they are very readable—I quickly came to see this body of women's "panic fiction" as deserving of much wider contemporary attention.[2] For one thing, its focus on economic anxiety resonates strongly with our own worries today about job loss, bankruptcy, and other facets of a long-term economic downturn. While many of the terms have changed and financial practices have become more sophisticated, the underlying concerns about how to get ahead safely and how to cope with loss have remained very much the same. Extravagant spending without the actual cash to pay for purchases is both reviled and actively pursued in today's American culture as well as in nineteenth-century panic novels, even though credit cards have replaced more informal credit arrangements. The reckless land speculation blamed in the novels for the crisis reminds me of accounts in our own media about risky securities based on subprime mortgages. Both raise the question of "real value" versus value on paper and illustrate discomfort with more abstract forms of investment. And while contemporary government bailouts of financial institutions with taxpayer money may have no direct parallel in the Bank War of the 1830s between Andrew Jackson and the Whigs, rhetoric about greedy bankers who care only about their own profits at the expense of ordinary citizens are strikingly similar in both eras. Reading these narratives from nearly two hundred years ago and seeing the parallels to our own time, one is struck not only by the consistency (and ingenuity) of human greed but also by the way human responses to both opportunity and catastrophe remain very similar despite different circumstances.

But for all their resonance with today, nineteenth-century women's panic narratives are very much products of their own time and circumstances, and as such, they make a perhaps more significant claim on our attention for their potential to enhance our understanding of both American literary history and America's economic development in the decades preceding the Civil War. It is crucial, first of all, to see women's antebellum panic fiction as a distinct genre, differing from male-authored panic fiction and from the broader category of domestic fiction by virtue of the explicit intersection between economics and domesticity manifested in the plots, themes, perspectives, and narrative styles of these texts. Reading the uncertainties of the antebellum marketplace—as captured in moments of panic and economic collapse—from the perspective of women and the home contributes to our understanding of what was at stake for at least some women (mostly white and middle class) in the massive economic and cultural transformations taking place during the 1830s, '40s, and '50s. Similarly, reading what are essentially domestic narratives in the light of the intense economic insecurity produced by panic helps to reveal the class-based identifications and anxieties that underlie the authors' concerns with maintaining the domestic space.

The fact that this outpouring of texts that were simultaneously domestic and economic came in response to the event of a panic not only speaks to the ways that financial crisis must have impacted the domestic realm but also highlights how "panic"—as an interruption in the patterns of exchange, a reversal of forward momentum—functioned to disrupt, or at least create some space within, emerging gender and class identities of the period in ways that were both anxiety producing and empowering. I am arguing here that female panic authors saw panic as both threat and opportunity, for the characters of their novels and also for themselves. On the one hand, the ramifications of a panic, including both the economic recklessness that precedes and precipitates it and the failure and loss that follow, are shown to pose very real dangers to national and to individual economic and social well-being. Moral integrity is corrupted, trust is violated, material comforts are sacrificed, and social identity is threatened. On the other hand, the disruption that panic causes to the normal workings of the marketplace offers an extraordinary chance for women who have been excluded from that marketplace to find, if not a foothold there, at least a voice. The potentially destructive effects of panic on the domestic domain evidently served as a point of entry for the female authors of panic fiction to authorize their own participation in the "public sphere" through their novels.[3] Similarly, panic becomes the impetus for female characters in these narratives to assume economic agency and to model economic reform through the domestication of economic behavior.

I am further arguing that while panic serves as the central locus of economic anxiety in panic novels, it also allowed their authors to engage in much broader financial commentary, extending their analysis to a host of larger questions about national economic growth, development, and regulation. This double agenda—focused on the specific moment of panic but also attentive to the broader social and economic contexts of their times—produced narratives that are simultaneously very much alike in their settings and rhetoric but divergent in the larger meanings that they draw out from the event of panic. The ways in which panic and failure were experienced and understood by nineteenth-century Americans depended on many factors, including region of the country, race, political affiliation, socioeconomic status, occupation, and specific time period. Boston merchants in the 1830s suffered different consequences from panic than New York laborers in the 1850s, for instance, or plantation owners in Georgia in either decade. Whigs and Democrats, Northerners and Southerners, all had different perspectives on the reasons and solutions for panic. Female panic authors themselves, while all white and predominantly middle class, reflect these diverse allegiances in their economic commentary even as they share with each other a domestic perspective that distinguishes theirs from male-authored discourse within their particular milieus. Thus, I will show that while the effect of panic on the home is the common denominator of these narratives, panic also serves as a focal point for a variety of rhetorical aims influenced by the circumstances of each author's specific time and place, as well as her own class affiliation and personal experience of loss. These aims are evidenced not only in the nature of their direct economic discourse but also in the use of narrative conventions.

What this book attempts to do is to tease out the ways these two levels of economic discourse work with (and sometimes against) each other in women's antebellum panic fiction—that is, to show how the authors' shared agenda of protecting the home from the ravages of panic and failure is intertwined with and colored by their distinct personal, regional, and class-based perspectives. By reading these texts along with other examples of discourse from the various milieus of antebellum panic—from newspapers, popular journals, economic treatises, advice manuals—we can see how women's panic fiction participates in these modes of rhetoric and where individual novels diverge from these sources and from each other in their particular concerns and analysis. By reading these novels in comparison with each other, we can see how even subtle changes in narrative structure, characterization, and emotional tone reflect each author's particular perspective and contribute to their economic commentary. Ultimately, I hope to demonstrate the value of these novels as a genre—as historical documents that reflect the economic, political, and social views of their particular societies, but also as attempts by marginalized voices of women to influence economic dialogue and the relationship between home and marketplace.

Panic and Its Discourses

What actually happened to spur the outpouring of panic fiction in the 1830s started not with the panic itself in 1837 but with the period of unprecedented economic prosperity that preceded it. Throughout the 1830s, new roads and canals had opened up the territory west of the Appalachians, resulting in a federal treasury surplus from the sale of public lands. Excited by the possibilities for development and hopeful of getting rich, merchants and speculators bought up land and stocks, causing prices to rise and spurring banks to offer increasing amounts of credit. By 1836, newspapers from New York to New Orleans were boasting of their regions' prosperity, reveling in the abundance of money and the pace of business.

Within months, all of that changed. Pressed by foreign creditors and new governmental monetary policies, banks began to call in their loans. By March of 1837, banking contractions had forced dozens of mercantile houses and other credit-dependent enterprises into bankruptcy; hundreds more were to follow in the next few months. On May 10, banks in New York stopped cashing their own notes, followed during the ensuing week by bank closures across the nation. For a full year banks remained suspended, during which time the panic evolved into a devastating depression that lasted well into the 1840s. Thousands lost property, businesses, and jobs; many more suffered wage cuts and a lowered standard of living.

The Panic of 1837 was not the first widespread financial crisis to hit the United States, nor was it the last. Panics of varying severity had already occurred in 1793, 1807, and 1819 and would occur again in 1857, 1873, 1893, 1907, and 1929, just to name the most prominent. But the crisis of 1837 was the most severe the nation had seen to that point and, occurring just as the nation's print culture was expanding dramatically, triggered an outpouring of discourse on the causes and consequences of panic.[4]

Much of this discussion appeared in newspapers, whose responses to the crisis varied according to their political leanings and regional perspectives. For instance, the *New York Herald*—a Democratic organ loyal to outgoing President Jackson and fairly hostile to his enemies in the commercial and financial worlds—sounded warnings about "reckless speculation" more than a year before the crash and blamed the panic on a combination of excessive credit, a bloated paper currency, and villainous bankers who, in recalling loans and suspending payment, "suck[ed] out the profits of the merchants, and squeez[ed] the last drop of blood out of the mechanic." A competing Whig paper, the *Morning Courier and New-York Enquirer*, defended both the soundness of the nation's paper currency and the actions of bankers, attributing the crisis instead to Jackson's "misrule" in removing federal deposits from the United States Bank and attempting to regulate paper money. Newspapers in the South and West, far removed from New York's financial center, tended to walk a fine line, blaming the panic on northeastern bankers while defending the plentiful credit that enabled development in their regions.[5]

A newly emerging national literary culture provided a different sort of outlet for economic discourse. While, as Maria Carla Sanchez has argued, few of the critically respected authors of that period engaged directly with the Panic of 1837 in their fiction despite its effects on their lives (5), one who did make bank failure a subject of his work was Edgar Allan Poe, whose story "Diddling Considered as One of the Exact Sciences," published in 1838, satirizes banking as simply a more sophisticated and larger-scale form of "diddling" or swindling. While Poe neither engaged in the typical moral rhetoric of the time concerning panic nor proposed solutions to current economic problems, Terence Whalen argues that the financial debates of 1837—particularly regarding speculation and "making money out of nothing"—were a major source for Poe's stories of hoaxes and swindles (199). Ralph Waldo Emerson's literary response to the panic was less direct even than

Poe's satire, but financial anxiety plays a palpable role in his essays of the period and furnishes him with memorable images. Although his later essay "Wealth" credits "speculative genius" for the building of American civilization (702), Emerson's earlier works often warn against the transience of money and commerce. In "The American Scholar," for example, presented as an oration just four months after the bank suspensions of May 1837, "ephemeral trade" is one of the distractions that divert the scholar from more worthwhile pursuits (56); four years later, in "The Transcendentalist," Emerson figures the illusoriness of materialism as a "banking-house" that, although built on a foundation of granite, proves as unstable and capricious as a balloon, "spinning away, dragging bank and banker with it at a rate of thousands of miles the hour, he knows not whither" (88).

But clearly the most direct literary response came in the flood of popular panic fiction that I have described, novels and stories produced very quickly and in great numbers even as the panic was still unfolding. Some of these were shorter narratives, published in popular journals such as *American Ladies' Magazine* and the *Lady's Book*; others were stand-alone novels or series of separately published volumes, often produced and sold cheaply by publishers such as Boston's William S. Damrell and New York's S. Colman and Harper and Brothers. Panic fiction was not the sole province of female authors; male authors such as T. S. Arthur and Charles F. Briggs also wrote and published novels centered on themes of economic failure, some of them quite popular. But judging by reviews and by what little information exists about sales, it was the fiction by women that most captured the public imagination and turned the genre into a way to engage in serious public discourse. This female-authored panic fiction, in which economic loss or the threat of it constitutes the principal thematic and dramatic content, continued to appear throughout the 1840s and, to a somewhat lesser extent, into the 1850s, when the nation was again caught up in a cycle of speculation leading to panic.

Although most of these texts are virtually unknown today—available, if at all, on microfilm or in the rare book vaults of university libraries—they were remarkably popular and well reviewed in their time. Some of the authors, like Catharine Maria Sedgwick, whose novels *The Poor Rich Man, and the Rich Poor Man* (1836) and *Live and Let Live* (1837) formed part of this genre, already had a major literary reputation. Elizabeth Oakes Smith, author of *Riches without Wings* (1838), and Emma Embury, author of *Constance Latimer* (1838), were also known to the emerging literary establishment. Maria Cummins, whose novel *Mabel Vaughan* (1857) responded to the panics of the 1850s, had already achieved fame with the best-selling *The Lamplighter* three years earlier.

Other authors of panic fiction were not well known but achieved at least a passing notice through the immense popularity of their stories of failure. Hannah

Farnham Sawyer Lee's short novel *Three Experiments of Living* (1837)—part of a five-volume series issued as *Stories from Real Life*—was a publishing sensation, going through at least twenty editions in the first year alone and reportedly as many as thirty editions altogether (Blain 642). Frank Luther Mott lists the novel as one of only four American best sellers for 1837—along with Nathaniel Hawthorne's *Twice-Told Tales* and Charles Dickens's *Pickwick Papers*—with sales equal to or greater than 125,000, roughly 1 percent of the national population during the 1830s (306). References to *Three Experiments of Living* crop up repeatedly in literary reviews during the late 1830s, and several reviews mention imitations of the novel, including a pamphlet entitled "Three Experiments in Drinking" (*Knickerbocker* May 1837, 530). In September 1837, the *Gentleman's Magazine* declares that "a host of 'experiments' have been exhibited to the public, but destitute of the merit of the original, they have failed in appropriating their wonderful success" (219). *Godey's Lady's Book* even mentions plans for a dramatized version of *Three Experiments* to be produced in a Boston theater, although there are no further references to such a production.

While few panic novels reached this culturally iconic status, many were favorably reviewed in the literary and popular journals of the day, including the *North American Review*, the *Knickerbocker*, *Southern Literary Messenger*, *American Monthly Magazine,* and *Godey's Lady's Book* and were clearly known to a sizable portion of the American reading public. The enormous success of *Three Experiments* and other panic novels points to the way in which the entire genre of panic fiction struck a chord with American readers, tapping into the financial anxieties of the period and offering commentary on economic practices as well as entertainment.

Making Sense of Panic

Historians have only recently begun to explore in depth the phenomena of periodic economic crises in American economic history.[6] While the cyclical nature of the nineteenth-century marketplace has been well documented, focusing more explicitly on these moments of crisis and the devastating losses that followed—what we might call breaks in the narrative of continuous economic progress—allows us to see more clearly the undercurrents of fear and anxiety that shadowed the rampant optimism that is more generally understood to characterize the time. Literary scholars also have only relatively recently recognized panic as both a recurrent theme in nineteenth-century American literature and a potent symbol for various kinds of disjuncture within American society—political, social, and cultural, as well as economic.

For many years the term "economic fiction" was applied predominantly to male authors of the later nineteenth century, such as William Dean Howells, Frank Norris, and Theodore Dreiser, who chronicled the rise and dominance of industrial capitalism in the United States.[7] Later scholars reinterpreted the meaning of "economic" and/or argued for the significance of previously unknown or little-read texts. For example, a number of scholars have explored the underlying economic preoccupations in the work of canonical antebellum authors such as Melville and Thoreau, while others have added female authors such as Rebecca Harding Davis and Elizabeth Stuart Phelps to the ranks of economic novelists.[8] More relevant to this project, several critics have also shown how domestic fiction engaged with issues of the marketplace, if not with the specificity of panic fiction, certainly with an eye toward reform and an awareness of the interconnectedness of home and marketplace. As both Jane Tompkins and Gillian Brown point out, Harriet Beecher Stowe's portrayal of idealized domestic scenes, marked by orderliness and sympathetic care, provided an alternative model for society in opposition to the chaos and exploitativeness of the existing male domains of politics and commerce. Not all domestic writing challenged the values of the marketplace, however. Both Brown and Lori Merish have persuasively demonstrated that despite a rhetoric of separate spheres, middle-class domesticity—in the home and in print—was, in fact, integrally connected to the emerging capitalist economic structure through consumerism and as a means of defining class identities.[9]

Making the case for an even broader employment of economic themes in American fiction, Karen Weyler argues that, in fact, "economic relations" is one of the two principal "axes around which virtually all early American novels revolve" (*Intricate Relations* 2). In her study of American fiction by both men and women from 1789 to 1814, Weyler finds that economic and sexual relations, as "sites of desire, expenditure, and exchange," were emblematic for the larger anxieties attendant on the creation of a new nation at a time when modes of exchange and patterns of personal relationships were undergoing massive changes (3–4). While female characters negotiate the terrain of sexual and moral self-regulation, male characters must face the pitfalls and temptations of the marketplace, learning to regulate acquisition and expenditure.

This theme of pervasive economic distress and uncertainty in literature of the late eighteenth and early nineteenth centuries is also taken up by Joseph Fichtelberg, whose *Critical Fictions* is one of the first critical texts to look specifically at panic fiction as well as other genres. Fichtelberg examines a number of panic narratives by both male and female authors as part of his exploration of how American fiction used sentiment to "explain and shape the market" during the economic turmoil of the early republic and antebellum eras. He sees the prevalence of resourceful, middle-class heroines of panic narratives as representations of "how weakness was the prelude to recovery" (Fichtelberg 144). At a time when masculine qualities of control and autonomy did not serve men well in a fluid, ever-shifting economy, Fichtelberg argues that feminine sympathy and adaptability suggested new "strategies for survival" (149). Rather than condemning market excess or attempting to reimpose republican notions of restraint, antebellum authors imagined a new, more pliable, model of economic agency in which female characters symbolized the qualities of "sincerity and suppleness, inner constancy and shrewd responsiveness" that (male) merchants would need to negotiate the changing marketplace (Fichtelberg 118).

Other recent studies by David Zimmerman, David Anthony, and Maria Carla Sanchez similarly focus on how panic has been represented and responded to in particular time periods and in specific genres, exploring the variety of ways in which "panic" has served as an emblem for a broader sense of rupture, crisis, or social turmoil throughout the nineteenth and early twentieth centuries. Zimmerman's *Panic!*, for example, examines Wall Street fiction and other panic-oriented novels published between 1898 and 1913, focusing on the public spectacle aspect of panics, manifested both in the hysteric behavior of "market crowds" and in the often sensationalist pages of male-authored panic fiction. Characterizing both financial panics and the novels written about them as "agents of revelation and reckoning," Zimmerman argues that panic novelists of that era employed a variety of narrative strategies to attempt to represent and even manipulate the "baffling excess" associated with panic and thus to shed light on what he aptly calls the many "forms of unanchoring" produced by modernity (2–3).

Anthony, who examines representations of manhood in the sensationalist media and in male-authored panic fiction of the antebellum era, is interested in how notions of professional manhood, in particular, changed as economic circumstances became destabilized by panic and speculative capitalism. In *Paper Money Men*, Anthony argues that modes of expression like cartoons, stage melodramas, the penny press, and even murder pamphlets allowed the extremes of desire and fear—economic as well as sexual—to be managed and even made pleasurable in ways that "rational" discourse could not (22). Depictions of the "debtor male," often seen fleeing from his creditors, became characterized by "excessive affective states of panic and hysteria and by postures of submission and humiliation" (Anthony 106). Like Fichtelberg, Anthony sees in these images evidence that crisis demanded a new version of masculinity, one that exchanged individualist self-reliance for a deeper emotional capacity and, ultimately, incorporation into middle-class gentility (108, 112).

Sanchez, in *Reforming the World*, emphasizes the moral dimension of antebellum panic fiction, reading the panic narratives of both male and female authors as a kind of "social reform" fiction with parallels to novels that promoted moral reform, temperance, and abolition. All of these genres were engaged in the "social work" of attempting to "alter the institutions, systems, and processes" of nineteenth-century life, Sanchez argues, and all of their authors distanced themselves from the very notion of "fiction" in order to emphasize their claims of truthfulness (5). Similar to the arguments that I am advancing here, Sanchez points out that much of the rhetoric in panic fiction about the immorality of speculation focuses on the dichotomy between fiction and reality and how this dichotomy relates to financial matters as well as purely moral matters. Because speculation relies on "fictitious" prices and imaginary assets—that is, credit—it is seen in panic fiction as a "practice of falsehood" and a "dangerous deviation from the country's inherited moral codes" (Sanchez 41, 58). As a result, Sanchez sees most of these texts as essentially conservative—leaning toward "restoration and not innovation," promoting the agrarian values of an older way of life (58).

My own study seeks to contribute to this vein of scholarship by considering women's antebellum panic fiction as a separate genre and examining how it performed the cultural work of making sense of economic change and crisis within narratives of home and family relationships, and in so doing, how it blurred the (imaginary) generic boundary between domestic and economic fiction. Like the scholars cited above, I am interested in the ways in which panic produced anxiety about social changes and disrupted certain kinds of identity, particularly that of gender and class. This project follows Fichtelberg, in particular, in seeing female characters as models for economic recovery, but whereas his work, like Anthony's, sees the feminine as symbolizing desired traits for men to embody in times when traditional models of masculinity were destabilized, I am looking at how these models represent possibilities for women themselves. I join Sanchez in seeing panic fiction as being more "restorative" than revolutionary—that is, seeking to return the economy to values of the past, such as restraint, rather than envisioning an entirely new system. But I propose that their mode of restoring moral considerations to the economy is by blurring the lines between home and marketplace, claiming the home as an economic space and therefore women as legitimate economic agents. In other words, the domestic enactments of women's panic fiction are not merely metaphorical representations of national crisis, nor are they simply a means of translating a public problem into a more solvable private one, although panic authors do advocate parallel solutions for national and individual failure.[10] Rather, women's panic fiction challenges ideological barriers between the domestic and the economic by showing panic as a genuinely domestic issue.

The implications of this claim are significant. Not only do panic authors stake their right to debate market operations on the domestic consequences of panic and failure, they also assert women's right—and fitness—to influence those operations as a means of protecting their domestic interests. Panic fiction remains more pragmatic than revolutionary, however: whereas Gillian Brown interprets Stowe as proposing to "abolish the marketplace altogether" and replace it with an economy based on "abundant mother-love" (23-24), I read panic authors as simply wanting to make market economics safer. The defining characteristics of the economy they envision are not love and abundance but rationality and frugality. They seek an economic system marked by slower growth, less greed, and less vulnerability to periodic downswings.

Because of this, the participation of women's panic fiction in the conventions of sentimentality is somewhat equivocal. The affective connotations of panic, as a time when people act from motivations of unthinking fear, suggest that fiction about panic might focus on emotional states, both representing the affective experience of panic and attempting to evoke an emotional response from readers. Just as sentimental fiction of the 1790s captured national fears of tyranny and disunity in emotional scenes and prompted social affiliation by producing sympathetic identification, one might think that panic fiction would attempt to heal economic wounds by similarly manipulating readers' emotions.[11] To some extent this is borne out, but I was initially surprised to find how little emotion is expressed in the pages of women's panic novels. I found that panic fiction does not so much *represent* panic as attempt to rationalize it, and it does not seek to arouse audience affect so much as to calm it.

The very nature of the problem that panic authors seek to solve—economic crisis produced by excesses of greed and fear—seem to make them wary of stimulating social action through sentiment. Their desires for social and economic stability prompt them to seek a balance between creating appropriate readerly feelings and regulating the excessive emotions produced by financial panic. Thus the affective states most commonly associated with panic—fear, apprehension, frenzy—appear almost exclusively in scenes depicting the economic boom before the crisis rather than at the occurrence of failure (a distinction that I will discuss more fully in chapter 1). Readers are led to feel a certain amount of suspense and anxiety, but once the crisis has occurred those feelings are put to rest. Unlike either gothic or sensation fiction, which revels in the affect it creates before containing it, women's panic fiction downplays both shock and fear, depicting such emotions negatively more than actually evoking them.[12] Similarly, while depictions of sudden impoverishment inspire sympathy for failed families and—in the tradition of eighteenth-century sentimentalism—even enjoin social bonds that supersede economic individualism, panic fiction resists the overt sentimentality of both eighteenth-century seduction texts and nineteenth-century tearjerkers.

Although Jonathan Elmer argues that sentiment itself functions to regulate excessive affect such as grief (96), panic authors often turn away from emotion-based solutions altogether, emphasizing instead rational means of bringing about recovery. Rather than seeking sympathy—an emotional response that implies distance between readers and characters—panic authors solicit admiration and imitation for their heroines' responses to panic from readers who might be experiencing similar circumstances. Predictable narratives and repeated scenes of economizing provide an accessible model for readers to follow. They also assure readers that economic and social recovery is achievable and position middle-class women as the rational agents through which such recovery will take place.

In short, panic fiction's project of voicing panic's effects on the home and envisioning rational reforms of an unstable economic system complicates its employment of sentimental conventions often associated with domestic fiction. Panic texts tread carefully around the representation and production of emotional response, tempering their appeals to sympathy with implicit pleas for a measured approach to economic decisions.

Precursors to Panic Fiction: Economic Loss in Early American Women's Novels

I would like to backtrack here for a moment to acknowledge that the theme of economic distress or failure in women's fiction is not, of course, confined to novels written between 1836 and 1857. In fact, a large number of American women's novels written both before and after that period feature such failure in some form. Nina Baym has noted in *Woman's Fiction* that economic losses typically form a part of the basic "overplot" in women's antebellum fiction, in which a young woman is deprived of support and has to make her own way in the world. According to Baym, a primary purpose of such fiction is to strengthen the female ego—to encourage female readers, through identification with the heroines, to see themselves as strong, capable, and self-respecting rather than as victims (16). The financial failure of the heroine's father or male guardian, often early in the novel, thus serves to test the heroine, forcing her to develop and use her own resources and thus become responsible and independent.

Another reason for the prevalence of economic loss in early American women's fiction—and the principal reason for it in fiction published prior to the 1830s—is that it reflects a very real cultural anxiety about economic instability. Two major wars, a crippling embargo of foreign trade, rapid territorial expansion, and largely unregulated currency, which often depreciated rapidly in value, all contributed to a sense of economic turbulence and uncertainty in the years between the American Revolution and the Panic of 1837. And although historians have challenged the common view that antebellum America, especially in the Jacksonian era, was a place of unlimited social mobility—where wealth was precarious and the line between rich and poor was easily breached in either direction—most Americans, as historian Edward Pessen notes, *believed* that their society was one of fluctuations; "social flux" was almost an "article of faith" (80). That belief, as Pessen frames it, focuses on the positive aspect of social mobility—the potential for the "common man" to rise to wealth. Yet it also carries with it the opposite potential—that of the wealthy man, or even just the comfortable one, to lose all that he has. Women, having little direct control over family or personal finances, and fewer opportunities than men for recovering from financial loss, may have felt particularly vulnerable to the vacillations of a chaotic economy. Add to this the fact that a number of women writers during this era had themselves experienced financial difficulties, and some took up authorship in order to help provide for themselves and for their families, it is perhaps not surprising that so many female-authored novels include economic loss as a circumstance with which their characters have to cope.

The body of work that I am specifically designating as women's "panic fiction," however, differs in several substantial ways from those novels that merely include failure as a circumstance to test the heroine or as a way to convey anxiety. First, the unprecedented concentration in the late 1830s of such a large number of texts focusing on economic loss signals a new level of engagement with specific economic events. Panic novels responded to actual panics, not just general economic anxiety. More importantly, the economic anxiety that lurks in the background of much antebellum fiction is brought to the forefront in panic novels. While most novels of the early republic and antebellum eras employ failure primarily as a device to establish the heroine as economically vulnerable, panic fiction gives it center stage, dramatizing failure in plots that revolve around the irresponsible economic behavior and decisions that lead to the brink of loss and the appropriate attitudes and actions to be taken once that loss has occurred. In other words, panic fiction is truly *about* failure. Finally, panic fiction uses these plots to explore the causes of economic failure and seek solutions for it, offering much more economic commentary and analysis than other fiction.

As a result, the panic fiction of the 1830s, in particular, can be seen as a kind of bridge between women's fiction of the first three decades of the nineteenth century, which tends to be strongly suffused with economic anxiety but populated with helpless and suffering female characters, and the domestic fiction of the 1840s and 1850s, in which women learn to be independent and resourceful but in domestic settings often nearly devoid of economic references. Panic authors' agenda of attempting to explain and manage financial crises necessitated the creation of strong rather than vulnerable heroines, which marked a break from the earlier fiction and provided a model for heroines of the later fiction. Their inclusion of explicit economic discourse, however, did not carry over into much of the later domestic fiction, as changing circumstances, including the diminished effects of panic and the increased use of domestic fiction to define the home as a noneconomic counterpart to the masculine marketplace, led to plots and settings in which the economic underpinnings of the heroines' situations were largely erased. Thus, the particular combination of strong, resourceful heroine and explicit economic commentary is unique to women's panic fiction, especially that of the 1830s.

In order to see more clearly how panic fiction offered a very different economic role to women than previous female-authored fiction, let us look closely at two very early novels by American women—Sally Barrell Keating Wood's *Dorval; or the Speculator* (1801) and Rebecca Rush's *Kelroy* (1812). Both portray economic failure as a circumstance that leaves family members, especially daughters, vulnerable to poverty, forced marriage, spinsterhood, and even the potential for rape or murder. In *Dorval*, two well-to-do gentlemen—a landowner and retired soldier, Colonel Morely, and a merchant, Mr. Dunbar—invest and lose all their property in a land speculation scheme urged upon them by a consummate villain named Dorval. Both men have daughters whose lives are nearly ruined as a result of their fathers' losses and their consequent powerlessness. Elizabeth Dunbar is kidnapped by the evil Dorval as part of a larger plan to ruin both families, and she only narrowly escapes a fate of rape and humiliation. Aurelia Morely, the heroine of the novel, endures a lengthy estrangement from her fiancé, the loss of all her family's property, the murder of her mother, and two attempts by Dorval on her own life—all set in motion by her adoptive father's disastrous investment. Through the rather gothic device of an utterly evil and seemingly all-powerful villain, who creates and manipulates the two families' misfortunes, the novel provides a melodramatic enactment of contemporaneous economic worries, expressing both a disapproval of risky speculation and a sense of female powerlessness in the face of male economic decisions. Although Aurelia has the common sense to know that Morely's scheme is ill-advised, he does not listen to her, and later on she refrains from advising him because that is not her place as a daughter.

Economic loss functions similarly in *Kelroy*; the female members of the Hammond family are left in economic dire straits when Mr. Hammond, a merchant, dies nearly bankrupt. To protect her daughters (and herself) from poverty and social humiliation, Mrs. Hammond devises a desperate scheme to orchestrate the appearances of wealth and thus attract wealthy husbands. While Rush's novel is clearly satirical about Mrs. Hammond's aims and pretensions, like *Dorval*, it illustrates women's economic and social vulnerability to the fluctuations of an unstable economy. Without their father's money, and lacking any legitimate means of recovering it, Lucy and Emily Hammond face a choice between possibly distasteful marriages (arranged through deception) or the loss of their social status—the primary basis for their identities—as well as the loss of material support.

Unlike panic fiction or the later domestic fiction that Baym discusses, economic loss in these earlier novels does not serve the beneficial purpose of forcing or allowing female characters to develop independence. *Dorval*'s Aurelia is psychologically independent from the beginning, but her physical and economic dependence upon men is, if anything, intensified by her father's losses. Without support, she is even more vulnerable to the machinations of Dorval and must ultimately be doubly rescued: physically by her real father and economically by her returning fiancé. In *Kelroy*, while the title (male) character actively attempts to recover his own father's lost fortune by embarking on a commercial venture to the Far East, his female counterpart, Emily, remains largely passive throughout the novel, eventually dying of heartbreak. The female character who best represents qualities of independence and resourcefulness, family friend Helen Cathcart, is one whose comfortable economic status has remained unthreatened. In these novels, at least, economic loss carries no connotation of an opportunity for women to build character; rather, it serves as a frightening evocation of the precariousness of money and social position in times of economic instability and of women's powerlessness either to preserve what they have or to regain what they have lost.

Women's fiction of the 1820s continues to manifest economic anxiety through the depiction of economic loss or failure but without quite the same sense of powerlessness. The female protagonists of such novels as Catharine Sedgwick's *A New-England Tale* (1822) and Sarah Josepha Hale's *Northwood* (1827) are still fairly passive, in the sense that they remain dependent upon relatives following their father's failures, but the novels themselves seem less rattled by economic circumstances and more able to imagine and construct economically stable fictive worlds. Both Jane Elton of *A New-England Tale* and Susan Redington of *Northwood* are left destitute and dependent when their fathers die bankrupt, and both survive and ultimately thrive by developing domestic skills and virtues. Jane becomes the moral center of her aunt's morally and economically mismanaged household, and she is later rewarded with her own secure domestic space through marriage to a worthy man. Susan is raised into prosperity through marriage to *Northwood*'s hero, Sidney Romelee. It is actually Sidney's loss of inherited fortune through his uncle's financial failure that is most significant in *Northwood*. Like the heroines of domestic fiction in the 1840s and 1850s, Sidney's deprivation of support forces him to make his own living through the hard work of farming, a process that also enables him to cultivate discipline, industry, and thrift.

Both novels thus pose economic loss as an adverse circumstance that threatens security and well-being, but one that can lead to personal triumph. This shift in attitude from earlier novels may be partially explained by different economic conditions in the 1820s. Although America's economy was still unpredictable, the most immediate cause of its instability had changed. In 1819 the nation suffered an economic panic that in many ways was a forerunner of the even greater crisis of 1837. The historian Andrew Cayton notes that while earlier widespread financial troubles had been attributed to either external factors such as war or political policies such as Jefferson's embargo, the Panic of 1819 was the first major economic upheaval to result from the internal workings of the newly emerging market economy (147). Daniel Feller attributes the panic to a sequence of interrelated factors, including explosive postwar growth, an accompanying expansion of credit, the failure of banks to maintain adequate specie backing for that credit, and consequent skyrocketing land and commodity prices. When European demands for American agricultural products suddenly dropped, prices fell and the entire economy contracted (Feller 39–41). Even if the triggering factor for the panic was, as Feller claims, partially external to the United States, the economic structure that permitted and fostered the economic events that led to the panic was to some degree internally constituted and thus theoretically responsive to reform.

Novels of the 1820s and later reflect this sense that the causes of economic disaster are knowable and thus potentially controllable. In contrast to the more gothic fictions of Wood and Rush, in which characters, especially daughters, are helpless against economic circumstances beyond their control, Sedgwick's and Hale's novels point the way toward economic recovery and stability.

It was, ironically, the panic fiction of the 1830s—produced in response to the deepest financial crisis yet experienced in the country—that most fully expressed this tendency toward imagining recovery and stability. The enormity of the Panic of 1837, and its disastrous consequences, is the most immediate explanation for the emergence of this bolder economic vision. As banks closed, prices plunged, and tens of thousands of people were put out of work, the outpouring of discourse about the crisis in sources ranging from newspapers to novels demonstrates that the panic forced people to reexamine their assumptions about the inevitability of America's economic expansion and to entertain alternative narratives about the nation's economic future.[13] Whether panics were seen as irrational ruptures in an otherwise seamlessly expanding system or as rational responses to a system out of control, they were clearly times of retreat in which even the most optimistic searched for explanations. In the context of such national soul-searching, the female authors of 1830s panic fiction seized the opportunity to offer their own narratives.

A more complete explanation for the sudden occurrence of panic fiction in the late 1830s must also take into account the larger processes of class and gender formation underway between 1820 and 1850. During those decades, the nation's rapid transition to a market economy created enormous changes in both socioeconomic class structure and conceptions of gender. As later chapters will describe in greater detail, a newly emerging "middle class" and definitions of femininity were both highly contested terrains in ways that were not the case in previous decades. In such circumstances, the event of panic, I argue, prompted the emergence of narratives whose explanations and solutions for the crises were deeply influenced by these changing class and gender definitions.

But while my description of panic fiction so far has emphasized its collective goals, the genre is by no means monolithic in its economic critique and vision. Individual novels manifest a wide variety of attitudes and positions with regard to such things as labor, social change, and the potential for domestic values to triumph in the world of the marketplace. Some of the novels identify clearly with a producing class, while others are firmly lodged in the world of the merchant; some authors demonstrate a desire to change the social order, while others hope to preserve it intact; most fervently proclaim the power of domesticity to solve the problems of economic instability, while a few signal reservations about its ability to overcome entrenched power relations.

In particular, as I have argued earlier, novels from different decades and regions demonstrate different rhetorical agendas, including their perspectives on class and gender, at the root of their economic critique. The Northern authors of the 1830s, who produced the critical mass of panic fiction, wrote with an overwhelmingly middle-class agenda, concerned with the potential loss of hard-earned status in an urban, commercial milieu. Paradoxically, these earliest of panic authors are also the ones most hopeful that panic can ultimately prove beneficial to society as a whole by serving as a warning against financial risk and by allowing women to assume greater financial responsibility. Southern authors of the 1840s and 1850s viewed panic from the perspective of the agricultural elite, depicting economic crisis as a threat from outside to Southern culture and ways of life. Thus their critique centers on comparing the stability and value of Northern and Southern economic sectors and labor systems. Women figure prominently in these narratives but are not agents of recovery. Northern authors of the 1850s similarly focused on issues of labor but, again, from a middle-class perspective, reflecting that era's concerns about a growing industrialized working class and exploring the implications of an increasingly industrialized and commercialized society for middle-class women.

In the first chapter, "Speculation and Failure: Panic Fiction's Common Ground," I examine two emphases that link panic novels across boundaries of region, class, and time, and form the common basis of the genre—denunciations of risky modes of economic gain such as speculation and expressions of anxiety about the effects of financial failure on the middle-class home. Within the context of nineteenth-century boom-and-bust economic cycles and debates over the role of speculation and credit in causing panics, the typical narrative structure of panic novels, in which escalating acts of frenzied and irrational investment lead inevitably to failure, is outlined. This chapter discusses panic fiction's treatment of speculation—whether in land, stocks, credit instruments, or human beings—at some length, detailing the genre's near-unanimous condemnation of speculation on moral, social, and economic grounds, but also its fascination with and anxieties about financial gain. Failure itself, the subject that is simultaneously the focal point for panic novels' fears and the destination that fictive speculation leads to, is also a curiously truncated moment in most panic narratives and fraught with ambivalence. While nearly every panic novel contains at least one instance of failure, the meaning invested in that loss—for example, who bears responsibility for it, how it should be responded to—varies widely, making failure the departure point for panic authors' specific rhetorical purposes.

Most of the fiction written in direct response to the Panic of 1837 came from Northern authors, such as Hannah Farnham Sawyer Lee, Catharine Sedgwick, Emma Embury, and Elizabeth Oakes Smith, and centered on expressions of anxiety about middle-class social identity in times of economic instability. Focusing primarily on a series of extremely popular novels by Lee, all published during 1837, chapter 2, "Domestic Constancy: Preserving Class Identity in 1830s Panic Fiction," examines the narrative strategies this early panic fiction employed rhetorically to shore up middle-class status in the face of threatened economic loss and the rapid social mobility produced by a speculative commercial economy. These authors assuaged anxiety and provided an accessible model of economic recovery through repeated use of a narrative structure in which the anxious and frenzied scenes of speculation and failure, discussed in the previous chapter, are followed and offset by the more restrained narration of a step-by-step process of retrenchment and recovery by competent domestic heroines. Thus the emotional aspects associated with panic—including sympathy, as well as fear and grief—are tightly contained within an overall narrative that privileges rationality and ties middle-class identity to domestic constancy rather than economic status. Middle-class dominance over the working class is rhetorically reinforced by recurrent scenes of middle-class women directing domestic servants or dispensing charity, which emphasize the paternalistic nature of such relationships and imagine only very limited opportunities for social mobility.

A second and related aim of most Northern panic novels was to lessen middle-class women's economic and social vulnerability by envisioning expanded economic power within domestic roles and by portraying women themselves as important agents of financial recovery. The third chapter, "Female 'Economists': Expanding Women's Financial Agency," outlines the multifaceted depictions of middle-class women's financial competence—as domestic managers, philanthropists, and economic advisers to fathers and husbands. Eliza Follen's *Sketches of Married Life*, published in 1838, presents perhaps the most ambitious vision of such female empowerment, depicting a husband and wife as equal partners in economic decision making and conceiving an economic system in which commerce and industry are pursued for the ultimate purpose of benevolence—an endeavor widely recognized as a feminine domain—thus opening the marketplace itself to women's participation. Panic authors were not of one mind, however, in their estimation of women's actual opportunities for wielding power in a male-dominated society. Anna Warner's *Dollars and Cents*, published in 1852, presents a decidedly less optimistic view of women's agency, depicting a rational and resourceful wife at the mercy of her hapless husband's continually failing speculations. This chapter places these disparate visions of women's potential role in the economy within the context of an ongoing process of defining gender and class in which women's relation to the marketplace played a major part.

My fourth chapter, "Threats from Outside: Defending the Southern Economy," turns to panic fiction of the 1840s and 1850s by Southern authors such as Maria McIntosh, who depicted anxieties about loss and employed calls for economic reform for very different rhetorical purposes. The principal concern of Southern panic fiction was not with protecting a commercial middle class from the social instability of unregulated economic practices but with defending an elite planter society and an economy based on slave labor from political attack and perceived economic domination by the North. Panic in these novels is thus not symbolic of internal disorder in need of reform but rather of a threat from outside that must be repelled. Similarly, Southern panic fiction does not, for the most part, promote women's economic agency but rather upholds a paternalistic, hierarchical societal structure in which white women occupy an intermediate position between white males and black slaves. Female characters display competence and courage, but the agents of economic recovery following failure are primarily male. I argue that these divergences from the common patterns of earlier Northern panic fiction reflect the authors' assessment of the South's particular economic needs—to actively develop its industrial and commercial resources and to cease being vulnerable to Northern economic hegemony. In keeping with these aims, Southern panic fiction employs sentimental—even melodramatic—conventions of heroines in distress, near calamities, and theatrical rescues in order to reinforce the categories of dependence and authority upon which Southern society rested.

In the final chapter, "Freedom and Order: Proposing Solutions to 1850s Labor Problems," I examine Northern panic fiction of the 1850s, which retained many of the elements of its 1830s forebears but also expressed anxiety about and proposed solutions for increasingly volatile class divisions and relationships between employers and employees. These novels responded in large part to the Panic of 1857, which, while not as severe for financial institutions as that of 1837, exacerbated problems of unemployment and labor unrest in Northern cities. Their economic discourse, however, is also colored by growing concerns in the North about slavery—not only that it posed a threat to the nation's ideals of liberty and equality but also that it undermined Northern attempts to resolve its own labor problems. Maria Cummins's novel *Mabel Vaughan*, published in 1857, proposes westward migration and settlement as a potential solution to the upheaval produced by panic, serving both as a release valve for displaced urban laborers and as a place to create a new (free) society based on merit and productivity rather than the sterility of rigid social categories. Alice Haven's narratives remain within the Northern urban milieu that Cummins abandoned but imagine a model for labor relations that steers a middle course between Northern class antagonism and Southern paternalism in slavery—a domestic labor model. Haven's novel *The Coopers; or, Getting Under Way*, published in 1858, also reflects the era's increasing acceptance of business and the risks of capitalism—presenting a panic narrative in which failure does *not* occur, and women's domestic role becomes a "business" in its own right.

one

Speculation and Failure
Panic Fiction's Common Ground

At the beginning of Hannah Farnham Sawyer Lee's novel *Rich Enough*, published in 1837, two brothers, Howard and James Draper, discuss their divergent investment philosophies. Howard, a thriving farmer, has come to James, a wealthy Boston merchant, with a small surplus of money that he would like his brother to invest for him. He is not interested in becoming wealthy but merely wants a safe investment that will "secure something for my family in case of accident" (4). James, on the other hand, scorns Howard's caution, proclaiming his own philosophy of taking risks in order to make a fortune. The remainder of the story develops this contrast between Howard, whose agricultural life and satisfaction with "moderate gains" bring him and his family health and contentment, and James, whose "feverish pursuit of wealth" brings misery to his wife and children without ever seeming to make him "RICH ENOUGH" (18).

Already wealthy as the story begins, James is never satisfied with what he has or with what exists. He sees his property and the landscape around him only in terms of its potential resale or development value. He is impatient, for instance, with his wife's love of their large city estate with its beautiful gardens and extensive grounds; he is unable to measure the aesthetic or emotional value it holds for her and can only gauge its worth by the amount of money it would yield if sold to developers. When he comes to visit his family at the farm that he bought for them as a summer place—a pastoral spot of meadows, woods, a lake, and waterfalls described by the narrator in idyllic terms—he sees potential waterpower and the perfect site for a textile mill. As each plan comes to fruition, James becomes more and more ambitious. The "spirit and enterprise" that Howard noted in him early on aid him in establishing a full-scale manufacturing complex on the site of Clyde Farm, complete with its own railroad line. When his wife, Frances, complains that he is not only ruining the view but also "injuring the cause of the country" by helping to convert an agricultural society into an industrial one, and farmers into "speculators," James defends his capitalist efforts as good for the nation. He is creating wealth through his business enterprises, he says. Leveling their former home for the development of smaller city lots and building the mills and railroad have helped others, as well as himself, to realize enormous gains, thus contributing to the "public benefit" (55).

But James's dreams of wealth, the narrator suggests, are like El Dorado, the city of gold that is perpetually sought but never found. Unable or unwilling to honor his promise to retire when he reaches a certain predetermined sum of money, he risks more and more to achieve some imagined pinnacle, even as his wife's health begins to suffer. Although Frances needs a change of climate, the excitement of a booming economy has James transfixed. He cannot leave town "when Eastern lands and Western lands, rail-roads and steam-boats, cotton, and manufactories, were in all their glory; when his own Clyde Mills were just going into operation! . . . Never had there been a season of such profits, such glorious speculations!" (48).

Even the possibility of economic collapse does not deter James: "Some *croakers* said it could not last; and some of our gifted statesmen predicted that an overwhelming blow must inevitably come. But all this was nothing to speculators; it certainly would not arrive till after *they* had made their millions" (49).

The increasingly frantic pace of James's speculations is mirrored by his wife's and daughter's worsening health. The family finally leaves New England in search of a better climate, but even the weather is unstable and seems to foreshadow a coming state of uncertainty—a snowstorm in New York, sunshine in Philadelphia, rain in Baltimore, storms in Charleston (50). The daughter dies, but James still does not heed the warning. Finally, James's world comes crashing down. Frances dies of consumption, and almost simultaneously, the nation's economy collapses, leaving James financially ruined. Although he is not alone in his plight—the narrator describes widespread destruction, a "desolation upon the community" that struck high and low alike—he is clearly held to be culpable for his part in this economic disaster, namely, his obsessive speculations and single-minded pursuit of wealth. The ever-content Howard, who bears his loss of invested capital with equanimity, is given the last word: he invites his devastated brother (and the readers of the book) to "come, and learn that, beyond what we can use for our own or others' benefit, wealth has only an imaginary value" (72).

This brief tale, only seventy-two pages, exemplifies the two elements that define the genre of panic fiction and unite its varied narratives across boundaries of region, class, and time: anxiety about loss and anxiety about appropriate modes of gain. While panic novels differ considerably in terms of their economic and political perspectives and the lessons they draw for readers from their stories of panic and failure, all arose ultimately out of fears of the economic and social consequences posed by widespread economic crises, and all focus considerable attention on the role played by risky modes of economic gain such as speculation. The narrative arc that *Rich Enough* traces—from a starting point of financial sufficiency, through an increasingly frenzied whirlwind of financial gain fueled by uncontrolled desire and marked by irresponsible risk taking, to a climax of collapsing fortunes and failed ambitions—encompasses the dramatic elements that form the common basis for the genre. Panic novels from the 1830s through the 1850s, from Northern and Southern authors representing multiple rhetorical agendas, all address themselves to a fundamental debate about gain and loss that marked the first several decades of the nineteenth century in America. In a rapidly growing nation with an expanding economy and seemingly unlimited natural resources, what was the appropriate model for that growth and expansion? Should the nation be content with the "moderate gains" of Howard Draper, achieved through steady industry, or should his brother James provide the model—one of boundless development, wringing maximum financial gain from every opportunity? The panics that occurred periodically throughout this era brought particular urgency to this debate. Were such crises related to the nation's rapid rate of economic growth and the methods by which such growth was achieved? And if so, what exactly was the relationship?

The authors of the panic fiction that comprises this book acknowledge the fascination and excitement engendered by speculation—the practice of investing in land or commodities not for use or income but in order to profit from rises in market value.[1] Characters like James Draper illustrate the powerful attraction not only of the immense profits to be had from speculation but also of staking one's success on one's own ability to accurately foresee such rises. But panic authors' emphasis on the emotional aspects of speculation, and on the apparent inability of the speculator to regulate his desires for gain or his economic behavior, clearly suggests their perception of speculation not as a reasonable response to abundance and opportunity but as a dangerous and corruptive model for economic growth. Endeavoring to explain and prevent recurrences of the economic devastation that accompanied antebellum panics, panic authors pointed to irresponsible wealth seeking as a principal cause for economic collapse. Speculation served as a particular target of their denunciation, seeming to encompass for them all of the wrongs and dangers of an unstable economy.

This chapter examines panic authors' shared opposition to speculation and the relationship between such an "anxiety of gain" and a pervasive anxiety about loss. One element of that relationship is simply the fear that speculative gain does not provide a stable economic foundation either for society as a whole or for the middle-class or elite home that is at the center of panic fiction. Speculation threatens material instability because its success is so theoretical, dependent upon unpredictable market forces that could produce loss instead of gain. The very volatility that promises rapid gain, and thus makes speculation more appealing to investors like James than the gradual profitability of farming, also makes it an unreliable source of income. Panic authors express their fears of such loss by characterizing speculative gain as illusory—having only the "imaginary value" that Howard Draper attributes to wealth. And because the gains resulting from speculation often exist only on paper, speculative investment is also represented as irrational—motivated by expectations that are founded on greed and wishful thinking rather than on any "real" or intrinsic value of the commodity being bought and sold.

As this link between irrationality and greed suggests, however, panic authors' condemnation of speculation runs deeper than simple fears of material loss. Whether speculative ventures lead to immediate financial failure or are—at least temporarily—wildly successful, they are depicted as both morally corruptive and socially dangerous: By offering gain without work, speculation destroys the moral value of honest labor and encourages fraud and exploitation. By promising gain without the production of anything tangible, it makes profit a goal in itself, promoting a system of values based solely on money rather than on Christian and republican virtues. And by sidestepping traditional avenues to success, it produces increased social mobility, thereby disrupting the social order.[2] Finally, and of particular concern to some of these female panic authors, speculation represents a new type of economic exchange that, because conducted in a financial arena inaccessible to women and largely divorced from tangible property, diminishes women's economic influence.

Panic fiction weaves this interconnected web of objections to speculation through a combination of didactic observations, illustrative plot lines, evocative imagery, and—most notably—a narrative structure that concentrates all the emotionality and irrationality associated with "panic" in the wealth-seeking segment of each story rather than in the failure that inevitably follows or in its aftermath. By contrast, the moment of failure itself receives relatively little narrative attention, serving principally as a turning point from the horrors of speculation to modes of recovery. The remainder of this chapter examines panic novels' multifaceted attack on speculation and the connections they draw between such gain and the threat of financial loss.

"A Speculative Spirit": Antebellum Booms and Monetary Policy

While clearly exaggerated for effect, James Draper's almost frenzied efforts to capitalize on every financial opportunity in many ways epitomize actual behavior during the periods immediately prior to each antebellum panic. Preceding each major economic downturn between the beginning of the nineteenth century and the Civil War were periods of unprecedented growth and prosperity, often characterized as booms. The years between 1815 and 1819, as well as the mid-1830s and mid-1850s, were marked by surges of opportunity for new investment in land, mercantile enterprises, transportation, and manufacturing. After the end of the War of 1812, for instance, renewed trade with Britain revived American commerce, which had languished during years of embargo and war, while the newly opened American Indian lands of the Northwest Territory and the "old Southwest" sparked an increase in western settlement (Feller 39). The "transportation revolution" of the 1820s and 1830s, in which hundreds of miles of new roads, canals, and later railroads made a market economy possible in a nation of such vast territory, created a much larger economic boom in the mid-1830s. Greater accessibility made western lands even more attractive to investors, who began to visualize the enormous wealth that could be made from the inevitable westward movement of a quickly growing population into regions of untapped resources. Land sales in areas such as Michigan and Illinois increased rapidly, as a burgeoning Eastern population looked for new opportunities, while in Alabama and Mississippi, the lure of fresh lands for growing cotton—increasingly profitable as America's incipient textile industry joined Britain's already booming mills as a market for the crop—drew many planters and their households westward. According to the historian George Van Vleck, such territorial expansion was still a major factor in the economic boom of the mid-1850s, aided by the discovery of gold in California in 1848 and an expanded European demand for American grains during the Crimean War. The consequent profitability of western agriculture and, to an even greater degree, of the railroads that transported those agricultural products produced a sharp increase in both American and European investment in American land and railroad securities.[3]

The prosperity of these three periods is generally characterized by historians in explosive or maniacal terms. The economy "boomed," and prices "skyrocketed." Daniel Feller reports that the availability of land and the doubling of cotton prices after 1815 led to "frenzied purchases of land and slaves" (39), while R. C. McGrane denotes the speculation of the mid-1830s as a "mad rush to destruction" (44). Whether placed in a positive or negative light, the periods of economic growth that preceded the major panics of the antebellum era are characterized not as times of gradual and orderly expansion but as periods of rapid, uncontrolled, even irrational growth, fueled by perceptions of enormous economic potential and the desire for wealth. Speaking of the Jacksonian era just prior to the Panic of 1837, the historian Edward Pessen contends that a "speculative spirit" pervaded the nation, enticing many with visions of fortunes to be made in land or transportation ventures (103).

"Speculation" is a key term with which to characterize these pre-panic boom periods, signifying both investors' obsession with seemingly unlimited financial gain and the increasingly abstract nature of their financial transactions. Originally derived from the Latin verb *speculari*—to see or look at—the word "speculation" had come to mean contemplation of an abstract or conjectural nature. Economic speculation, like the philosophical kind, "looked" to the future; it conjectured about what was going to increase in value and by how much. Speculative investors, trusting their own or others' predictions of future rises in value, purchased land or stock shares at low prices and sold when increased demand caused prices to rise. Unlike traditional economic exchange, in which goods traded are of roughly equal value, speculation offered investors the promise of far greater returns on their investment as long as others continued to invest, driving prices ever upward.[4]

Although many Americans took advantage of available western lands as settlers, to farm or to start small businesses, the antebellum land booms were created largely by land speculators who bought large tracts of land from the government in order to resell at a profit to smaller buyers. Competition for land and the prospect of profit drove up land prices, creating a self-perpetuating phenomenon, as land often changed hands numerous times within short periods. Speculation also took place within the realms of commerce and industry, since merchants required investors to finance imports and exports, and manufacturers needed capital to establish America's first factories and mills.

Both the risk of speculation and its fundamentally abstract nature were compounded in nineteenth-century America by the fact that most speculative transactions were based on credit rather than actual wealth. A credit-based economy had already developed in England and continental Europe in the late seventeenth and early eighteenth centuries and had extended into colonial America as well, but credit became a particular issue in the United States in the early national period as Americans struggled to create and sustain a viable national economy. Legal tender in the form of "specie," or gold and silver, was in short supply in the young nation, so most business was transacted on the basis of some form of "paper money." Goods and services were commonly purchased with bank notes, representing a bank's promise to redeem for specie, while larger and more speculative investments were carried out with bank loans or lines of credit.

As the nation's potential for economic growth stimulated speculative desires far beyond the nation's actual possession of wealth, speculation and credit became virtually synonymous. Speculators' needs for capital spurred rapid increases both in the number of banks and in the amount of credit extended during the antebellum boom periods. Between 1811 and 1818, for instance, the number of banks rose from 88 to 392, more than a fourfold increase in only seven years. Between 1830 and 1835, during Andrew Jackson's war against the Bank of the United States, the number of state banks doubled. Another rapid increase took place in the 1850s, when the number of banks again doubled between 1850 and 1857 to more than 1,500.[5] Most of these new banks, established not as recipients of investments themselves but as sources of credit for those wishing to invest elsewhere, issued notes and supplied credit far beyond their actual specie reserves. In the mid-1830s, some banks issued anywhere from ten to fourteen paper dollars for every silver dollar they possessed, while one bank in Pennsylvania reportedly extended credit at a ratio of 30:1 (McGrane 16). While the historian Peter Temin argues that an influx of specie during the 1830s kept banks' reserve rates fairly steady throughout that decade, he also acknowledges that such plentiful credit boosted speculation (76). According to Van Vleck, the "pressing question" of antebellum American banking was "how to attain a maximum circulation with—and unfortunately in many instances without—the greatest possible security for its redemption" (23). By the 1850s, speculation was such a pervasive force throughout the American economic system that many financiers traded on the credit systems themselves, reinvesting annually in commercial paper for the interest without ever seeing a tangible return (37).

Following each of the major antebellum panics, considerable debate arose among politicians and economists about the role American monetary policy played in causing or exacerbating these crises. Most historians today see the banks' overextension of credit and the unsustainable cycles of speculation that followed as only the most proximate causes of panic, set into motion by a much more complex economic situation that also included such factors as agricultural yields, European banking pressures, and the international balance of trade.[6] In the 1830s and 1850s, however, most commentary on the panics centered on questions of banking and credit—a continuation, basically, of an ongoing quarrel between those who favored and those who opposed a credit economy. One faction, which Daniel Feller broadly labels "inflationist," contended that America's dynamic economy required an abundant money supply, and since gold and silver were scarce, paper currency and other forms of credit were necessary to develop the nation's industrial, commercial, and agricultural potential (42). Credit advocates such as economists George Tucker and Henry C. Carey emphasized the promise of America's future growth and defended the role of banking in providing opportunities for the creation of wealth through the extension of plentiful credit (Conkin 152, 277).

On a purely practical level, the defenders of credit often pointed to the convenience of paper instruments such as bills of exchange and bank notes, noting, as the economist Samuel Newman did in an 1835 treatise, that "the remittance of large amounts of specie from one section of country to another, is attended with expense and risk," making the exchange of paper a preferable alternative (110).

But philosophically as well, many economists of the era and those involved in commerce viewed bank notes and other paper instruments as legitimate forms of currency, even when issued in excess of the amount of specie backing that banks possessed. According to Newman, for instance, "the basis of the whole system of credit currency is mutual confidence" (111). In other words, as long as people believe bank notes to be "representations of value," then they are; trust in the banking system permits continued development and prosperity. Confronted with the wild market fluctuations of late 1836 and early 1837, even diehard inflationists conceded that banks had overextended credit and that some speculators had imprudently "wade[d] beyond their depth," as the commercial journal *Niles' Weekly Register* put it, but even then advocates promoted the "reasonable" extension of credit. As late as mid-April of 1837, in the midst of numerous reports of commercial failures, Mr. Niles continued to publish items on the perfect safety and "wholesome" condition of the nation's banks and to promote the credit system as "the sure foundation of our prosperity."[7]

Directly opposed to such views were many who were suspicious of paper money as "fictitious representations of value" and who believed that the nation's currency was sound only as long as it remained specie-based (Feller 133). Economists such as John Taylor and William M. Gouge voiced such "contractionist" views in their condemnation of "paper wealth" and banking excesses. Gouge begins one of his treatises on paper currency with the flat declaration that "all the Banks in the United States are bankrupt" (5). Although this particular book was published in 1837, he was not referring to the panic but to banks' practice of lending beyond their specie reserves. "The only legal tender is gold and silver," he announces, and "whoever cannot pay, on demand, in the authorized coin of the country, a debt actually due, is, in point of fact[,] *bankrupt*" (5). After having thus made his point rather dramatically about the illegitimacy of any currency other than gold or silver, Gouge goes on to detail why he objects to paper money and credit and how the United States could, without the inconvenience alleged by inflationists, function with a strictly specie-based currency. In particular, he contends that allowing banks to issue notes beyond their actual possession of specie leads to reckless speculation, inflation, and the subsequent depreciation of currency value. Unlike specie, of which there is always a quantifiable supply, credit is subject to "every wind that blows," extended or withdrawn at the whims of the bankers (9). Gouge also argued that when low specie reserves made banks unable to redeem their own notes, they caused panics by calling in loans and suspending payment of specie (Conkin 209). Ultimately, Gouge's target is the banks' use of "public money"—federal funds—to offer credit to speculators, giving them an unfair advantage over those Gouge characterizes as hardworking farmers and mechanics who ask for no favors. Many paper money and credit opponents similarly objected to the perceived favoritism inherent in the credit system, contending that a specie-based currency better preserved a level playing field for all.

Although Gouge makes his arguments in largely pragmatic and economic terms, many antebellum hard-money advocates opposed credit for moral reasons—in particular, that it was dishonest and fraudulent because it allowed speculators to invest money they did not have. The popular lecturer and reform advocate Theophilus Fisk represents this view at length in an oration he delivered in Charleston in July 1837, equating "artificial money" with "artificial morals and laws" (4). According to Fisk and his like, paper money and credit aided the lazy and the greedy to get rich without labor and also corrupted the innocent by tempting them to purchase articles they could not afford (14–15). Such moral arguments seem to have resonated with an American public that looked for religious answers to economic problems. In the wake of crisis, speculation fueled by greed became a popular target of blame in newspapers as well as in fiction. At the same time, however, the growth promised by credit was a powerful incentive to a nation defined by opportunity, assuring that speculative ventures would be repeatedly revived despite rhetorical opposition.[8]

"Imaginary Value": Speculation as Illusion

Earlier representations of speculation in the literary arena were not as negative toward it as the panic fiction of the 1830s. While American advocates of credit and speculation largely framed their arguments in terms of the necessity for such instruments rather than their attractions, there existed a tradition of writing by some Europeans that was marked by much greater frankness about the appeal of speculative economics. From the beginnings of the credit economy in late seventeenth-century Europe, observers noted a tension between speculation's dangers and its enticements. A number of early eighteenth-century writers—including, most notably, Daniel Defoe—exploited the inherent drama of such tension, personifying it in both essays and fiction in the figures of "Lady Credit" or "Dame Fortune." In his *Review*, for example, Defoe describes Lady Credit as a "coy Lass" and writes that "'tis a strange thing to think, how absolute this Lady is; how despotickly she governs all her Actions: If you court her, you lose her, or must buy her at unreasonable Rates; and if you do, she is always jealous of you, and Suspicious; and if you don't discharge her to a Tittle of your Agreement, she is gone, and perhaps may never come again as long as you live; and if she does, 'tis with long Entreaty and abundance of Difficulty." Speculative economics are thus characterized by the supposedly feminine traits of instability and fickleness but also by desirability and fecundity. Successful speculative ventures had to be courted like a woman, Defoe suggests, with the outcome always in doubt. The speculator might be blessed by Lady Credit's powers of creating wealth out of nothing, or he might fall out of her favor, losing everything.[9]

This tension between danger and enticement appears in American panic fiction as well but with several crucial revisions. Significantly, the female panic authors of this study did not personify credit or speculation as feminine. There is no "Lady Credit" or "Dame Fortune" in their novels, an omission that allows panic authors to portray women as economic agents in their own right rather than merely symbols of economic transactions performed by men. Like their male counterparts, female characters in panic fiction have the capacity either to be seduced by or to resist the attractions of speculation. Although female characters do not purchase land or stock certificates on credit, they do engage in patterns of consumption that parallel marketplace speculation. Panic fiction portrays women's extravagant purchases of apparel and household furnishings beyond what they can afford as the feminine equivalent of speculative investing, not only because such spending on credit contributes to debt and financial failure but also because it represents a similar expectation of future gains. Just as the appearance of wealth encourages the further extension of credit in the financial realm, it also promotes social credit and ascension to higher social circles within the domestic sphere. Female characters who aspire to a higher social position dress, furnish their homes, and entertain beyond their means in order to establish their fitness for, and to be accepted into, that elevated status.

Panic authors further revise Defoe's and his colleagues' characterization of credit by not celebrating its seductive aspects. There are a number of fairly obvious reasons for this—for example, their inclusion of women as potential "speculators," the circumstances of their writing during times of panic, and American puritanical suspicion of seductiveness. For all of these reasons, American women writing about panic align their fiction largely with contractionist, hard-money economic arguments, and thus they cast the enticements of speculation almost entirely in a negative light. Speculation becomes, in their novels, as much the faithless seducer as the object of desire. The hope of profit does indeed fascinate and enthrall the speculators of these novels, but speculation proves to be (ironically) consistently untrustworthy, tempting its victims into dangerous economic behavior with false promises of quick wealth and luxury. Such desires in themselves signal danger to a readership steeped in Puritan and republican ideals, but it is the unstable means of attaining those desires that ensures the speculator's fall. Because of speculation's lack of solid financial basis, any gains produced by speculation on credit are either temporary or even illusory, merely serving to lure the speculator into further ventures that ultimately prove deadly to both fortune and integrity.

Textually, panic authors represent this danger through repeated narratives in which the attractions of speculation or spending on credit lead inevitably to economic ruin. The most typical plot in panic fiction is that of a merchant who either borrows beyond his ability to repay or overextends credit to others in speculations that have no clearly defined purposes other than making money. In Hannah Farnham Sawyer Lee's *Three Experiments of Living*, for example—which will be more fully discussed in chapter 2—the male protagonist is a physician named Frank Fulton who is enticed by the prospects of the wealth he can make as a speculator and abandons his medical profession in order to speculate full time. Tempted by the lavish lifestyles of social acquaintances, he also builds and furnishes a house upon borrowed money. Neither his home nor his business are founded on real assets, however—only on credit and on Frank's hopes of financial and social advancement—and thus when market changes occur, requiring immediate repayment of loans, both home and business are completely lost.

Panic fiction's imagery reinforces this sense that speculative wealth is not real or will not last. Like the hard-money advocates who feared the ultimate worthlessness of paper money not securely based on gold and silver, panic authors express their anxieties through images of impermanence and insubstantiality. The title of Elizabeth Oakes Smith's 1838 novel, *Riches without Wings*, employs an image that recurs throughout panic fiction—that of the tendency for speculative wealth to "fly away" rather than remain permanently in one's possession. Speculative schemes are frequently represented either as "dreams"—existing only in the speculator's mind—or as fragile, liable to be destroyed by a mere touch. In Anna B. Warner's *Dollars and Cents* (1852), for instance, Mr. Howard's plans for his property take shape only on paper, suggesting an analogy to the unfulfilled promise of paper money: "coloured and uncoloured, lithograph, pen and ink, and pencil. Here a road going smoothly through impassable places,—and there an imposing row of stone cottages about which a fine young forest had suddenly sprung up—but that might have been the lithographer's fancy. Then the scene changed to wheels and timber and foaming torrents,—a half-finished mill-dam, with a cart and horse comfortably carrying out gravel;—and at the bottom a long string of units and tens and hieroglyphics—'wheels—say so much,' and 'mill-stones—say so much'" (38). In reality, the cottages remain unroofed and the mill is twice destroyed. Planning more than his actual finances can carry out, Mr. Howard's overreaching results in a dream unfulfilled.

Similarly, James Draper's speculations in *Rich Enough* are not only referred to as his "El Dorado," but his sister-in-law also says they remind her of the "Jack and the Beanstalk" folktale, in which the castle at the top of the beanstalk proves to be illusory, "made of vapor," and Jack comes tumbling down. She says she will tell the story to her children in order to "teach them to train their beans in the good old-fashioned way, near the ground" (46). Repeated images such as vapor, spider webs, and bubbles convey the lesson that wealth gained or sought through speculation is fragile and ephemeral. In contrast, images of solidity signify wealth and status that are secure and unchanging. Ownership of plain but "massive" furniture, suggesting immovability, signifies the possession of unthreatened wealth in Hannah Farnham Sawyer Lee's *The Harcourts* (1837), while such surface decorative techniques as gilding, veneer, japanning, tinsel, and glitter are frequent markers of wealth that has nothing behind it—either in terms of "real" assets or moral qualities—and thus will not last.

This opposition of "real value" versus the mere appearance of value is frequently extended to human behavior, as is most clearly seen in the subtitle of Maria McIntosh's novel *Two Lives; or, To Seem and to Be*, published in 1846. Here the overarching metaphor for financial gain that cannot be trusted is that of acting. One of the "two lives" of the title is Grace Elliot, an heiress who has no deeply founded moral principles and thus acts according to societal expectations. She also literally acts in private theatricals, shocking behavior that symbolizes her inauthenticity as well as her lack of modest virtue. Grace's "skill in artifice" produces its first negative consequence when her fiancé finds he cannot trust her avowals of love after having seen her feign love for another man in a play. But Grace's propensity to merely "seem" loving, virtuous, and repentant—and other characters' inability to distinguish between her real feelings and her false ones—models an uncertainty about value in general and financial value in particular, given the novel's overall focus on speculative loss and gambling. Grace herself becomes a gambler, eventually losing her fortune and dying in moral and financial disgrace. Throughout the novel, McIntosh intertwines questions about moral and monetary substance, suggesting that both can be illusory, merely seeming to have value rather than actually having it.

"The Prevailing Epidemic": Speculation as Mental and Physical Illness

If speculative gain was, at best, ephemeral and, at worst, entirely illusory, as panic authors suggested, then one logical conclusion to draw would be that the pursuit of wealth through speculation is not a rational endeavor, but one motivated by forces outside the realm of reason and logic. Panic fiction was written during a time of much cultural contention over what constituted rational economic behavior. Eighteenth-century republican thought had linked reason with virtue—

suggesting that rational consideration would naturally prompt behavior in accordance with public welfare—but by the second quarter of the nineteenth century, what was considered "rational" in economics was being separated from virtue or morality and linked instead with individual self-interest. Expansionist economists such as Henry C. Carey were particularly prone to citing Adam Smith's principle of enlightened self-interest, as in a passage in his 1835 "Essay on the Rates of Wages," where he dissuades the capitalist from investing in "good works," or the redistribution of wealth, and enjoins him rather to invest his surplus "in such manner as would be profitable to himself" (254). An anonymous writer in the *Lady's Book* of July 1837 decries the "money-loving spirit" and "grand business of accumulation" that he or she claims is "every day . . . mentioned under the name of 'practical value,'" but the author goes on to attribute that prevalent pursuit of individual self-interest to the unique (and cherished) circumstances of American society: among them, "unfettered freedom of thought and action," a "boundless field of enterprise," and "inexhaustible materials of profitable labor" ("Moral Culture"). While this author clearly disapproves of the disappearance of moral considerations from the economic equation, he or she also sees rampant self-interest as a logical consequence of American conditions and one that had arisen, in particular, from the ability of Americans to think and act freely—that is, to apply their reason to their circumstances, independently of traditional moral teachings.

Whatever the truth of how capitalism worked in early nineteenth-century America, many observers made similar claims, noting that rational economic behavior was being equated with that which produced the largest gain for the least investment, regardless of its consequences for other investors or the community as a whole. For those who truly espoused such a view, speculation was supremely rational, at least during a time of rising prices, since it could bring enormous profits for the investor who could find a buyer for his inflated property. For them, the term "panic," with its connotation of unreasoning fear and emotional response, described the moment when investors abandoned their rational belief in continuous market growth and rushed to withdraw their investments. Even as companies were failing in domino fashion in April of 1837, defenders of the economy in commercial journals denigrated those they termed "panic makers" and "assassins of credit," associating panic with a fearful and unfounded lack of trust in the vast resources of the country.[10] Common usage of the word "panic" from the eighteenth century to the present day to denote such acts of "de-investing"—epitomized by the "run on the bank" or a hasty sale of a previously hot commodity for whatever it will bring—suggests the strength of this strain of economic thought. In panic fiction, however, it is buying rather than selling that lends itself to irrational economic behavior, shifting the emotional connotations of "panic" from divestiture to acquisition. Panic novels depict the individual and national rush to expand and become wealthy during the antebellum boom periods as driven not by reasonable expectations of profit, much less carefully thought-out plans for achieving security and prosperity, but rather by passion—an uncontrolled and uncontrollable desire for wealth, even a kind of "fever" that got into the speculator's blood and urged him into ventures that had no hope of success. In associating speculation thus with an antirational passion, panic authors tap into an earlier republican rhetoric that placed high value on both self-control and industry as vital to the survival and health of a newly established, self-governing republic. Karen Weyler quotes Benjamin Rush, a prominent early American physician and public figure, as blaming speculation for a rise in cases of insanity around the turn of the nineteenth century: "In the United States, madness has increased since the year 1790. This must be ascribed chiefly to an increase in the number and magnitude of the objects of ambition and avarice, and to the greater joy or distress, which is produced by gratification or disappointments in the pursuit of each of them. The funding system, and speculations in bank scrip, and new lands, have been fruitful sources of madness in our country" ("'Speculating Spirit,'" 221).[11] Theophilus Fisk echoed this language of madness in his address of July 1837, declaring that thousands of ordinary farmers and workers had been drawn into the folly of speculation, "plunged into the maddening vortex with the vain hope of growing rich in a day." His allusions to not just the "golden dreams" of speculative wealth but also to "hallucinations" link his imagery of illusion to that of complete loss of touch with reason and reality (Fisk 8, 19).

Elizabeth Oakes Smith's *Riches without Wings* illustrates this common association within panic fiction between speculation and lack of rational self-control. Smith's novel contrasts the middle-class Cleveland family, whose gentility and status derive from "taste and intelligence" rather than money, with the rich but vulgar Masons, who lose their fortune due to "bad speculation" and "an indolent way of doing business" (119). While reason and perfect order reign in the Cleveland household, uncontrolled displays of emotion rule the Masons. Young James Mason reveals his lack of self-control when he slams down his gun in a fit of rage after being hindered from getting what he wants; his mother and sister indulge in repeated scenes of tears and quarreling following the family's financial collapse. In such scenes of personal disorder, panic authors echo the fears implicit in Rush's complaint—that speculation is both product and producer of unregulated human passions, an economic practice that defies the rational control needed to ensure national harmony and prosperity.

Reinforcing this link between speculation and unrestrained passion or irrationality, the narrative structure of panic novels concentrates both the emotionality of characters and emotional appeals to readers within the portion of the narrative that depicts speculation or similar economic practices. In Hannah Farnham Sawyer Lee's novels, for example, characters engaged in speculative investment or extravagant spending on credit express considerable anxiety. Rather than giving them the peace of mind they seek, their increasing wealth or possessions make them either irritable or verging on manic, as illustrated in James Draper's frantic enthusiasm over the booming economy in the opening vignette of this chapter. In a much later novel, Maria McIntosh's *The Lofty and the Lowly* (1853), a character whose gambling is explicitly compared to speculation experiences a whole gamut of negatively inflected emotions, from an "intoxication of pleasure" to a "craving for fiercer excitement" to "uncontrollable anger," while at the gaming table. Such descriptions of the characters' states of mind paint a vivid picture of speculators' emotionality and of the dominant role that emotion plays both as motivation for and consequence of their behavior.

In addition to making the reader associate speculation with negative emotional states, the affective intensity of these sections of panic novels also seems designed to stimulate the reader's own emotional response. Looking again at Lee's passage in *Rich Enough*—quoted earlier in this chapter—which depicts James Draper's excitement about opportunities for profit, we can see how its breathless phrasing and repeated exclamations create a narrative tone that mimics the emotion of the character. Readers are compelled to mentally enact that emotion and thus invited to either experience some degree of the character's emotional state or react against it. The resulting response might thus be a shared sense of anxiety over impending gains or losses, sympathy for the sufferings of a victim like Frances Draper, or even anger toward a character's weakness. By encouraging such responses to the portrayal of speculation, panic authors undoubtedly acknowledged and played upon the anxieties already present in their readers in times of panic, but they also directed that existing emotion specifically toward speculation. Their own feelings aroused by these depictions, readers would more readily make the association between speculation and irrational economic behavior.

Several panic novels carry this sense of speculation as divorced from rationality, or as an unthinking act impelled by forces beyond the control of the will, even further by associating it with the body rather than the mind and, in particular, with bodily illness. Images of speculation as either an illness in itself, or a cause of disease, intensify the sense of danger and harm associated with such economic acts—to the individual and to society. Figured as disease, speculation is seen not only as not rational but also as potentially productive of systemic decline; just as illness may lead to death if not cured, speculation could result in national economic collapse if not tamed or regulated in some fashion.

Often it is speculation itself that panic fiction depicts as a disease infecting the individual investor and, through him, the body of the nation. James Draper's obsessive speculations not only cause harm to others but are also manifested within himself as a kind of fever. Narrative descriptions of James's face as "flushed" and his eyes as "unsettled and flashing" suggest that his reportedly "feverish pursuit of wealth" is more than simply an analogy for haste or enthusiasm. James's speculation becomes a condition beyond his own will, one that clouds his rational faculties and overheats both his desires and his imagination, driving him toward ultimate collapse.

An even more graphic representation of speculation as debilitating physical condition appears in Emma Embury's 1838 story "The Son and Heir." Embury's first-person male narrator is a bitter man who has spent his life in the obsessive pursuit of wealth through speculation, only to lose both wife and son. In several key scenes in the story the narrator reacts to moments of emotional violence with bursting blood vessels and bleeding from the mouth and nose. Following one distressing encounter with an acquaintance, he recalls: "My brain reeled—my eyes swam—all the blood in my body seemed rushing with torrent-like fury to my head, and bursting with irrepressible violence from every possible vent" (121). Analogous to James Draper's feverishness, these bleeding episodes, occurring whenever the narrator is impassioned with rage or grief, signify the passion and lack of rational control associated by panic authors with speculation. The narrator's inability to conduct his financial affairs within reasonable or moderate bounds is thus figured as an involuntary physical condition, wracking his body as his speculations ruined his life.

Embury's novel *Constance Latimer; or, The Blind Girl*—originally published in one volume with "The Son and Heir" as a benefit for the New York Institution for the Blind—links speculation with scarlet fever as parallel causes of a family's devastating losses. The title character's father, Charles Latimer, is a wealthy merchant who goes bankrupt due to imprudent speculations in a period of global "commercial distress" (50). As a result, the family must give up most of its possessions and learn to live in relative poverty. Before the bankruptcy, however, the Latimers have already experienced a misfortune that tests their courage and endurance, the scarlet fever, which leaves Constance blind and kills her younger brother. Just as Constance's blindness serves as a physical symbol of loss and foreshadows the family's loss of fortune, the disease that caused it is linked with the irresponsible financial behavior that results in the family's failure. Mr. Latimer's speculation is thus symbolically equated with the scarlet fever that ravaged his children's health. Both cause enormous suffering and endanger the well-being of home and individual, respectively.

If speculation is a "disease," then of course there is the problem of contagion. Lee captured this fear in her introduction to *The Harcourts*, published just a few months before *Rich Enough*, right at the height of the Panic of 1837. Tracing the origins of the crisis from its immediate cause of speculation to a "fearful increase of luxury and ostentation," she said that tendency "has left us in so enfeebled a state as to fall ready victims to the prevailing epidemic" (v). It is unclear whether "epidemic" here refers to the contagiousness of speculation itself—one successful investment spurring another, as bids to buy cause prices to rise—or whether it signifies the frenzied sell-off of a panic after the speculative bubble has burst. Either way, the phases of a speculative economy are characterized by a term that connotes the spreading of disease, or a condition of ill health that is progressively contaminating a larger population. The crowd mentality of both speculation and panic lends the metaphor of illness increased power, suggesting that the dangers of speculation are not confined to the individual speculator.

And as we have seen in *Rich Enough*, the "disease" of speculation can sicken non-speculators as well. Frances Draper's consumption is directly connected to her husband's business enterprises, even though she herself never buys a share of stock and, in fact, overtly discourages James's projects as injurious to both her and his well-being. She is an innocent victim of speculation, literally made ill by worry and her husband's neglect—his refusal to leave his business to give her a change of climate, for instance—while serving as a symbol of all that is corrupted and destroyed by the speculator's single-minded attention to profit at any cost. As Frances's cough becomes "deep and hollow," her skin transparent, and her nights sleepless, her deterioration parallels the less visible corruption of James's character—progressively blighted by greed, the inability to be content with what he has, and a failure of compassion toward those he loves. The fact that Frances's death occurs simultaneously with the nationwide panic that bankrupts her husband underlines Lee's use of her disease as a metaphor for national as well as individual decline. Just as a consumptive's flushed cheeks may falsely appear to signal robust health, Lee suggests, the rapid development and sharply rising prices of a speculative economy are false signs of economic strength, foreshadowing instead a looming crisis.

By portraying speculation as a symptom or cause of illness, panic fiction suggests that the American economy is in need of healing. And just as physical health is restored by reducing fever and bringing the body's systems under regulation, panic authors propose that the fever of speculation needs to be cooled and order imposed on the means and pace of economic gain in order for national prosperity to be regained.

Controlling the Means of Gain: The Importance of Labor and Social Value

I have been arguing in the previous two sections that panic authors' characterization of speculation as illusory, irrational, and unhealthy stemmed from fears of loss and served to warn readers of the economic dangers of speculative investment. Such imagery is also tinged with moral condemnation, however, and linked to fears of social as well as purely economic instability. Exhortations against "imaginary wealth" and demands for the return to what is "real," for instance, not only function to protect against loss but also to uphold moral values of honesty and sincerity and to defend against the uncertainties of disguised economic position. Similarly, images of speculation as a disease not only remove it from the realm of rational behavior but also represent it as corruptive, metaphorically destroying the soul as illness destroys the body.

This blending of the "economic" and the "moral" denotes a complex agenda on the part of panic authors. In part, their moral condemnation of speculation can be seen as reflecting the nation's legacy of both Puritan and republican thought. Although by the 1830s American religious belief had splintered into numerous denominations with widely divergent modes of expression, Protestant Christianity remained a predominant influence on American society, strengthened by the evangelical enthusiasm of the Second Great Awakening.[12] Ann Fabian notes that much of the popular response to the Panic of 1837 was couched in religious terms, bemoaning the societal sins of greed and extravagance that had brought such divine wrath upon God's people ("Speculation" 131). The political tradition of republicanism similarly served as a source for panic authors' language of virtue in response to increasing economic self-interest. Many writers and political leaders during the revolutionary and early republican eras had emphasized the need for "republican virtue"—the exercise of qualities such as self-restraint, frugality, industry, and willingness to sacrifice self-interest for the common good—in order to maintain national independence and resist a return to tyranny. While some historians have seen republican influence as waning by the early nineteenth century, others claim that its values remained pervasive and became intertwined with those of Protestant Christianity, particularly in the rhetoric of antebellum reform movements.[13]

Even as panic authors' emphasis on morality and virtue reflect these influential societal discourses, their focus on "social climbing" or outsiders' use of money to intrude into a closed social world as the epitome of immoral behavior suggests that moral concerns were also intimately tied to secular anxieties about status. As Karen Halttunen notes, the antebellum "cult of sincerity" that deplored all forms of pretense had a social as well as religious basis. Halttunen writes that middle-class demands for external appearances to conform to economic realities, however couched in moral terms, arose from desires to be able to gauge the status of one's neighbors and associates in a time when increased social and geographic mobility were disrupting previously fixed social hierarchies (xv).

I turn now to a more detailed examination of panic fiction's moral arguments against speculation—but with an understanding that the genre's moral framework and its interest in social class stability are intimately connected. I do not suggest that panic authors cynically clothed a class-based resistance to speculation in the moral discourse of Christian and republican ideals but rather that their genuine moral critique was perceptibly shaped by class-based experiences and needs. It is important to note here that, since the class (and regional) perspectives of Northern and Southern panic authors differed substantially, their moral critiques of speculation overlap but are not identical. While Northern panic novels overwhelmingly represent a middle-class perspective, their Southern counterparts tend to reflect the elite worldview of the planter. Regional social and economic differences also contribute to distinct types of social anxiety, with Northern panic fiction focused on threats to middle-class stability from the working class and an unpredictable market economy (as developed more fully in chapter 2), and Southern panic fiction concerned with threats to the slaveholding class from "outsiders"—including Northern financial institutions (see chapter 4). As a result, Northern panic fiction appears much more occupied in policing the economic behavior of all its characters in order to distinguish between acceptable and unacceptable modes of entering the middle class, while Southern panic novels focus more on the impact on the home of immoral economic behavior from the outside.

The most prominent aspect of Northern panic fiction's condemnation of speculation, and the one in which the ideological nexus of morality and middle-class interest is most visible, is its challenge to gain without labor. Both a republican model of virtuous citizenship and the Puritan ethic that permeated early northeastern American culture emphasize the moral value of labor. While wealth bore dangerous connotations of luxury and worldliness, it had traditionally been respected as a sign of worth and godly favor if gained through the character-building and purifying means of hard work. Acquired without work, wealth was seen as corrupting. From economists of all stripes, who praised the "honest labor" of the nation's farmers and mechanics as the source of all real wealth, to religious writers, who quoted Genesis as the basis for a universal imperative for all men to live off "the sweat of their brows," public discourse of the 1830s joined in nearly unanimous praise of gain through hard work (and condemnation of its opposite).[14] Typical was a Fourth of July address by one S. G. Goodrich, reprinted in the August 1835 *American Ladies' Magazine*, in which Mr. Goodrich proclaimed: "Toil, then—bodily toil—is no curse; it is a blessing. It is alike salutary to the body and the soul. It is ordained of heaven, as giving vigor to one, and wholesome discipline to the other. Let no man spurn it—let no man deem himself degraded by it—let no man feel elevated, by being placed in a situation which does not require it" (468).

But the very concept of prosperity through labor is inherently middle-class, as evidenced by Goodrich's closing declaration that American "truth of character" is most frequently found in "the middling class, who are kept by that admirable regulator of society—industry—between the extremes of poverty and riches" (469). Since an aristocracy does not need to labor in order to be wealthy, and the working poor rarely prosper from their work, the moral valuation of that regulator, industry, reflects a distinct middle-class bias. Furthermore, labor assures that gain will be gradual and therefore that changes in social status will take place slowly, giving those on the rise time to assimilate the values of their new class. Speculative gain, on the other hand, can be achieved suddenly, propelling the uneducated or the uncultured into middle-class or elite status without any period of assimilation. In morally condemning gain acquired without labor, then, Northern panic fiction simultaneously favors a slower mode of economic growth that maintains greater class stability.

As American commerce and industry expanded, however, definitions of what constituted "labor" were contested. Occupations that required physical effort—such as farming, factory work, or artisanal production—clearly counted as genuine work. Some made the case that occupations pertaining to the nation's growing capitalist infrastructure of commerce, banking, and financial services were also forms of labor. Daniel Feller quotes the Massachusetts statesman and orator Edward Everett, for example, as defining workers "not by calling but by character." In a speech made in 1830, Everett claimed that capitalists as well as laborers, if they worked "in an honest way and for a lawful object," should be considered working men (quoted in Feller 136). Those at the opposite end of the economic spectrum disagreed. Organizers of trade unions and the Workingmen's political parties during the 1820s and 1830s declared that bankers, brokers, and speculators were not truly workers because, as Feller puts it, "they wielded no tools, produced no wealth" (130). They made money for themselves by manipulating prices and instruments of credit but returned nothing to society in the way of either labor or product. Panic authors fall somewhere in the middle, accepting commerce and other nonmanual occupations as legitimate labor but privileging occupations that produced a tangible product or provided a recognizable service. While Southern authors place less emphasis on the need for labor—maintaining the legitimacy of inherited wealth—they do implicitly condemn young heirs who neglect the plantation for frivolous pursuits and older landowners who turn to speculation for a quick profit rather than developing their land. Thus labor is not an essential component of their characters' class identities, but the willingness to labor does reflect the possession of personal qualities necessary for continued success.

Panic fiction as a whole, then, attacks the concept of gain without labor on three moral grounds. The first of these is that gaining wealth without working for it demonstrates a lack of character and integrity. Since the work ethic exalts industry as a primary virtue and one that builds character, anyone who attempts to become wealthy or to restore waning prosperity without being industrious loses the opportunity to develop character. Typically, panic fiction presents young male characters faced with decisions about how to pursue prosperity—through steady labor or through some get-rich-quick speculation scheme. The young man's choice determines whether he becomes a man of strong principle and integrity or one whose weak character cannot sustain him in times of difficulty. In Hannah Farnham Sawyer Lee's short novel *The Log-Cabin, or the World before You* (1844), the protagonist Henry Green sets out for the West with one hundred dollars in his pocket. A former friend shows up and offers to "turn [his] hundred into thousands" through a speculative venture, but Henry rejects that offer in favor of his fixed intention to "be really useful and obtain a living" (61). Rather than accepting vague and perhaps shady promises of rising instantly, Henry prefers to "gradually rise in the world," developing industry and honesty as a farmer, while his speculative friend bounces in and out of jail for various money-related crimes.

Panic authors' second strike against gain without labor is that it inevitably involves the corruption or exploitation of others. If money is not being earned in fair exchange for labor, then its acquisition must be at the expense of someone else's loss. Henry Green's unscrupulous friend in *The Log-Cabin* is basically a swindler. He makes money for himself by promising fantastic returns on his victims' investments, then simply pocketing their money. The land speculators that Caroline Kirkland describes in *A New Home, Who'll Follow?* similarly make their fortunes by exploiting others. They misrepresent and then sell plots of land at greatly inflated prices, knowing that the purchasers may never recover the value of the land, much less realize a gain. This fear of the exploitive nature of speculation is captured by Eliza Dupuy at the very beginning of her 1858 novel *The Planter's Daughter*, as Gertrude Harrington warns her brother Charles (the planter of the title) about the dangers of trusting a speculator: "Brother, beware of that man. . . . He is reckless, and, I am afraid, unprincipled. As a capitalist, he probably seeks you; but after he has fairly obtained the control of your means, I am sadly afraid he may be unscrupulous in the use of them. Under any circumstances, they will be used to his own advantage, whatever the result may be to you" (12–13). As panic authors suggest, the very nature of speculation, in which paper transactions between strangers replace the tangible exchange of goods and property among neighbors, encourages exploitation; the lack of an ongoing relationship between buyer and seller as well as the invisibility of the investment provides ample opportunity for fraud.

Finally, panic authors condemn gain without labor because it does not produce any tangible goods or social benefit. Acquired simply by profiting from repeated purchases and sales, speculative gain is neither the legitimate profit from an agricultural or manufacturing enterprise that furnishes the community with necessary goods nor income earned by providing useful services such as education or medical care. Which specific occupations are regarded as producing such benefits and which are not varies from novel to novel, and sometimes even within novels. Catharine Sedgwick makes the clearest contrast between appropriate and inappropriate ways of earning a living in her 1836 novel *The Poor Rich Man, and the Rich Poor Man*. Sedgwick's model couple, Harry and Susan Aikin, is engaged in actual productive work for their money—Harry as a cart driver, Susan as a "tailoress." Both have chosen their occupations specifically because they are "honest," useful ways to earn a living. Their wealthy counterparts, the Finleys, engage in no perceivably productive work at all. The son of a speculator who believed that "money should work," Morris Finley is a "businessman" who apparently operates according to his father's philosophy, making money from money rather than from a trade or profession.

Many panic novels focus on the occupation of merchant, one of the most vulnerable modes of employment in times of economic crisis and thus particularly pertinent to the genre's critique. The role of the merchant occupies an ambiguous position in panic fiction, since he provides society with the valuable service of transporting and marketing agricultural and manufactured goods, but his work always involves a certain element of risk, which is sometimes equated with speculation. In addition, the merchant's close association with the exchange of money marks him, at least potentially, as one who desires money for its own sake. Karen Weyler, writing about representations of speculation in earlier American fiction, contends that authors sought to distinguish between "virtuous trade" and immoral speculation in order to defend one of the new nation's only means to prosperity as conforming to republican ideals of civic virtue (208). In many panic novels, including *The Harcourts*, *Constance Latimer*, and *Mabel Vaughan*, the merchant is an essentially honest man who either carelessly allows his debts to extend beyond his assets or gets caught up in risky business ventures that he believes will pay off. Thus, panic authors approve the general role of merchant while condemning the specific mercantile practice of speculating beyond one's existing capital. Other panic novels are not quite so affirming of mercantile legitimacy. Before he turns to manufacturing as an avenue for speculation, *Rich Enough*'s James Draper is a merchant, importing merchandise from China and India, as well as cotton from the Southern United States. Although Lee's specificity about his enterprises bestows some legitimacy upon them, James's risk taking and excessive desire for wealth show just how fine a line there is between merchant and speculator.

The moral criticisms aimed at speculation resembled those leveled at gambling, and the two were often, in fact, equated in public discourse by those opposed to speculation in order to stress the nonproductive and reckless risk-taking qualities of speculative enterprises. While most Northern panic fiction merely implies that speculation is a type of gambling, several Southern panic novels use the cards and dice as either a substitute form of economic risk or as an explicit parallel to the speculative ventures of another character. In McIntosh's *The Lofty and the Lowly*, for example, young Donald Montrose's progressive entanglement in gambling, with its consequent endangerment of his family's entire fortune and estate, stands in for the speculation that attracts and ruins men in most other panic fiction. He experiences the same "feverish" desires that consume James Draper in *Rich Enough*, and he repeatedly attempts, like speculators, to recover his losses with yet another futile bet or toss of the dice. At one point, a fellow gambler makes an explicit comparison between gambling and stock investment, arguing that the former is every bit as legitimate as "brokerage" because both require skill; the fact that neither involves real labor (one of Donald's initial objections to gaming), combined with the heavy losses that Donald is incurring during this conversation, cement the connection between speculation and gambling and suggest the equal disapproval with which readers should look upon both activities.

In Dupuy's *The Planter's Daughter*, Victor Harrington's gambling serves as a parallel to his father's simultaneous speculative schemes—more obviously risky and dissolute but sharing enough characteristics to demonstrate the dangers and moral wrongs of the elder man's ventures. For example, when Mr. Harrington chastises his son for his gambling losses, it is because Victor "risked what [he] knew [he] had not the means of paying" (278), not because he considers gambling intrinsically bad. Similarly, Victor is depicted as successful for a time when he develops a kind of card-counting scheme—an "infallible means of winning"—but ultimately loses when a more skilled stranger defeats him with his own trick (299). In both instances, Victor's experiences illustrate principles that apply equally well to his father's disastrous attempts at speculation—that one should risk only an amount that one actually possesses and that financial ventures that involve the unknown cannot, by definition, ever be a sure thing.

Southern panic authors' frequent use of gambling as either a substitute for or parallel to speculation may simply reflect regional realities. Various forms of gambling had been traditional among young men of the planter class in the South since colonial days, and thus gambling losses may have posed a similar threat to families' economic stability that speculation appeared to pose in Northern mercantile circles.[15] Nevertheless, as economic behavior, the results of which are beyond the control of the gambler, gambling possesses a potent symbolic value that simultaneously works to condemn speculation through association and to define the limits of acceptable economic risk taking. Ann Fabian, in her book *Card Sharps, Dream Books, & Bucket Shops: Gambling in Nineteenth-Century America*, contends that American opposition to gambling arose largely in concert with the development of speculative capitalism. Communities in colonial and early republican America, Fabian notes, often sanctioned certain forms of gambling, such as lotteries, as ways of financing public works (1). But as the means of acquiring wealth became more speculative, gambling came to be seen as at once the embodiment of American wealth seeking and risk taking—an analogue to land and commodity speculation—and a threat to an orderly society based on rational gain. That is, while it participated in the same spirit that was fueling America's economic expansion, gambling also represented the irrational, uncontrollable, potentially destructive aspects of speculative economics.

Reformers' objections to gambling, as Fabian outlines them, closely resemble panic authors' criticisms of speculation—reflecting both anxiety about a capitalist, profit-driven society and a desire to define appropriate economic behavior in circumstances of increasing social mobility. But Fabian argues that as the acquisition of wealth shifted from the realm of a small elite to the province of the middle classes, middle-class attitudes toward money making began to change. By isolating "gambling" as a marginal or extreme form of economic behavior, often attributed to the very rich or the very poor, reformers helped to legitimize and ease anxieties about middle-class wealth seeking, even that of a speculative nature. Gambling, Fabian says, became "the one form of gain that made all other efforts to get rich appear normal, natural, and socially salubrious. To condemn gambling was to condone the speculative profits generated by the transfer of land and stock and by the sale of contracts for agricultural commodities. While such speculative profits had once appeared dangerous and destructive, they were surely less so than the illusory profits of gambling" (4–5).

The authors of panic fiction are not so quick to legitimize speculation, nor in fact to make clear distinctions between speculation and gambling. Nevertheless, they do take pains to distinguish dangerous acts of speculation from legitimate mercantile business (just as McIntosh and Dupuy distinguish destructive gambling from friendly games of chance), thus exhibiting a similar desire to define appropriate economic behavior without condemning all avenues of gain. The principal difference is in where they draw the line. Panic authors' inclusion of speculation as a dangerous practice appears to reflect a greater fear of loss than that of gambling opponents a decade later but also a sharper sense of exclusion from the potential advantages of a speculative economy. Whereas the mostly male (and Northern) antigambling activists may have at least imagined their own successes in the market, panic authors, as women, had little access to such opportunities, while Southern authors, in particular, may have seen certain types of speculation as benefiting primarily the financial infrastructure centered in the North rather than their region's agricultural economy.

The Inhumane Extreme: Speculation in Slaves

For the most part, moral condemnation of speculation centered on the manner in which such economic transactions were performed and not on the commodity being traded. Land, bank stocks, commercial cargo, and shares of manufacturing enterprises were all seen as able to be legitimately purchased and sold as well as speculated in. One exception to this in the antebellum economy was speculation in slaves. Slave trading added a whole new dimension to the moral condemnation of speculation, beyond its effects on the character of the speculator or the integrity of his transactions. Here was a category of trade seen as intrinsically wrong, even by Southern authors intent on defending slavery, because the commodity was a human being. In fact, the sharpest critique comes from Southern authors. Northern panic novels of the 1830s ignore slave speculation almost entirely, focusing instead on the economic practices that most directly affected their own communities and homes. A few refer to slavery obliquely in making comparisons with Northern class relations but not to the purchase or sale of slaves. Later Northern fiction more overtly addresses slavery as a labor system (see chapter 5), but it also largely ignores human trafficking as a source of speculative profit. One Northern novel that does recognize the speculative aspect of slavery is not a panic novel but Harriet Beecher Stowe's *Dred: A Tale of the Great Dismal Swamp* (1856), which includes the commodification of enslaved people as an integral part of its overall critique of slavery. Mr. Jekyll, a Southern lawyer, explains to a Northern visitor why slaves, and not land, are the most profitable investment in the South: "Why, sir, if a man has a knowledge of human nature, knows where to buy and when to buy, and watches his opportunity, he gets a better percentage on his money that way that any other. . . . Say, now, that you give one thousand dollars for a man,—and I always buy the best sort, that's economy,—well, and he gets—put it at the lowest figure—ten dollars a month wages, and his living. Well, you see there, that gives you a pretty handsome sum for your money" (191). Other characters in *Dred* refer frequently to slaves' market value or to the sale of slaves to pay off creditors, clearly illustrating abolitionists' awareness of the financial roots of slavery.

Among panic novels, it is those by Southern authors, published during the 1840s and 1850s, that cite the trade in slaves as a form of speculation and condemn it as inappropriate profiteering in human beings, even though these same novels openly acknowledge slaves as financial assets for plantation owners and defend the practice of enslavement on a variety of grounds. Slave-owning protagonists in panic novels are portrayed consistently as having inherited their slaves ("in the family" for generations) or as having acquired them wholesale along with a purchased estate. Slaves are sold only under the direst economic pressures and only to settle debt, not to make a profit, while every effort is made to keep families intact and to sell to owners in the neighborhood rather than to a trader. Slave speculation and trading of any sort is displaced onto the "outsider"—a uniformly despicable character, often depicted as being from the North, whose only relation to the slaves he buys and sells is economic. Thus "owning" is separated from the acts of buying and selling and thereby divested of its most crass financial aspects, allowing the owner to be characterized as a benevolent patriarch and caretaker. In McIntosh's *The Lofty and the Lowly*, for example, the Montrose family agonizes over the possibility of having to sell slaves to settle Donald's gambling debts and, even then, only contemplates local sales. When a slave trader arrives uninvited—and accompanied by the Northern merchant Mr. Browne—Donald recoils, as, "there, before him, in the home of his fathers, stood one whose presence tainted the air he breathed, and soiled the earth on which he trod" (2: 33).

This portrait of Southern abstention from speculation in slaves is contradicted by the actual historical record. The historian Michael Tadman, for instance, refutes the proslavery propaganda claims that owners sold slaves only reluctantly and in extreme circumstances, contending instead that slave trading took place on such a massive scale throughout the South that the chance of the average slave being sold to another region before the age of forty was about 30 percent (112). Traders' records show a relatively small percentage of sales due to owner death or debt; in fact, the heaviest sales from planters to traders tended to come during economic boom periods, such as the mid-1830s, prior to the Panic of 1837, and again in the mid-1850s. Furthermore, sales of slaves from the upper South to the expanding lower South tended to increase when slave prices were higher, suggesting that upper South planters typically took advantage of price fluctuations to profit from the sale of "surplus" slaves—those not needed for their own agricultural production (Tadman 115–17).[16] In addition, Tadman contends that there is little evidence that planters were reluctant to do business with traders or that slave traders were the reviled outsiders that panic novels and other proslavery texts depict them as. On the contrary, Tadman finds much evidence that slave traders were prominent and accepted businessmen in their communities, serving as city aldermen and bank directors (193). Some even came from prominent Southern families. The famous Confederate cavalry leader Nathan Bedford Forrest, for example, reportedly made a ninety-six thousand dollar profit in one year by trading slaves in Memphis (Stampp, *Peculiar*, 265).

Although panic authors' condemnation of slave trading centers on the moral repulsiveness of breaking up families and profiting from human beings, speculation in slaves appealed to the same economic desires and entailed many of the same risks as other forms of speculation. Tadman finds evidence of a "feverish interest" in "Negro speculation" during the booming mid-1830s; he quotes Allan Gunn, a North Carolina trader, as writing, "Negro fellows are a selling here for $600 and every man that can get credit in the bank and his situation will let him leave home is a Negro trader" (54). Other sources apparently confirm this excitement: a Quaker reformer named J. J. Gurney had heard that "two-thirds of the funds of the Bank of North Carolina were invested in loans to slave merchants; and that no less than a million dollars had been expended the year before [1836] in the single county of Caswell for the purchase of Negroes on speculation" (54). A similar wave of slave speculation swept the South in the 1850s, according to Kenneth Stampp, who quotes a Georgia planter commenting on $1,500 slaves: "Men are demented upon the subject. A reverse will surely come" (*Peculiar*, 417). In fact, Stampp contends that even in good economic times, slave trading was highly competitive, and many lost money at it. In addition to the risks that attended other types of speculation—buying inflated goods, being forced to sell during a price decline, and being defrauded by unscrupulous sellers—slave traders faced the costs of transportation and support; losses through sickness, death, or escape; and the heightened risk of fraud in dealing with property that is neither stationary (like land) nor durable (like minerals) nor traceable (like stock certificates) (Stampp, *Peculiar* 264–65; Tadman 137). As a result of these risks, many traders apparently preferred cash transactions rather than credit for both buying and selling slaves. They could thus also avoid paying interest on their purchases and were able to pay cash because they expected a very quick turnaround (Tadman 52).

By completely ignoring these aspects of slave trading—the enticement of rapid gain to be made from the purchase and sale of slaves, the financial risks such ventures shared with other forms of speculation, and the heavy involvement of Southern traders—Southern panic authors were able to join their counterparts in the North in condemning speculation as a dangerous and immoral financial practice without implicating slave owners or the institution of slavery itself. In fact, while absolving their region of responsibility for speculation in slaves, those authors actually intensified the critique of speculation in general by suggesting, however mutedly, the inhumane extremes to which the desire for quick wealth could be taken.

"Value" vs. "Values": Opposing the Financial Yardstick

Encompassing all of these moral critiques of speculation was a broad resistance to what panic authors throughout the antebellum era and across regions saw as its promotion of a financial yardstick by which all value would be measured. Echoing a widespread cultural apprehension that economic individualism was shaking the nation's moral foundations, panic authors suggest that speculation replaces traditional values with a value system based solely on money.[17] Rather than measuring land's value according to the opportunities it provides for industry and independence, or even by the aesthetic value of its physical features, for instance, the purely paper transaction of a land speculation deal invites investors to measure worth by purchase price and potential resale value alone. Such a pecuniary way of thinking, panic authors imply, tends to permeate society, governing not only investment but the valuation of all things, from consumer goods to men's and women's character and success.

In order to show the moral inadequacy of a money-based system of value, many panic authors set up a contrast between such a system and a counter-philosophy that measures value according to usefulness or moral good. Catharine Sedgwick's *Poor Rich Man* opens with just such a contrast and lesson in value. When the young Morris Finley claims that his bird book is worth twice as much as Harry Aikin's Bible because it could be sold for twice as much money, Harry's future wife Susan May chides him: "Ah, then I've caught you, sir; Harry would not sell his Bible for any sum, so by your own rule Harry's is worth the most!" (13). Although Susan pretends to measure the worth of Harry's Bible by Morris's rule of resale value, she is actually asserting its worth in terms of its moral value to Harry. Harry will not sell the book because its real value for him lies in its ability to provide moral and spiritual guidance. By the same token, the narrator sees both the Bible and the bird book as being worth more in moral terms than the pink silk handkerchief that the children's classmate Paulina exchanges her book for at the store, since both promise mental elevation in contrast with the handkerchief's mere decorative function. A few pages later, Morris propounds his capitalist philosophy of value in even more explicit terms: "[W]hen one knows the value of money, one does not like to have so much lying idle. Money should work, as father says. If you could reckon interest and compound interest as well as I can, Miss Susan, I guess you would not like to have your money lying idle on a book-shelf!" (13). Money's value to Morris and to speculators like his father lies in its ability to replicate itself through interest; its value lies essentially in itself. To Susan, the value of money lies in the useful things it can buy—books, as well as good medical care for her invalid sister.[18]

Panic fiction portrays this conflict between a singular financial "value" and plural moral "values" for the most part as an either-or proposition. The desire for wealth, these novels suggest, is a single-minded obsession, incompatible with the cultivation of spiritual, mental, or emotional qualities. Morris Finley's love of money for its own sake, for example, does not coexist in his character with moral qualities such as honesty or compassion but instead displaces them. As he grows to adulthood, his obsession with wealth leads him to engage in less than perfectly honest business dealings and to value material possessions at the expense of human relationships. In contrast, Harry and Susan Aikin's utilitarian view of money—choosing a job that allows time for family and charity rather than maximizing income—leads to a life of domestic virtue and benevolence. Sedgwick suggests that Harry's and Susan's actions—seeking opportunities for benevolence, being productive and independent, and implanting good morals in the next generation—signify their possession of "true wealth." This wealth of spiritual and moral values not only cannot be purchased with material wealth, but it is actually hindered from developing when material wealth is sought. One of the principal evils of valuing according to wealth, Sedgwick suggests, is that it detracts from the development of the inner qualities that enable people to achieve real satisfaction and fulfillment in their lives.

The values that panic novels defend against the usurpation of speculation and financial gain are clearly a diffuse set. Characterized variously as moral, spiritual, intellectual, emotional, and personal, they are difficult to define precisely. Virtues such as charity, honesty, and humility are clearly part of Christian teaching, while qualities of simplicity, independence, and intellectual striving resonate with republican ideals. Subordinating one's own interests to those of others or of the community as a whole is a tenet of both Christianity and the republican concept of virtuous citizenship. "Refinement," on the other hand, and the capacity for aesthetic appreciation—qualities that frequently crop up as lacking in those who measure worth by money alone—are more attached to class definitions than to either philosophy or religion.

One reason for this advocacy of diffuse values is that panic fiction arose during a time when national values were in transition, as republican ideals gave way to liberal individualism and already-relaxed Puritan strictures yielded to a more sentimental Christianity. Situated in this era of change, many panic novels look back to the past nostalgically while simultaneously participating in the creation of ideologies that transform those older value systems. Thus while they defend traditional religious and political values against the incursions of a rising economic value system, they also incorporate elements of individualism—such as the notion of private virtue—into their worldviews.

But a more fundamental reason it is difficult to pin down the precise value system of panic fiction is simply that its values were contingent upon the individual authors' own class and regional affiliations, as well as the time periods and specific circumstances in which they wrote. Thus, early stories of failure tend to be more rooted in republican values than later ones. Similarly, some panic novels have a spiritual bent, while others lean more toward secular values. Northern novels tend to privilege qualities associated with middle-class women and the home—private, domestic virtue—while Southern panic fiction showcases more public, "masculine" forms of virtue such as physical courage and independence. But while the particular values espoused by individual panic authors reflect their circumstances and rhetorical agendas, all were united in opposing a value system ruled by money and promoted values that they saw as protecting and preserving the domestic sphere, however differently that might be defined.

Economic Ambivalence: Speculation that Strengthens the Domestic Sphere

Although panic fiction clearly portrays speculation as a threat to social stability and moral values, under certain specific circumstances it appears to be not only tolerated but even approved. This seeming contradiction reveals an ambivalence toward capitalism and the marketplace, especially the literary marketplace, that was shared by many nineteenth-century authors. While often deploring a market-oriented culture of wealth that threatened to displace values that gave women power, female authors also looked to the emerging literary marketplace as a potential new avenue to power or, at least, income. As Susan Coultrap-McQuin has documented, increased literacy created an expanded reading public, and women seized on authorship as a respectable and often profitable means to economic security (23). And because financial need served as one of the few socially acceptable justifications for women to enter the public sphere, female authors often publicly embraced the commercial aspect of writing even when their male colleagues sought to distance themselves from it. Emma Embury evinces such an embrace when she declares in the preface to *Constance Latimer* that the novel was "written, not for fame, but for money" (vi).[19]

Given such an often frankly commercial relationship to writing, it is not surprising that the authors of most panic fiction distinguish carefully between acceptable and unacceptable aspects of a market economy rather than denouncing it outright. Panic authors do not condemn the marketplace itself but rather economic practices that threaten to destabilize the middle-class or elite home through sudden loss, sudden gain, or a shift in focus away from domestic values. Although speculation is generally seen as just such a practice, and thus a danger to the stability of American society, occasionally it serves to either establish or strengthen a domestic environment, leading to some curious contradictions. While most panic novels depict the appropriate mode of recovery from loss or building of prosperity as a gradual process brought about by steady hard work, in a few cases fortunate speculations speed up that process.

In *Constance Latimer*, for instance, Constance's father conscientiously travels abroad following his financial failure, visiting each of his mercantile "agencies" personally and working hard to pay off each of his outstanding debts. His declaration that he will subsequently "devote [himself] entirely to [his] family, and relinquish all attempts at commerce"—signaling a shift from market to domestic values—is clearly an author-approved sentiment. But the means that enable Mr. Latimer to relinquish commerce and enjoy his domestic life in comfort turns out to be a "successful speculation, which presented itself at the moment when he was preparing to embark"—and which triples the value of his remaining fortune (Embury 72). Similarly, in Maria Cummins's *Mabel Vaughan*—following chapters in which Mr. Vaughan's failed land speculations nearly destroy him before bringing about a change of heart and values—a minor character, the urban laborer Owen Dowst, moves west and quickly becomes prosperous by investing his small amount of money in land that doubles in value within a couple of years.

In both cases, these "happy endings"—provided by an act of speculation—appear to contradict their respective novels' overall condemnation of speculation. But what distinguishes Mr. Latimer's final investment from his earlier business practices and Owen Dowst's land speculation from that of Mr. Vaughan is that both enable, rather than take the place of, domestic life. Mr. Latimer's final speculation creates rather than destroys domestic security for his family, and Owen Dowst's investment in land is for purposes of settlement and cultivation, as opposed to Mr. Vaughan's sole interest in profit. Thus, even the most anti-speculation of panic fiction succumbs to the lure of a quickly turned profit when the purposes for that profit are explicitly domestic or promise to uphold appropriate values.

Anxiety of Loss: The Role of Failure in Panic Narratives

In the vast majority of panic novels, however, speculation is followed by financial failure. Since most panic fiction was written specifically in response to the actual occurrence of widespread failures during and after panics, and was intended to explain such events, the actual loss of money, property, and position is the second crucial element common to the genre. While the actual moment of failure tends to play a much smaller role, in terms of narrative space and authorial emphasis, than speculation and other forms of financial irresponsibility, it is nevertheless an important turning point in the typical panic narrative.

In Lee's *Rich Enough*, for example, all of James Draper's financial ventures—his fevered speculations in real estate, cotton, textile mills, and railroads—narratively lead toward and culminate in the economic collapse that brings about James's ruin and closes the novel:

> New scenes were opening upon Mr. Draper. It became evident that a dark cloud hung over the business atmosphere. Unexpected failures every day took place. Some attributed the thick-coming evils to the removal of the deposits, others to interrupted currency; some to overtrading, and some to extravagance. Whatever was the cause, the distress was real. Mr. Draper's cotton became a drug in the market; manufactories stopped, or gave no dividends. Eastern lands lost even their nominal value, and western towns became bankrupt. Ships stood in the harbor, with their sails unbent and masts dismantled. Day laborers looked aghast, not knowing where to earn food for their families. The whirlwind came; it made no distinction of persons. (70)

Lee's description of the effects of the crisis evocatively captures the devastation reported in other accounts. Records of depleted bank reserves, bankrupted businesses, and unemployed workers fill the newspapers of the time. One article in the *New York Herald* immediately following the New York bank suspensions in May of 1837, for example, lists 239 businesses that had failed in the city so far that year. A letter from a committee of merchants to President Van Buren that was reprinted in the rival *Morning Courier* around the same time complains of depreciated real estate, failed commercial houses, declines in stock and merchandise values, and at least twenty thousand people thrown out of work.[20] Historians have similarly emphasized the material impact of antebellum panics, confirming unemployment rates in the tens of thousands in both 1837 and 1857. Edward Pessen estimates that somewhere between one-third and one-half of urban workers in the Northeast "suffered unemployment for substantial periods" between the panic of 1837 and the mid-1840s (84, 147), while Kenneth Stampp puts the 1857 figure in the hundreds of thousands nationwide, with forty thousand in Philadelphia alone, and between thirty and one hundred thousand in New York City (*America* 226). Following both panics, banks suspended their payment of specie for considerable periods of time—for more than a year in 1837–38 and for two months in 1857.[21]

Given the fervent anti-speculation rhetoric of panic fiction and its emphasis on the dangers of such "illusory investment," it would be reasonable to assume that panic authors propose a simple cause-and-effect relationship between speculation and failure. In fact, though, their treatment of failure turns out to be much more complex. Just as Lee offers a variety of explanations for the collapse at the end of *Rich Enough*—"the removal of the deposits . . . interrupted currency . . . overtrading, and . . . extravagance"—panic authors reflect the very divided views of their times over both the causes of failure and its meaning. At issue, principally, is whether economic failure signifies moral failure and, if so, whether the blame belongs to the failing individual or to the economic system that permitted or brought about his loss. While James Draper's greed clearly fueled his "overtrading" and thus his personal downfall, Lee's references to currency policies and banking practices beyond his control, as well as the nationwide nature of the collapse, suggest a mingling of individual and systemic culprits. While Martha Banta is largely correct in observing that failure of any kind has been seen as the "greatest shame" in a nation that defines itself by success, blame for financial failure has varied over the course of American history according to religious belief and economic circumstances.[22] The Puritans, despite their distrust of rapid economic gain and abhorrence of ostentatious displays of wealth, attributed economic failure largely to individual moral weakness. Because they interpreted virtually all events and circumstances as signs of divine providence, they tended to see prosperity as a mark of God's favor and failure as evidence of his displeasure. As nineteenth-century American society gradually became more secular, moving away from a worldview that saw divine purpose in every event, failure eventually became less directly linked with moral behavior. This change was reinforced by the market fluctuations that accompanied the rise of capitalism; as Americans endured a succession of severe economic crises in which financial failure was widespread, such loss came to be seen more as a natural occurrence in a commercial society than as a consequence of moral weakness.

Divine Wrath or Commercial Downswing?: Changing Understandings of Failure's Causes

As noted earlier, modern historians have attributed the antebellum panics to various interrelated factors that include changes in European economic conditions and

American governmental policies as well as overexpansion of credit, irresponsible banking practices, and frenzies of land and commodity speculation. These combinations of factors created unstable business climates that needed only some triggering event to virtually topple the nation's economic establishment. In 1837, that event came on May 9, when, according to the historian R. C. McGrane, "$652,000 in specie was withdrawn from the vaults" of New York's banks; the following day, all the city's banks suspended further payment of specie—that is, they refused to convert bank notes into gold and silver (97). The crisis had really begun in March of that year, when shortages of specie forced many mercantile houses and other businesses to close. Lee's "dark cloud" covered the entire nation that spring, from New Orleans cotton traders to the East Coast mercantile elite to the entrepreneurs and farmers of the western frontier towns.[23] Unable to stem the outward flow of their reserves and fearful of collapse, the major banks finally closed their doors in May, resulting in what McGrane calls "a general suspension of business" (98).[24]

The Panic of 1857 followed a similar pattern, with widespread business reversals triggering bank suspensions and resulting in a nationwide depression. A number of historians have credited the August 24, 1857 collapse of the Ohio Life Insurance & Trust Company as the proximate cause of a series of bank suspensions that started in Philadelphia on September 25, spread throughout Pennsylvania and New Jersey, and finally culminated in the closure of New York banks on October 13.[25] But while the Ohio Life failure—due in part to fraud and embezzlement and in part to heavy railroad losses—undoubtedly made bankers throughout the nation nervous, Charles Calomiris and Larry Schweikart argue that a better explanation for the panic's origin lies in the collapse of railroad securities. As Kansas and Nebraska opened to thousands of new settlers, the mid-1850s had seen a boom in railroad stocks as well as land sales. The "perceived profitability" of westward expansion fueled a new fever of speculation. But by the late summer of 1857, western land values dropped—the result, Calomiris and Schweikart argue, of the March 1857 Dred Scott ruling and subsequent strife in Kansas between pro-slavery and free-soil interests. With reduced immigration, railroad earnings declined sharply and a number of rail companies went bankrupt. The subsequent failures of railroad investors who had borrowed from eastern banks strained the capacities of those banks and led to their suspensions.

Early nineteenth-century attributions of blame for the panics acknowledged some of these causal factors—others are clearly the products of a later historical perspective—but continued to intertwine marketplace explanations with moral and religious ones. Scholars of nineteenth-century American culture propose differing theories about when beliefs about the causes of failure began to change and the extent to which moral blame was still attached to economic failure during the first half of the nineteenth century. Ann Fabian, in her study of antebellum panic discourse, locates this shift in the period between the Panics of 1837 and 1857. Popular discourse in 1837, Fabian contends, still centered on religious explanations for the widespread disaster. Economic advice books mimicked sermons in their condemnation of the panic as divine wrath for the sins of greed and extravagant consumption. Failed investors were called to moral repentance as the basis for renewed commercial integrity (Fabian, "Speculation" 131–32). By 1857, Fabian argues, God's role in the panic was seen as more remote, as both religious and economic advice literature cast financial failure in terms of natural disasters such as storms and floods. Such weather metaphors acknowledged the destructive forces of the market but depicted them as natural, inevitable, and ultimately necessary for prosperity and beneficial to long-term growth (133). In Fabian's reading, the individual moral agency assumed and promoted in the 1837 discourse had virtually disappeared twenty years later, as acceptance of market and industrial capitalism overshadowed earlier moral concerns.

Daniel Feller, reading not economic advice or religious writing but legal documents and court decisions pertaining to debt and property rights, sees moral attitudes toward financial failure as having begun to change already by the turn of the nineteenth century. Between roughly 1775 and 1825, Feller contends, changes in U.S. law that increasingly favored commercial uses of property over agricultural claims and permitted seemingly unequal business contracts "both reflected and furthered Americans' emerging perception of competition and innovation as positive social values" (36). Such increasing openness to and encouragement of commercial risk at the legislative and judicial levels, Feller suggests, signals a declining moral stigmatization in relation to failure among the population at large.

Scott Sandage, on the other hand, in his treatment of the cultural history of failure in America, finds evidence of moral disapproval of failure throughout the antebellum period and beyond. Although the nation pursued structural solutions such as bankruptcy laws and the establishment of credit agencies to protect both individuals and society from the consequences of failure, even mid-nineteenth-century rhetoric, according to Sandage, continued to depict the individual who failed as marked by moral deficiencies, including greed, extravagance, dishonesty, laziness, or drunkenness (22, 61). One reason for defining failure in moral terms, Sandage notes, is that it enabled nineteenth-century society to blame loss or poverty on individual faults rather than on a flawed economic system or misguided policies (1). By the antebellum era, America's predominant self-image was that of a land of opportunity—a nation where boundless territory, inexhaustible resources, and unprecedented liberties made success possible for everyone. Failure threatened to undermine such cultural narratives of opportunity and success, belying the promise of perpetual growth and prosperity for all. As long as failure could be characterized as an individual's inability to benefit from the nation's promise, however, the American Dream remained intact. Discourse that attributed economic failure to individual failings such as greed, dishonesty, or laziness—what Sandage calls "moral masterplots" (60)—functioned thus to defend the market economy and maintain belief in the national narrative of progress and success. In times of panic, however, when failures became widespread and clearly not confined to a few easily scapegoated individuals, such moral masterplots tended to lose force and had to be combined with other explanations.

Increasing sectional strife over slavery in the late 1850s added a further dimension to the treatment of failure as a moral issue. Kenneth Stampp and James Huston note that Northern abolitionists portrayed the Panic of 1857 as God's punishment for the national sin of slavery. Many Southerners, meanwhile, blamed the crisis on Northern industrialism and "rapacious Northern merchants" (Stampp 230; Huston 59–62). Both sides seized upon the occasion of widespread failure to condemn their opponents' political and economic actions in moral terms, while justifying their own.

Panic Fiction's Attributions of Blame

What becomes clear from these accounts is that attitudes toward economic failure were in the process of changing precisely during the time that antebellum panic fiction was being written. Political rhetoric and the ideological needs of capitalism, as well as genuine cultural contention between religious and secular worldviews, made the role of moral responsibility for failure a matter of much debate. The panic novels in this study reflect a wide variety of attitudes, and while most panic authors cling to some form of moral explanation for failure, many also acknowledge financial and commercial factors outside the individual's control.

Lee's *Three Experiments of Living* makes one of the most direct correlations between individual immorality and failure. Although the Fulton family is not exactly villainous—that is, they do not seek to do wrong or harm others—they do abandon the virtuous path of charity and simplicity and commit the sins of greed and extravagance. Most significantly, their failure is also individualized: no national crisis sweeps their neighbors into failure; only the Fultons suffer loss, brought about directly by foolish investment practices and "living beyond the means" (as the novel's subtitle proclaims).

More frequently, as in Lee's *Rich Enough*, moral failings combine with economic circumstances beyond the protagonist's control to produce either individual or communal failure. Elizabeth Oakes Smith, for example, targets immorality in her *Riches without Wings* but stresses the national scope of the problem. While the wealthy Mason family clearly goes bankrupt as a result of their numerous vices—laziness, vanity, and lecherousness, as well as devotion to money—they are portrayed not simply as individuals but as embodiments of a materialistic spirit that Smith sees as a national shortcoming. In the introductory chapter, Smith's narrator laments that the entire "restless and enterprising" American population responds to the country's untapped potential by engaging in the accumulation of wealth rather than "intellectual, benevolent, or domestic pursuits" (12–13). Thus, while Smith does not absolve the failing individual from moral responsibility, she does suggest that failure, no less than the desire for wealth that brings it about, is systemic as well as individual, related to national circumstances and economic policies.

A number of panic novels attribute economic failure to the fraud, injustice, or simply the imprudence of others, making the failed individual a victim rather than the agent of their own loss. Such is the case with Eliza Dupuy's Mr. Harrington in *The Planter's Daughter*, a decent but naïve landowner who is enticed into a speculative scheme that goes awry by a professional speculator deliberately intent on ruining him. Emma Embury's merchant Charles Latimer in *Constance Latimer* is brought to failure in less melodramatic circumstances, by trusting his business affairs to agents who prove faithless and imprudent, but the portrayals are similar. Although both Mr. Harrington and Mr. Latimer are guilty of misjudgment (and Harrington also guilty of extravagance), their failures are not depicted as the consequence of their own moral lapses. Such a characterization of failure, by blaming "others," allows panic authors to absolve of moral culpability those who have experienced loss without completely removing the moral dimension of economic failure. For the Harrington and Latimer families, failure is indeed seen as divine visitation, but it is in the form of trial rather than punishment.

While adhering partially to the traditional link between failure and morality, Embury's explanation for failure also encompasses a more secular acceptance of economic loss as a natural occurrence. Mr. Latimer's financial position, weakened by the debts incurred by his agents, is ultimately brought to ruin by "one of those seasons of commercial distress which occasionally occur in all mercantile countries, and are felt in every quarter of the globe" (50). By naturalizing panic as a "season" and universalizing it as a worldwide phenomenon, Embury distances economic loss from the individual moral agency that she had previously invoked. "Commercial distress" is depicted as something that just happens, not a consequence of particular actions. An excerpt from *The Young Lady's Home*, an advice manual for young, unmarried women published just two years after the Panic of 1837, demonstrates this mode of viewing failure as resulting from purely economic rather than moral causes. Preparing to advise the young woman whose father has just failed, the author asks, "Has a change come over his prosperous days? and has the wealth that patient industry or daring enterprise had gained, or that had been inherited from honored ancestors, passed away like the dew of the morning? What will you do to comfort him, during the heat and burden of this day of trials?" (Tuthill 116). The neutrality of the word "change," as well as the suggestion that wealth can simply dry up like dew in the sunshine, represents economic loss as occurring virtually without human agency. The author's emphasis is on neither cause nor blame but on how young women should respond when economic failure occurs.

One of the striking things about panic fiction, in fact, is that even those novels that do assign moral blame for failure focus relatively little narrative attention on the financial details or the immediate circumstances of the crisis, but instead they move quickly from a climax of failure to the narration of recovery. Lee's description of the crisis in *Rich Enough*, succinct as it is, pays unusual attention to the actual "moment" of failure; many novels simply report the occurrence of loss or the family's "ruin," while in others, the actual crisis of failure occurs "off-page" before the novel begins or in the first few pages—serving thus not even as the story's climax but as its setting.[26] Thus, despite the crucial role of failure as the raison d'être for these novels and the narrative climax to their anti-speculation discourse, in terms of narrative space and emphasis it takes a backseat to portrayals of the economic practices that precede it and the ways in which characters respond to the challenges of its consequent losses.

One reason for this seeming gap in panic narratives may be that the financial manipulations surrounding the actual event of failure—for example, commodity pricing, the calling in of loans, and bank suspensions—are features of a masculine marketplace over which women, the principal protagonists of these novels, had little control. Part of the anxiety surrounding speculation and failure derived from the lack of control the female characters (and authors) of panic fiction had over any of the financial practices in a speculative economy and thus their vulnerability to sudden loss. Middle-class and elite women were intensely involved, however, in the formation of attitudes toward money, and they were certainly affected by the consequences of failure as much as men were. Thus it is in the events leading up to crisis and in responses to loss that panic authors locate the primary meanings of failure. Tellingly, it is the male characters in panic fiction who "fail," while the women, whether they are suffering victims or equally irresponsible spenders, seek ways to adapt and respond.

But the diversity of attitudes toward failure described above, especially given the nearly unison voice with which panic authors treat speculation, points again to the differences in rhetorical agenda among panic authors as a further explanation for this lack of focus on the moment of failure. While financial failure was a very real occurrence for many individuals and for American society at large during this period, and panic authors were clearly concerned with the literal effects of loss, failure also served in these novels as a way to represent other, broader sources of anxiety that varied according to region, time period, and individual author. Nationwide panics and the devastating financial losses they produced were traumatic occurrences in themselves that also intensified a variety of economic and social phenomena that were perceived as dangerous or harmful to particular segments of society—for example, increased social mobility, unstable class relations, economic disparities between regions of the country, and violent labor conflicts. Because panic tended to exacerbate or cause increased anxiety about such problems, it functions usefully—for readers today as well as for panic authors themselves—as a lens through which to view these other causes of anxiety.

Thus, the differences we might see in the depictions of failure's causes and its overall meaning can be attributed to panic authors' very different situations of writing and different rhetorical aims—that is, the particular economic and social circumstances that concern them in addition to panic itself and the visions of reform or action that they want to convey to readers. And the fact that they *have* such agendas—that they are writing to convince readers of particular courses of economic action—suggests why their focus tends to move rather quickly from the moment of failure to more detailed depictions of financial recuperation. Panic authors' rhetorical agendas are most clearly displayed in their representations of characters' responses to failure: what kind of recovery or ideal economic circumstance is imagined, how is that recovery achieved, and who are the agents of that recovery are all questions whose answers reveal much about the respective authors' fears, solutions, and overall economic and social philosophies.

The following four chapters examine the variations in panic fiction, demonstrating the ways in which political and social concerns, as well as differences among authors' regions, time periods, and class affiliations helped to produce distinct accounts of the meaning of failure and diverse models of behavior for responding to panic and economic loss.

two

Domestic Constancy

Preserving Class Identity in 1830s Panic Fiction

Hannah Farnham Sawyer Lee's *Rich Enough*, discussed in the previous chapter, was just one of a series of short novels about speculation and failure that Lee produced in rapid succession in 1837 as the economic crisis worsened. Her first novel, *Three Experiments of Living*, published several months before the bank closings in May, apparently hit a chord with readers' anxieties about financial instability. Although it seems initially to have escaped the notice of the major literary journals, many of whom did not review it until several months later, the novel proved phenomenally popular, selling more than one hundred thousand copies and ultimately going through as many as thirty editions.[1] While all of the novels targeted speculation as an irresponsible and dangerous practice, Lee's agenda clearly extended beyond simple moral warnings about the evils of risky investment. Repeated scenes in which female characters struggle with the changes brought by social mobility, as well as the models of response to panic that she presented for middle-class women threatened by loss, suggest that one of Lee's principal aims was to demonstrate in her fiction a middle-class female identity less vulnerable to the destabilization produced by speculation and failure. Many of the dynamics of Lee's larger agenda are illustrated in the following scene from *The Harcourts*, which appeared just prior to *Rich Enough* and was probably written during the height of the panic.

Like *Rich Enough*, *The Harcourts* narrates the story of a family bankrupted by a general panic brought on by a speculative economy, although in this case the merchant, Mr. Harcourt, is a man of integrity ruined by the actions of others. Lee represents the monetary inflation, financial irresponsibility, and frenzied emotionality of speculation symbolically here, shifting the focal point from mercantile machinations to a female world of fashion and gossip. Midway through the novel, young Anna Harcourt receives the gift of an expensive cashmere shawl from her uncle, just as her father is declaring bankruptcy. Despite her older sister's admonition to dress in accordance with their new circumstances, Anna is unable to resist showing off her new acquisition, wearing it to a wealthier acquaintance's house, where she exaggerates its eight-hundred-dollar cost to a thousand dollars and brags that "it was imported for me," without saying by whom. Gossip soon inflates the gift further to three one-thousand-dollar cashmere shawls (one each for Anna's sister and mother as well) and mistakenly attributes the largess to the bankrupt Mr. Harcourt. Spreading quickly, this rumor soon reaches a carpenter to whom Mr. Harcourt owes money, who, believing that Mr. Harcourt is buying expensive luxuries for his relatives rather than paying his workmen, erupts in a fury that the narrative likens to a "hurricane." He rushes to Mr. Harcourt's countinghouse and threatens that if he is not paid within a day, he will "warrant" Mr. Harcourt or have him arrested for nonpayment.

Before this confrontation can develop further, however, Anna's sister Sophia steps in to calm the storm and restore financial, emotional, and social order. First she sells an expensive gift of her own, a five-hundred-dollar set of cameos, in order to give her father enough money to pay the angry carpenter. Then she systematically traces the course of the rumor, explaining the true value and source of the shawl to each participant in this drama. Upon hearing the truth, the carpenter is "heartily mortified" by his behavior and begs Sophia to intercede with her father—a "true-born gentleman"—to reestablish their harmonious relationship. "Thus Sophia," the narrator concludes, "by the exercise of a little decision and prompt action, put a stop at once to a false gossip, which, trivial as it may appear, might yet have operated to the serious injury of her father" (85).

One source of anxiety demonstrated in this scene is clearly the perceived vulnerability of a speculative economy to rumor and action based on emotion rather than real knowledge. The rapidly increasing value assigned to the Harcourts' supposed shawl collection, based on misleading information and false assumptions, mimics the wild inflation of credit-spurred land and commodity values that preceded the Panic of 1837. In both cases, reported price does not correspond to any inherent value but is a product of imagination, of hearsay, of exaggerated desires and expectations. Mr. Harcourt's reputation for integrity proves fragile under such circumstances, as any notion of fixed truth or value is swept away.

A second and equally potent source of anxiety that surfaces here is a perceived instability in class relations. The middle-class Harcourts are shaken first by the values of the nouveau riche, whose materialism and snobbery tempt Anna into her boastful exhibition. Anna's attempt to emulate this rapidly rising class not only places her father in a false position but also grants precedence to a social grouping competing with the Harcourts for status. The family is then more seriously challenged by the economic dispossession of the working class, represented in this scene by the carpenter, and by its emerging consciousness of rights and power. Just as the carpenter's mindless fury at supposedly being cheated of his pay poses a potential physical threat to Mr. Harcourt, his apparent knowledge of, and willingness to exercise, his legal rights endangers the merchant's freedom, livelihood, and standing in the community. Both types of threat signify a blurring of the lines of hierarchy, a breaching of the unwritten rules of deferent behavior. Before he is placated, the carpenter's potential for destroying Mr. Harcourt seems to represent a fear that working-class anger could erupt uncontrollably in the wake of panic hardship, threatening the clear social demarcations that order urban society.

The solution that Lee provides to all of these anxieties is Sophia—the young middle-class woman whose exemplification of scrupulous truthfulness, self-sacrificing care, and calm rationality makes her the epitome of constancy in a world marked by unpredictable change. She is swayed neither by the false values that her sister falls victim to nor by her family's changing economic circumstances nor by the storms of passion that threaten her father's name and well-being. It is significant that Sophia's ability to assuage anxiety about fluctuating value and to restore the enraged laborer to a sense of subordinate position is based not primarily on sentiment (although she does certainly possess sympathy) but on competence and rationality. Both goals are achieved by her own ability to take economic action (selling the cameos) and by her knowledge and circulation of accurate financial information, which returns true value to the shawl and removes the carpenter's motivation for disrupting social order. Through her actions, Sophia restores her father's financial reputation, the community's accurate assessment of value, and patriarchal relationships between the middle and working classes.

This vignette from *The Harcourts* not only captures the essence of Lee's agenda but also typifies the anxieties, solutions, and narrative structure found throughout Northern panic fiction of the late 1830s. Novels such as Catharine Sedgwick's *The Poor Rich Man, and the Rich Poor Man* (1836) and *Live and Let Live* (1837), Elizabeth Oakes Smith's *Riches without Wings* (1838), and Emma Embury's *Constance Latimer* (1838)—all written at a time and within a society widely identified with a rapidly expanding commercial and industrial economy—similarly interwove their narratives about panic and failure with questions of social status and class identity. The perspective in these novels—undoubtedly reflecting the authors' own predominantly middle-class backgrounds, as well as that of their readership—is almost uniformly that of middle- or upper-middle-class women, often the wives and daughters of merchants or businessmen, whose fears of lost social position correlate with reported anxieties of the time regarding changing class relations and growing class antagonism between employers and employees.[2]

As discussed in chapter 1, speculation further raised the specter of social anarchy, as much contemporary commentary dwelt on the phenomenon of fortunes rising and falling without respect to traditional avenues of advancement, with the consequent social status of both speculators and non-speculators in constant flux. Although the reality of social mobility was much less dramatic than such reports would indicate, clearly the potential for relatively prosperous families to lose their position due to failure or to lose status relative to rising speculators was a source of some concern to many middle-class Americans in the 1830s.

One solution that Lee and her fellow panic authors employed to assuage such anxieties was to redefine female middle-class identity according to supposedly noneconomic qualities that comprised "domestic constancy" rather than by actual economic level. Qualities such as Sophia Harcourt's moral adherence to truth and courteous manners, for example, signal her middle-class status despite the family's loss of assets and thus reassure readers that failure does not automatically force one into the ranks of the "poor." A second mode of reassurance was the model such domestic constancy provided for a process of economic recovery. As Sophia's successful endeavor illustrates, women could be instrumental in guiding their families' return to prosperity through financial competence and rationality. Yet another—and very key—strategy for easing middle-class fears was to play up supposedly "natural" distinctions between the middle and working classes, often through repeated scenes of charity and the direction of domestic labor by middle-class mistresses. The carpenter's return to deference following Sophia's explanation typifies the kind of paternalistic interclass relationships constructed throughout 1830s panic fiction.

All of these ways of declaring middle-class stability were presented and amplified through a common narrative structure that contained the representation of emotion within sections devoted to speculation or some equivalent form of the desire for gain. When the novels turn to the narration of failure and efforts to recover from failure, they shift markedly in tone, allowing only minimal sympathy and discouraging the tears that sentimental novels would have promoted as the desired response to such hardship. Panic fiction heroines' consistent display of calm rationality, as they model the conduct necessary for economic recuperation, tends instead to elicit a similar calmness in the reader. The audience is thus invited to admire and imitate panic heroines rather than to weep over their difficulties. Such revisions of the sentimental tradition point to the overall rhetorical purpose of this era's panic fiction—the stabilization of middle-class identity, particularly for women. Rather than portraying middle-class women as suffering victims of panic to be sympathized with in their weakness, panic authors created models of strength and constancy, whose personal qualities, capabilities, and relations to the poor preserve their social identity even in the face of panic and failure.

From Middling to Middle Class: Antebellum Class Formation

Historians have documented that the development in northeastern cities of distinct middle and working classes, with clear-cut occupational and ideological differences—out of what had previously been simply "middling" and "poorer" sorts—occurred in conjunction with the rise of industrialism and modern capitalism in the early nineteenth century. More efficient methods of manufacturing and improved modes of distribution of manufactured goods disrupted the traditional artisanal system and, with it, traditional relations between master artisans and their journeymen. The historian Sean Wilentz explains that one of the major consequences of the shift from small shops to large factories was that division of labor—prompted by a primary concern for profit—replaced an artisan ethos of developing skill in a trade. Masters became foremen and owners rather than fellow workers and teachers, while journeymen were transformed into wage laborers making mass-produced items (30–33).

Throughout the 1820s and '30s, exploitation of Northern urban wage laborers through such means as piece-work systems, unhealthy factory conditions, and wage cuts led ultimately to a distinct working-class consciousness—an awareness by wage laborers of themselves as a group with separate, even antagonistic, interests from their employers. Politically and economically, workers expressed this consciousness through the organization of short-lived political parties and the trade union movement. A "labor critique" of America's economic system attacked the growing inequality between exploited workers and the employers who got rich off their labor and condemned those who profited without producing—speculators, bankers, capitalists of all stripes.[3] Working-class consciousness also manifested itself culturally from the 1830s on, as working men and women acted out the differences they saw between themselves and the employer class with dress, speech, and leisure activities.[4]

At the same time, a separate middle class was also emerging. Less definable than either the wealthy elite or the mass of wage laborers, America's middle class consisted loosely of those who worked in what Stuart Blumin calls "the nonmanual sector" (67). Middling merchants and professionals, not wealthy enough to be classed among the elite, as well as traditional nonmanual workers such as retailers and bookkeepers, were joined by men whose occupations developed from the increasing specialization of industry—including supervisors, distributors, and contractors. Many master artisans, especially those who owned larger shops, became part of this growing middle class as their labor shifted from production to supervision. Yet another sector arose from the expanding economy's increasing need for financial services—bankers, brokers, and insurers, among others.[5] Although the occupations making up what we now call the middle class were diverse, and although many former artisans continued to identify themselves with their trade, one thing that linked members of the middle class was their separation from manual labor. Blumin notes an "enormous disjuncture between public rhetoric [about the value of work] and the actual economic, social, and cultural circumstances surrounding manual work," including low pay and low status (109). Consequently, the status of nonmanual labor rose as it became increasingly distinguished from manual work—through physical separation within the workplace and mode of pay (salary), as well as by higher earnings.

Even more than such workplace distinctions, women and the domestic space they inhabited became the most significant symbols for an emerging middle-class identity. Many historians consider the rise of the middle class and the ideology of domesticity to be inseparable, since increasing affluence and the shift from home to factory production made new, noneconomic roles for middle-class women necessary and desirable, while domestic practices of child rearing and conservation of resources helped to maintain and perpetuate middle-class position. Blumin argues, in addition, that as public spaces became less marked by social deference, class distinctions began to be manifested more in the controllable, private space of the domestic interior as well as in social relations (179). From the 1820s onward, middle-class families established their differences from the working class through increasing residential segregation within cities and through the types and quality of furnishings inside their homes. Possession of specific kinds of furniture, carpets, or knickknacks, then, distinguished the banker's or business owner's home from that of the wage laborer, as well as the home's size and neighborhood.

More importantly, the middle-class (and especially the upper-middle-class) woman became both a marker and an enforcer of class divisions through her own separation from manual labor, her emphasis upon the emotional aspects of domesticity, and her display and expectation of proper manners. Whereas working-class women, even married ones, frequently had to supplement family earnings or support their families on their own through some form of wage labor—as well as attending to their own household work—middle-class women were increasingly defined, and defined themselves, by *not* working, thus affirming their freedom from financial need. Even within the home, household labor became the province of hired domestic servants, with the middle-class mistress serving as supervisor. The ways in which middle-class women performed their roles as wives and mothers also distinguished them from poorer women who did not have the time or resources to devote to domesticity. Christine Stansell, in her history of working-class women in nineteenth-century New York, notes a growing contrast between a middle-class emphasis on the home as private space and a more public working-class home life. While poor women often depended on their neighbors for material and emotional support and were obliged to send their children into the streets on errands, middle-class domesticity was increasingly marked by self-sufficiency and intimacy. A close relation between mother and children, wife and husband, separated from all others within the privacy of the home, became part of the middle-class domestic ideal, one not available to poorer women (Stansell 41).

The increasing class divisions in American antebellum society—both economic and ideological—did not entirely square with the nation's traditional ideals of equality and independence. By the mid-1830s, working-class advocates and the trade unions were attacking this disjunction between philosophical ideal and economic reality head on, accusing employers of promoting an unequal society by exploiting workers for their own gain, thus threatening the nation's republican foundations. Such direct critiques were largely marginalized within a narrow reform discourse, however, while the majority of Americans—and visiting foreigners—continued to characterize American society as egalitarian. Middle-class and wealthy Americans, in particular, reconciled obvious disparities of condition with ideals of equality through a rhetoric of easy social mobility. Such a rhetoric argued that class lines were not fixed but fluid and emphasized, as Blumin notes, "unlimited opportunities for workers to rise out of the working class to become entrepreneurs and even wealthy capitalists" (119). We can see the established nature of this belief in socioeconomic fluidity in repeated assertions by economic writers in their arguments about wages and wealth creation. Henry Carey, in a typical example from his 1835 "Essay on Rates of Wages," notes the lack of impediments to advancement, saying, "the people have the confidence that they will have the enjoyment of almost the whole product of their labour undiminished by taxation, and that moderate exertion, with economy, will lead to independence" (145). Samuel Newman, also writing in 1835, goes even further, declaring that "the road to wealth is alike open to all" who are willing to be industrious and frugal (91).

But claims of unlimited opportunity for social and economic advancement were probably more fiction than fact. Barriers between classes were in fact quite rigid by the 1830s already, and movement between the lowest and highest classes was rare. A few men, including Andrew Jackson himself, were genuinely "self-made men," having risen from poverty to wealth by their own exertions; most of the wealthy during the Jacksonian era, however, had inherited their fortunes. According to Edward Pessen, "only about 2 percent of the urban socioeconomic elite were born poor," with 6 or 7 percent from middling families and the vast majority "descended of parents and families who combined affluence with high social status" (86–87). The wealthiest Americans were also seemingly the most immune from downward social mobility, despite common claims that rich and poor frequently exchanged places. Even during the Panic of 1837, few of the wealthiest Bostonians suffered losses, and many even became richer. In contrast, more than one-third of those with modest property—the emerging middle class—suffered serious losses in the panic. Pessen concludes that social mobility, both before and after the Panic of 1837, was actually quite circumscribed. The middle and working classes faced the possibility of lost property or jobs in economic downturns, but the majority could expect to rise only modestly and usually within their class and "between closely related occupations" (89).

Nevertheless, social mobility remained a commonly held assumption and a source of considerable anxiety as well as hope. If the working class bore the brunt of physical suffering during and after the antebellum panics, the middle class surely was the site of the greatest uncertainty regarding social and economic status. Even before 1837, what Blumin calls "the elusive middle class" was contested terrain, still in the process of being formed and defined (1). As nonmanual workers increased in number, they defined their social position largely in opposition to those both above and below rather than according to any specific criteria. Just who belonged to this emerging social formation was an open question, especially when individuals' economic circumstances fluctuated. Were retail and office clerks, who initially earned less than skilled manual workers, part of the middle class by virtue of their nonmanual duties and potential for advancement? What about small master craftsmen who owned their own shops and employed workers but still participated in the manual aspects of their trade? Those of established middling status and a relatively high degree of education coexisted uneasily in this social terrain with newly prosperous manufacturers and businessmen.

Even the term "middle class" and the history of its usage suggest the elusiveness of the concept it purports to define. Karen Halttunen contends that whereas the eighteenth-century term "*middling class* referred to people who occupied a static social position between the extremes of peasantry and aristocracy," by the 1830s, "to be middle-class was to be, in theory, without fixed social status,"—to be, in effect, on a steady upward path to prosperity (29). Blumin notes further that while the term "working class" was used frequently as early as the 1820s, "middle class" did not appear unequivocally as a descriptive label until the 1850s, suggesting that middle-class identity remained relatively unfixed throughout the antebellum decades (242–49).

While periodicals of the 1830s carry many laments about the destabilization of money seeking, and complaints about threats to national order posed by the uneducated poor, one essay in particular, published in the March 1836 edition of *American Ladies' Magazine*, captures the uneasiness of many toward what the anonymous author calls "the spirit of enterprise"—that is, widespread striving for social and economic advancement. While acknowledging such a spirit as a natural human desire and even, when "rightly directed and duly controlled," potentially beneficial to society, the author confesses "fears for the result" if the spirit of enterprise and progress is not balanced by an equal tendency toward "permanence," epitomized in the "abiding place" or home. Without such balance or control, the author concludes, "the spirit of enterprise, when it becomes the predominant and all-controlling influence in any community, is hostile to the stability of that community, and therefore unfavorable to its best interests. . . . It labors not so much to keep what is in possession, as to obtain what is not. It attributes too much to time, place, circumstance; and not enough to truth and a contented mind" ("Spirit" 133). While the notion of home as a restful counterpoint to the hustle of the marketplace was already emerging as a commonplace of domestic rhetoric, what strikes one in this passage is the anxiety expressed about instability to the "community." Relations among community members are seen to be threatened by uncontrolled efforts to "obtain what is not." While the wording of the essay makes it unclear whether the author has greater fears of the discontentment of the already independent (the middle class) or the social strivings of a lower class, either or both have the potential to disrupt the social status quo. Significantly, the author here employs the concept of home as a check to the constant pursuit of gain and a means of protecting community stability.

Given this pervasive anxiety about class position and social stability even before the panic, the economic losses that occurred as its result, and which fell disproportionately on the middle and working classes, made this already unstable middle-class identity seem even more vulnerable. If to be middle class was, by definition, to be rising, then panic and failure threatened the very basis for such identity, while loss of property and income removed or diminished purely economic distinctions between middle and working classes. Those class distinctions centered in the domestic domain thus took on even greater importance, and, as the above-cited article suggests and panic novels illustrate, women were seen as particularly responsible for maintaining the stability of their families' class status.

Redefining Class Identity: The Fiction of Hannah Farnham Sawyer Lee

Part of the cultural work of defining and maintaining class boundaries within societies has traditionally been done by literature. Historians of the novel such as Ian Watt and Nancy Armstrong laid the groundwork for our understanding of the novel as a genre that simultaneously reflected, promoted, and legitimated the rise of the middle class. Armstrong, in particular, calls attention to how the genre's emphasis on personal qualities advanced a middle-class agenda, arguing in *Desire and Domestic Fiction* that eighteenth-century English domestic novels established the middle-class household as culturally desirable by redefining what was desirable in the female. By portraying personal qualities achievable by middle-class women (such as domesticity, purity, and strength of mind) as more desirable than attributes available only to aristocratic women (such as wealth, position, title, and family), domestic novelists helped to construct both the modern concept of the individual and a middle-class system of values.

The panic fiction of the 1830s operated in much the same way in its narratives of loss and recovery, although nineteenth-century American authors, not challenged for cultural supremacy by an aristocracy, tended to be more concerned about contestations of middle-class identity and the potential threat from an increasingly visible and vocal working class.[6] Panic authors sought a kind of rhetorical stability for their middle-class heroines by binding their social identity to personal qualities rather than to economic status. To be "respectable" or "genteel"—adjectives associated with the emerging middle class—depended not on material possessions or money, these novels suggested, but on the possession of correct manners, education, and domestic values. Once these had been acquired, a woman would retain her middle-class identity even if she lost the original economic basis for her status. By divorcing these attributes from an economic basis, panic authors reassured readers that their own social status could remain intact despite financial fluctuations. Significantly, however, panic authors did not suggest that such noneconomic markers of gentility were therefore available to those of no economic means—that is, the working class. Nor, for that matter, were they necessarily accessible to the very rich or those whose middle-class status was due to money alone. Indeed, even as they insisted upon the irrelevance of financial status to class identity, panic authors continued to invest middle-class identity with very particular relations to and attitudes toward money and possessions.[7]

To get a better idea of these relations and attitudes, let us turn once again to the novels of Hannah Farnham Sawyer Lee and examine them in greater detail. Little is known about Lee, despite the enormous popularity of her fiction. She was born in Newburyport, Massachusetts, in 1780, married a naval officer, and was widowed at age thirty-six with three daughters. She apparently did not start writing until the age of fifty but was quite prolific from that time until her death in 1865, producing about twenty books of fiction, history, and biography.[8] Although Lee was perhaps initially the least well known among those who wrote panic fiction in the 1830s—Smith and Embury both had literary connections, while Sedgwick was one of the most respected authors of the time—her novels, especially taken as a group, best capture the full range of the genre's concerns, from the deceptiveness of speculative gains, to the uncertainties of class position in a fluctuating economy, to appropriate relations with higher and lower social classes. In these novels, we can see both the undercurrents of anxiety and explicit proposals for warding off and recovering from economic failure.

Three Experiments of Living and *Elinor Fulton*

Lee's first foray into panic fiction, *Three Experiments of Living*, is the story of Frank and Jane Fulton, a young Boston physician and his wife, who start out poor, become prosperous, then are "ruined" by commercial and domestic debts. The three subtitles, which also serve as part titles within the novel—*Living within the Means*, *Living up to the Means*, and *Living beyond the Means*—foretell the direction of the narrative and provide its structure.

Part one introduces Frank and Jane, whose very names suggest honesty and plainness, as living out a republican ideal of simplicity, independence, industriousness, and concern for the public welfare. When Jane's uncle Joshua questions Frank about his ability to support a wife on his small income, Frank replies that "our greatest security for a living, will consist in our moderate desires and simple habits" (14). Perhaps intended to suggest a nineteenth-century Ben Franklin, Frank begins his career as a physician with neither money nor patients, gradually building up a practice through steady industry and the cultivation of a reputation. In order to attract patients, he advertises his willingness to treat the poor for free—a move said to combine "true New England calculation" with genuine benevolence (18). In the meantime, Jane displays equal virtue and resourcefulness, visiting Frank's destitute patients and procuring for them food, clothing, and fuel. The narrator suggests that they are indeed partners in the work of benevolence or, as Frank phrases it at one point, "consulting physicians" (20). In time, Frank's successes attract paying patients, including some of the city's leading citizens. His business increases until "the close of every year left them a small overplus, which was scrupulously invested for capital" (42). Frank and Jane are able to move out of their boardinghouse into a small home of their own, where they start a family and create a cozy domestic paradise.

Throughout this first section, Lee creates a compelling image of the ideal middle-class life—the Fultons' class status established by their progressive rise—as centered in the domestic realm and rooted in traditional republican values. Frank and Jane's "freedom" from debt and their simple lifestyle mark them as inheritors of the revolutionary legacy—an association reinforced by the narrator's insertion into the text of a supposedly actual letter describing President Washington's first public dinner as consisting of boiled mutton and a single shared glass of wine. The incompatibility of independence and luxury was a common theme of republican rhetoric seeking to diminish European cultural influence in America, and

Lee taps into that sentiment: "Shall we, who so much prize our independence, give up, what, in a political view alone, is dross, compared to independence of character and habits? Shall we, who can call master spirits from every portion of our land, to attest to the hard-earned victory of freedom and independence give up the glorious prize, and suffer our minds to be subjugated by foreign luxuries and habits? Yet it is even so; they are fast invading our land; they have already taken possession of our sea-ports, and are hastening towards the interior" (44). For Lee, however, the real threat of such "subjugation" is not its foreign origin but rather the tendency for a desire for luxury to disrupt social stability, as the remainder of the novel demonstrates. The Fultons' "independence" in part one contrasts sharply with their later subjection to the tyrannies of social aspiration and economic desire.

Jane comments early on in the first part of *Three Experiments* that she and Frank will "graduate" their needs to "what is around" them (16)—by which she implies that they will be content with what they have, but which her savvy uncle takes as meaning they will adapt their lifestyle to that of their neighbors. In the second part of the novel, "Living up to the Means," Uncle Joshua's prediction proves true. As Frank's practice and income continue to grow, the Fultons begin to acquire the trappings, the manners, and, most importantly, the values of the class of wealthy merchants whom Frank now serves. Whereas at first their principal use of their new affluence is to provide the best schooling for their children, under the tutelage of a social-climbing acquaintance, Mrs. Reed, Jane learns the importance of silver forks and a "centre-table" (63). In order to afford these household luxuries, and to do "justice" to her now successful husband by dressing fashionably, she is advised to pay her servants less and send her children to cheaper schools. While Jane makes these changes only reluctantly, Frank embraces them. He "pride[s] himself" on Jane's stylish appearance rather than appreciating her "virtues and amiable qualities" and takes pleasure in the "piquancy" of witty jesting in place of the sincerity that had once marked their intimate conversations. Most strikingly, Frank discourages Jane from giving to charity almost in the same breath as he encourages her to emulate her wealthier friends.

With each change that Frank and Jane make, they drift from the domestic and republican values that had marked their earlier life together toward a value system in which money is the ultimate measure. In place of caring for others—children, servants, the poor—and nourishing such inner qualities as sincerity, kindness, and appreciation for education, the Fultons increasingly value the material possessions that display their wealth, along with social relationships that help to advance it. Lee explicitly pits these competing value systems against each other, showing the choices that Frank and Jane make—between schools and bonnets, between charity and the "centre-table." Frank and Jane's new monetary concerns soon stifle their integrity and benevolence.

At the very end of part two, the Fultons' extravagance and new values finally draw them into actual speculation. Unable to meet their rising expenses, and finding that there is "nothing they could give up" (83), Frank decides to increase their income by investing their life savings in an "enterprise" that promises to yield 20 percent. The final section of the novel, "Living beyond the Means," traces the course of the Fultons' speculations—both financial and social—along the typical panic fiction pattern of boom and bust. For several years, the narrator tells us, Frank's speculations are successful, and the family's expectations soar. Frank borrows money from Mr. Bradish, the wealthiest merchant in the city, in order to buy and furnish a new house for his family, upon the assumption that its value will increase. Lee emphasizes the danger of such debt and the illusory nature of purchases made on credit in a series of conversations that question whether the house is actually theirs. Uncle Joshua, who serves as the novel's voice of reason and conscience, asks Jane whether the house is "paid for," and she assures him that it is; but later she repeats the question to her husband, forcing him to equivocate about the meaning of "paid" (102). Frank becomes increasingly obsessed with speculating, eventually giving up his profession in order to become a full-time partner in Bradish's mercantile concern. Simultaneously, the Fultons' social prospects widen and flourish as a result of their lavish spending. But just as they reach the pinnacle of their financial and social success—an elaborate coming-out ball for their oldest daughter, Elinor—the unstable foundation for that success collapses. "Mercantile speculations," the narrator reminds us, are subject to "sudden changes," and Frank's speculative empire, built almost entirely upon borrowed money and carefully cultivated appearances, comes crashing down (134). In disgrace, Frank heads west to attempt to recover his lost fortune and honor, while Jane and her children are left to survive on a small legacy from Uncle Joshua.

We see in this brief outline the same concerns about speculation that were discussed in the previous chapter: Frank's dependence on borrowed money makes him vulnerable to commercial downswings and thus to failure, while Frank and Jane's desire for money and status, which fuels Frank's speculative drive, goes hand in hand with their loss of moral virtue and republican values. Lee also emphasizes the contrast in social value between Frank's original profession as a physician, which requires hard work and results in the tangible benefit of healed bodies, and his later occupation of speculator, which promises relief from his "laborious life" but produces literally nothing. Lee reinforces such arguments against speculation with the same emotional, even frantic, tone that would later characterize *Rich Enough*. As she tries to keep up with her husband's colleagues in maintaining a stylish establishment, for example, Jane is frequently "feverish, anxious, and unhappy," while Frank is described variously as "dismayed," "harassed," and "anxious" about money. Both are often "peevish" and irritable with each other, in contrast with their earlier harmonious partnership.

But what is perhaps most striking about *Three Experiments* is its conjunction between speculative economics and the instability of class identity. The restless discontent that the Fultons display throughout the latter two-thirds of the novel not only deliberately links Frank's speculation with a negative emotional state but also signals anxiety attendant upon constantly shifting social status. At first, the Fultons' rise from newlywed poverty is clearly depicted as desirable, demonstrating the rewards of their industry and benevolence. A comfortable income allows Frank and Jane to furnish a home and educate their children—that is, to acquire, enjoy, and pass on the essential elements of middle-class life and identity. Up to that point, they are contented and productive members of their society. But just how far they should rise, by what means, to what ends, and how fast, are the questions that drive the plot and are ones that Lee was evidently wrestling with. It is when the Fultons' income begins to be generated rapidly through speculation, for the purpose of emulating the wealthy and maintaining an upper-class lifestyle, that we see the changes in their behavior, emotional states, and relationship with each other. Some of these changes—in particular, Frank's growing admiration of fashion and his vanishing concern for the poor—simply signal Lee's disapproval of speculation, illustrating the correlation she makes between speculators' desire for rapid gain and their loss of moral values. Other, more subtle, alterations in the Fultons' behavior suggest, however, an attempt on Lee's part to represent the psychological toll imposed by rapid social mobility. Jane's initial reluctance to adopt fashionable spending priorities and the shame she feels when her upright uncle catches her avoiding his company mark changes to her originally open and content personality that are just as significant as the overt shifts in the Fultons' values or lifestyle. Jane is clearly uncomfortable with their changing social position and uncertain about what is required of her. Initially self-governing in preferences and behavior, Jane's growing reliance upon Mrs. Reed's tastes and opinions signal a loss of self-confidence and a sense of treading on foreign territory, being in a place where she does not belong. While Frank seems much more at ease and welcoming of their new circumstances, his increasing secretiveness about his financial affairs, in contrast to his previous openness with Jane, suggest that he also is experiencing some discomfort with their new status. The speed of their advancement, combined with being confronted with such a different set of values, has a disorienting effect on the Fultons, propelling them to a position in society that Jane, in particular, feels unprepared to occupy.

It is important to note here that the person who most directly leads the Fultons astray into a life of extravagance and material values is Mrs. Reed, the socially ambitious wife of a newly rich businessman, not the even wealthier and more established Mr. and Mrs. Bradish. Anxious to be received into elite society herself, Mrs. Reed aids Jane with decorating advice when she sees the Fultons as similarly rising in social status. But she proves to be a fair-weather friend, the first to abandon and defame the Fultons when crisis hits. Mrs. Reed's obvious social falseness marks her material values as similarly hollow and inscribes the "social climber" as the principal purveyor of moral corruption. Her encouragement of unwise spending and her later verbal disparagement of Frank and Jane do literally jeopardize the Fultons' social position, embodying the threat to social stability that panic authors see in speculation. In fact, Mrs. Reed serves simultaneously as a figure for the uncultivated speculator who crashes genteel middle-class society and for the lure and the danger of speculation itself. Her enticement of the Fultons, followed by rejection and ridicule, mimics the volatile behavior of a speculative venture. Thus her threat to social stability is twofold—changing the character of the middle class through her own entrance into it and bringing about the ruin of other members who emulate her greed and extravagance.

Frank and Jane's own social mobility proves dangerous primarily to themselves, their eventual ruin depicted as an individual failure that does not bring down other merchants. But Lee briefly acknowledges here the devastating consequences of panic and failure for the working class as well. When Jane seeks to comfort herself after the crash with the remark that "we have injured nobody but ourselves," a wiser friend reminds her that the merchant's failure is felt by the tradesmen—and women—who go unpaid for their services. The "women who go out to daily labor, and who have families of children depending upon them for bread" suffer the most from economic failure when the middle and upper classes are unable to pay their bills, this friend suggests (137). Such attention to the working class as victims of panic is rather unusual in panic fiction for reasons that are discussed later in this chapter. One reason for its inclusion here, I would argue, is to forestall any reader's potential response of sympathy toward the Fultons for their losses, redirecting that sentiment briefly toward the working class, but also signaling that a different kind of response is being called for.

The moment of failure itself is characteristically brief in *Three Experiments*. On the eve of his daughter Elinor's coming-out ball, Frank simply announces to Jane, "We are ruined!" (132). She has seen that he is worried, but neither Jane nor the readers are provided with any specific information about what is happening to Frank's investments or any explanation in financial terms for the ultimate collapse. Perhaps this is because the preceding narrative told readers all they needed to know about the reasons for Frank's failure, or perhaps Lee was not conversant with such details. In any event, one effect of such limited narrative space being granted to the description of failure is to reduce a reader's emotional response to it. Following the lengthy buildup of suspense and anxiety engendered by the narration of Frank's speculation, the announcement of ruin is almost anticlimactic, turning the reader immediately toward the practical aftermath—what will they do now?

Jane's own response to Frank's news is certainly emotional—she cries "seas of tears" and is later depicted feeling sorry for herself and her children—but the narrative gives Jane little chance to wallow in self-pity and gives readers even less chance to indulge in sympathetic sorrow. Immediately following her husband's announcement, Jane must pull herself together to carry on with the planned ball, acting as if nothing has happened. Once the news has become public, none of the book's other characters provide a model of sympathy. Some of Jane's supposed friends pretend sympathy but denigrate her behind her back; the only truly kind friend rebukes Jane's self-pity by calling her attention to the unpaid tradesmen and women. Readerly sympathy for the victims of financial failure is thus blunted by this character who treats pity as an inappropriate response.

The abrupt end of the novel immediately following Frank's failure and the ball reinforces this curtailment of emotional response. The story picks up again in a sequel, *Elinor Fulton*, which finds the Fulton women coping with straitened circumstances after some time, perhaps a period of months, has elapsed. Failure thus becomes essentially a turning point in the Fultons' saga—a moment that allows Lee to turn from narrating the dangers of speculation to outlining the necessary steps in the process of economic recovery. The grief and fear accompanying financial loss are not completely erased from either text—Jane Fulton's anxiety and self-pity provide poignant moments. But such representation of emotion is cut short, allowed only limited expression before the narrative moves into its next phase. Readers' responses are similarly managed, quickly redirected from sympathy to identification with the practical agents of recovery.

The principal agent of recovery for the Fulton family, as the sequel's title indicates, is their oldest daughter, Elinor. Lee executes her narrative move from speculation and failure to recovery, and from frenzied spending and investment to rational economizing, in part by shifting her focus from the characters who speculate, overspend, and fail to others who are capable of bringing the family economy under control. Specifically, she gives the responsibility for maintaining the domestic values that others are to emulate and for establishing the domestic arrangements that will ensure economic and class stability to the daughters of speculators—younger, middle-class female characters like Elinor Fulton and

Sophia Harcourt of *The Harcourts*. By endowing young women like Elinor and Sophia with the steadfast moral character and domestic competence that their mothers have either lost (Jane Fulton) or apparently never possessed (Mrs. Harcourt), Lee suggests that hope for a more stable future lies with a younger generation, untouched by the speculative economics that have corrupted their parents.

Significantly, it is daughters rather than sons who play this role in Lee's novels. Just as the disruptive event of panic provided authors like Lee with an opportunity to engage in economic discourse, within panic novels a father's failure offers the chance for daughters to wield social and economic influence that their youth and gender would otherwise make impossible. While their moral strength and domestic capability make them admired during times of prosperity, these same qualities enable their possessors to assume family leadership when crises occur. With the fathers of panic fiction generally absent from home attempting to repair their financial affairs and reputations, daughters like Elinor step out of assigned roles of subservience and rise to the challenge of guiding their families to a moral and economically rational lifestyle.

One of Elinor's tasks is the practical work of implementing a systematic plan of scaled-back expenditure and the repayment of debt. Having moved from the large house that Frank had been buying on credit to a much smaller home bequeathed to them by Jane's Uncle Joshua, the family's living arrangements have been greatly simplified. In addition to doing most of the housework in order to save money on domestic servants, Elinor directs both their clothing supply—mending and altering hand-me-downs for the younger children rather than purchasing new garments—and their diet, described as akin to the austere "Graham system" (38). To support the family in her father's absence, she gives piano lessons. Throughout this process of adaptation, Elinor maintains a calm and cheerful decisiveness, functioning as her mother's voice of reason and conscience, discouraging Jane's repeated yearnings for a renewed social life by insisting that the family live scrupulously within its slender means. Elinor's efforts do not produce immediate financial rewards, of course, since a dramatic return to prosperity would run counter to the message of slow and steady growth that Lee's fiction promotes. Instead, her fiscal measures are marked by self-restraint, in desires as well as in actual spending, suggesting a model of restrained growth for the national as well as the household economy.

Elinor's management also extends to the affective as well as to the domestic. Brief scenes of emotional display are quickly contained in this phase of the narrative, serving as models in miniature of the containment effected by Lee's panic narratives as a whole. When Jane Fulton confesses to her daughter that she has "shed many tears over" her unpaid household debts, for example, Elinor's own eyes fill with tears momentarily, but her next response is to take the roll of bills from her mother, pay each creditor in turn from her earnings as a piano teacher, and return the receipted bills. While this is certainly a sentimental moment for the reader, Jane's tendency to cry over her problems is implicitly reproved by Elinor's practical response. Such emotional reactions to panic are thus exposed as inappropriate and replaced by rational and systematic action.

Elinor's most important function in the novel, though, is to embody the constancy, or stability of middle-class identity, that Jane Fulton could not maintain in the course of her husband's successes and failure. In contrast to Jane's self-doubt and emotional disintegration, Elinor sustains the family's integrity through her own unchanging character. Although the family's smaller home in an unfashionable neighborhood signifies their fall, her even temperament, genteel manners, and dutiful housekeeping remain enduring symbols of the family's status. This is particularly emphasized in a scene in which Mrs. Reed stops to call at the Fulton's new home after months of neglect. As Jane trembles in anticipation of the shame of being seen in such humble circumstances by her former acquaintance, Elinor reassures her mother with a "quiet self-possession" (43). "What if it is Mrs. Reed?" she asks, "she is nothing to us; you know we are in our own house" (44). Elinor's reminder establishes their domestic proprietorship as a claim to social equality. Throughout the visit that follows, she remains polite in the face of Mrs. Reed's patronizing compliments on their "pleasant snug little room" but is never servile and, in fact, displays a sense of moral and intellectual superiority to Mrs. Reed's shallowness and insincerity (45). When Mrs. Reed attempts to buy her piano, Elinor refuses the offer without explaining the instrument's role in their daily survival. Despite their financial disparity from the wealthy Reeds, the Fultons retain their claim to gentility on a variety of grounds provided largely by Elinor—a neatly cared-for home, courteous manners, moral authority, and the possession of such symbols of culture and learning as the piano.

The Fultons' social constancy is later confirmed by their younger daughter Julia's engagement to young Henry Bradish, the son of the city's wealthiest merchant. Although by this time Frank has returned from the West with the means to pay his creditors, and the Fultons' economic circumstances are looking up, Lee makes it clear that this relationship began during the Fultons' period of poverty. But rather than depicting the engagement as a social leap or even a fortuitous return for the Fultons to the social world they had previously inhabited, Lee treats it simply as the natural alliance of two people with compatible tastes and character. Despite their lack of money, the Fultons maintain a middle-class status throughout the novel that allows them to move easily back into social intercourse with wealthier families. A social constancy based on moral character, education, and domesticity successfully counterbalances the family's economic loss and makes future prosperity possible.

The Harcourts

The third of Lee's panic novels, *The Harcourts*, covers much of the same ground as *Three Experiments* and *Elinor Fulton*. It depicts a merchant's family living beyond their means, aspiring to a higher social status within a society that measures value according to wealth. When Mr. Harcourt's business fails, the family is forced to abandon pretensions and return to a simpler lifestyle. In *The Harcourts*, however, the principal culprits are women; extravagant household spending and vain pretenses of wealth—such as Anna's ill-advised display of the cashmere shawl, detailed earlier in this chapter—replace financial speculation as targeted forms of irresponsible economic behavior. Although Mrs. Harcourt's spending is not blamed for her husband's collapse—that is attributed to the failure of another mercantile house that owed him money, causing him to be unable to pay his own commercial debts—her extravagance appears as a form of speculation in that it is supported not by present economic reality but by the appearance of wealth and hope for future gain.

As in Lee's earlier novels, *The Harcourts* centers on anxious questions of social identity: What makes one middle class or upper middle class? What is (or should be) the relationship between money, manners, and social position? How can one negotiate the ever-changing terrain of social status in a world where fortunes are won or lost daily through speculation? The Harcourts occupy a very tenuous position within a clearly upper-middle-class social circle, supported by a much lower level of actual income than those with whom they socialize. Mr. Harcourt was the son of a wealthy man and, we are told, began his married life in a "style of living better suited to his father's wealth than his own" (16). Since he inherited only a small portion of his father's money, however, the family's expenses soon outstripped his income, and they were forced to economize. But because Mrs. Harcourt is "fond of style" and wants to retain her position in society, she has devised numerous ways to scrimp while maintaining an "appearance of wealth" (18). As the novel opens, for instance, Mrs. Harcourt and her two daughters are sewing in the only warm room in the house, when some fashionable visitors arrive. Although the family room would clearly be the most comfortable place to receive guests, Mrs. Harcourt insists that a fire be made quickly in the parlor, and she entertains the guests there despite the lingering chill, which she blames on a servant. She does not want to reveal that they have been doing their own sewing and heating only part of the house in order to save money. Similarly, she sells the family's horses but keeps the private carriage and hires horses of the same color to fool any spectators (17).

Mrs. Harcourt's annual dinner party, which combines excessive expenditure with the pretense of wealth, displays her greatest folly. Attempting to equal, if not outdo, a recent party given by the newly wealthy Winwoods, she overspends her budget on a fantastic array of confectionery and ices, including "The Fairy Tree," a vision of candy "jewels" hung upon branches of sugar. If these "mock gems," so quickly consumed, serve as a subtle emblem of ephemeral wealth, Lee reiterates that message more forcefully when a clumsy guest demolishes the "beautiful Russian palace of ice" before it can be served (52). For all her efforts, Mrs. Harcourt is left with nearly ninety dollars in bills she cannot pay and, the narrator informs us, has failed to fool her guests, some of whom are overheard making disparaging remarks about people who give parties when they can't afford to "have every thing as it ought to be" (51).

Thus, we can see that Anna's attempt to pass off her uncle's gift as a signifier of the family's wealth and prestige is part of a larger pattern within the novel. Both she and her mother misrepresent the family's financial position in order to maintain a social identity unsupported by economic assets. Such recurrent imagery of appearance, illusion, and misrepresentation in relation to money certainly suggests some anxiety on the author's part about potential loss. Wealth "gained" through extravagance and pretense is no more stable a basis for permanent prosperity than that acquired through risky investment. In fact, the Harcourts' affectations of wealth make more concrete the claims Lee and other panic authors of the 1830s made about speculation as producing only "imaginary value" and thus exposing families of speculators to the threat of collapse and poverty.

But the imagery of illusion also serves to comment on the legitimacy of class status, distinguishing between those who truly "belong" in the middle or upper-middle class and those who claim membership without proper title. In the eyes of Mrs. Harcourt's fashionable dinner guests, she is the imposter, staking her claim to class status through false appearances of wealth. Even before the family's bankruptcy, Sophia and Anna are snubbed by guests at a party given by the nouveau riche Winwoods, a family made wealthy by Mr. Winwood's "daring speculations." Young gentleman acquaintances do not ask them to dance for fear of damaging their own standings in society, while the elder Miss Winwood pronounces that people in reduced circumstances "are no longer on an equality" with their wealthier neighbors (36, 26). Sophia, on the other hand (presumably speaking for Lee), advocates a standard of value that judges people according to qualities of character, such as grace, manners, and wisdom. Again, while such qualities clearly are associated with middle and upper socioeconomic classes, they are not tied to a monetary scale. In fact, Sophia's comparison of the "innate" grace of her old friend Mrs. Stanley with the "assumed gentility of the Winwoods" implicitly strikes out against a society in which wealth alone, without education or culture, can purchase status.

Sophia's role throughout the novel is very similar to Elinor Fulton's. Her own possession of moral character, domestic competence, and genteel manners anchors the family's claims to middle-class status and serves as a corrective to her mother's and sister's reckless extravagance and excessive emotionality. In short, she demonstrates the proper way to maintain class identity without economic backing. In the early scenes of the novel, for instance, Sophia repeatedly counsels honesty and simplicity, advising her mother to entertain guests in the comfortable but unpretentious family room rather than in the cold parlor and warning Anna not to wear the expensive shawl that gives a false impression of the family's financial standing. Had Sophia's family followed her moral example and embraced the simple home life that they could afford over the world of fashion to which they aspired, Lee suggests, the Harcourts' financial fall might have been lessened and their sense of social displacement alleviated. After the family's bankruptcy, which prompts Mr. Harcourt to declare a need for retrenchment, it is Sophia who takes charge of the family's economizing efforts. She helps her father to find a smaller rented home to replace their three-story mansion, dismisses the hired cook, and chooses the furniture to be moved to the new house. She also systematically culls through the household items, deciding which are unnecessary for their new circumstances—for example, the blancmange moulds, large preserving kettles, chandeliers, and Persian carpets—and helping her father to arrange their sale. Once the family is established in their new home, Sophia assumes the role of domestic manager, her economizing symbolized by serving Indian-meal cakes at tea that require "neither eggs, milk, nor butter" (97).

Even more than Elinor, Sophia functions as the narrative's emotional regulator, her rational imposition of order on the household and her personal unflappability, as demonstrated in the shawl episode, counteracting the emotional excess produced by panic in the forms of middle-class grief and working-class rage. In addition to calming the enraged carpenter, Sophia comforts her mother and sister, reconciling them to a humbler lifestyle. At one point, Mrs. Harcourt implies that Sophia is able to accomplish the tasks required by the transition because she is sentimentally deficient—"not capable of feeling" the family's loss. Lee suggests, however, that Sophia does indeed *feel* for their plight but that she also *knows* that retrenchment is the only rational solution—that is, she places reason above sentiment as a solution to the problems of panic and failure.

By placing characters like Sophia Harcourt and Elinor Fulton—agents of recovery rather than victims of loss—at the center of her narratives, Lee subtly rejects sentiment or sympathy as an adequate response to an event as catastrophic as panic. Because Elinor and Sophia show little evidence of suffering, and instead succeed admirably in restoring their families' psychological and financial well-being, the intended responses from readers seem likely to have been admiration and emulation rather than sympathy. Rather than a sentimental outpouring, in short, Lee's novels call for readers to protect their own households from financial loss through similarly rational steps.

Unlike *Elinor Fulton*, however, in which the title character is a sufficient model in herself for the kind of domestic constancy that keeps middle-class identity intact in the face of loss, *The Harcourts* reinforces Sophia's example with two additional models of social and economic behavior for readers to admire and/or emulate—one that might loosely be considered "republican," the other specifically Christian. The first is personified by the Wentworths, a family of old and established fortune, whose entitlement to "respect and attention," according to Sophia, is based on their "intellectual refinement and moral worth" and not for any "extrinsic possessions" (114–15). In contrast to the tinselly, imitative luxury of the speculating Winwoods, the Wentworths represent all that is "real." Their wealth, presumably inherited, is not subject to the whims of the market; their furniture is plain but "massive"; most important, their manners are genuine, arising from true feeling, not the hypocritical fawning of fashionable society. Despite their wealth, the Wentworths value simplicity; they prefer their country place to all the excitement of the city and choose to become acquainted with the Harcourts only after the latter have given up their pretensions to wealth. Thus the Wentworths appear to represent both a nostalgic vision of a time before economic self-interest and competitiveness permeated American society and a kind of dreamed of financial security that can afford to disregard the outward manifestations of money. Their way of life and mode of social relations offer legitimacy to a middle-class or even upper-middle-class identity far removed from the fashionable lifestyles of a speculative economy's new moneyed classes.

But the Wentworths' withdrawal from society cannot adequately exemplify appropriate economic behavior in a world seemingly governed by turbulent market forces, nor can their untouchable wealth provide an adequate model for the vast majority of middle-class readers whose assets were all too vulnerable in economic downswings. As a more accessible guide, Lee introduces in the last three chapters the Harcourts' new next-door neighbor, Mr. Morven. Described by Mr. Harcourt as one "who carries the unbending morality of the gospel into his business,"

Morven possesses "credit" in its original sense—a sound reputation for integrity and dependability (131).[9] Where old family and educated taste evince the Wentworths' solidity, the Morvens' values are undergirded by the bedrock of "Christian principle" (133). It is this Christian merchant who teaches Mr. Harcourt how to resume his business safely, successfully, and virtuously, while his daughter Ellen provides Sophia with a spiritual grounding for the independence and virtue that had previously derived from "her own reason" (134).

Curiously, while the majority of *The Harcourts* centers on household economics—both the culpable extravagance of Mrs. Harcourt and Sophia's economizing—Lee shifts rather abruptly in the final chapters to the most explicit exposition of commercial principles and investment advice to be found in any of her novels. This shift and the fact that *The Harcourts* was published just two months after the bank suspensions of May 1837 raises the possibility that the panic struck while Lee was in the midst of writing the novel, causing her to change her focus from prophesying the dangers of overspending and insincerity to detailing the causes of business failure. In any event, with Mr. Morven as her mouthpiece, Lee lays out at some length a manifesto for appropriate engagement in market economics. In answer to Mr. Harcourt's inquiry as to the "secret" of his "impregnable safety" throughout periodic downswings, Morven replies:

> There is no secret or mystery in it, my friend. It is so plain, that "he who runs may read." I commenced a moderate business in proportion to my capital. As my profits increased, I increased my business, but not in an equal ratio; for it has been my rule to lay by a portion of the profits every year in some safe investment as a security against unforseen losses. This was always the fund which I had recourse to in times of commercial distress, and this has often enabled me to assist those who were worth twenty times as much as I was. I have resisted all temptations to take advantage of my credit by extending my business, for I always preferred small but certain profits to magnificent probabilities that might never be realized. . . . This, my dear Mr. Harcourt, is the history of my past course; and my plan for the future is to retire from commercial life during the present year, as I have realized a competency. It is my belief, and I have drawn it both from revelation and from reason, that it is the duty of every man who has acquired a moderate sufficiency to withdraw from the field and give place to others. No man ought

> to take more than his reasonable share. Like the manna in the desert, every man should gather according to his need, for all that is gathered over will corrupt and be corrupted. (138–39)

Through Morven, Lee recommends caution, gradual growth, and only moderate ambition. Morven's philosophy, stated elsewhere, that a merchant ought never to "extend his credit beyond his capital," espouses opposition to speculation, since such investment does not require future gain to pay for itself (132). The daring speculator Winwood, who finds Morven's business practices "plodding" compared to the "glorious excitement" and "noble game" of million-dollar deals, voices the opposite philosophy (141). In the end, of course, Winwood ironically loses everything, while the Morvens and the Harcourts retire comfortably on their moderate "competencies."

Lee's dual focuses in the novel—Sophia's domestic constancy and Mr. Morven's business principles—suggest the need for a partnership between masculine restraint in investment and feminine agency in household management. Middle-class stability, the author proposes, depends upon both commercial and domestic practices that follow a rational course and adhere to moral precepts. *The Harcourts'* happy ending, notably, rewards those who embrace such practices with the capacity to maintain a middle-class existence rather than with fairy-tale wealth.

One of the most noticeable features of 1830s panic narratives is their predictability. Acts of speculation will build upon each other until the resultant "paper fortune" collapses, bringing failure and disgrace. Once fallen, the family will revert to a simpler lifestyle, relinquishing symbols of its former falsely assumed status and moving step by logical step toward recovery through the repayment of debt and the reform of spending habits. A modern reading sensibility tends to reject such predictability as unoriginal and dishonest—contending that it warps actual experience to fit a pattern designed to engineer a particular response. But for panic authors, such didacticism was precisely the point—repetition and familiarity in panic fiction were designed to shape readers' ideas about panic and to influence how they responded to it. Readers' learned anticipation that speculative ventures will lead fictional characters to financial ruin presumably led them to oppose speculation. Similarly, repeated associations of thrift with contentment theoretically encouraged readers to practice economy in their own homes.

In a time of economic turmoil, however, predictable narratives played an even greater role. They not only helped to shape readers' economic opinions and behavior but also provided reassurance that it was possible to negotiate the frightening upheaval of a national panic and the threat of personal failure and still arrive safely at a place of economic and social stability. The ability to predict a sequence of economic events suggests a corresponding ability to control such events in one's own life. By imitating the rational steps taken by Elinor Fulton and Sophia Harcourt during their crises—their acts of domestic downsizing, revisions of household expenditures, repayment of creditors through personal sacrifice, and maintenance of middle-class values of order and gentility throughout the ordeal—one could, these narratives implicitly promised, achieve a measure of economic recovery and retain a middle-class social identity. Predictable narratives further served as a kind of model for the transparency that panic novels advocated in both financial affairs and social relations. Stories that could be "seen through," or understood at face value, ran counter to the kinds of pretense that *The Harcourts* exposes and rejects; characters like Elinor and Sophia are what they appear to be, and there are no surprise endings to unsettle the social worlds of the novels. The particular character of panic fiction's predictability—that is, its culmination in happy endings versus the perhaps equally predictable heart-rending deaths of sentimental tales—arises, of course, from one of panic fiction's ultimate purposes, to calm anxiety and encourage rational economic behavior.

Undermining Character: Exposing Domesticity's Economic Basis

Such strategies as predictable narratives, happy endings, and redefined notions of what constituted middle-class female identity were not always enough, however, to erase the traces of economic anxiety that pervade panic novels of the 1830s. Despite authors' implicit claims about the ability of domestic character to stabilize middle-class identity, their texts often betray the fact that neither domestic space nor the personal qualities that comprise domestic character are ever completely independent of economic circumstances. The underlying economic basis for the middle-class home and its values poses an often unarticulated, but still quite discernible, threat to panic authors' claims of constancy.

The concurrent rise of an American market economy and the development of domestic ideology have been well documented by historians such as Mary Ryan and Stuart Blumin, who argue that domesticity functioned as a necessary corollary to capitalism, enabling the propagation of middle-class marketplace values within the home. Gillian Brown furthers this connection between the capitalist marketplace and the domestic sphere, contending that characterizations of the home as a place of stable value—separate from and even opposed to the turbulence and competitiveness of the market—actually made it complicit with economic expansion by allowing greater economic risk in the marketplace. "Maintaining a site of permanent value," Brown argues, "the domestic cult of true womanhood facilitated the transition to a life increasingly subject to the caprices of the market.

The confidence of encomiums to the virtues of womanhood and home simultaneously sublimated and denied anxieties about unfamiliar and precarious socioeconomic conditions and about the place of the individual within those conditions. In the midst of change the domestic sphere provided an always identifiable place and refuge for the individual: it signified the private domain of individuality apart from the marketplace" (3).

If the domestic sphere provided a fixed basis for masculine individuality, however, Brown's reading of Catherine Beecher suggests that it functioned somewhat differently for women. Noting that women were paradoxically excluded from the selfhood rooted in the private sphere they were responsible for maintaining, Brown turns to Beecher's *Treatise on Domestic Economy* for expressions of the relationship between women's identity and domestic stability. In her most famous work, Brown reports, Beecher "advanced an ideology of womanhood that also matched the expanding economy and the changing fortunes of individuals" (22). She admired women's ability to "harmonize with fluctuations," claiming that the exemplary woman's desires expand and contract with her husband's economic gains and losses. In Beecher's formulation, that is, the stability of the domestic sphere is largely predicated upon a fundamental *instability* in middle-class women's individual identities—their ability to adapt their economic desires to changing economic circumstances. Louisa Tuthill, author of an 1839 advice manual titled *The Young Lady's Home*, demonstrates a similar belief in women's adaptable identities when she admonishes her young readers to accommodate their mode of dress to their fathers' "worldly condition." When the father is wealthy, they ought to dress "splendidly," Tuthill says, in order to gratify his pride; when suffering loss, they are to be "indifferent" to appearance (116–17).

While a contingent level of expenditure and varying modes of dress might not be seen as determining or altering a woman's identity—and in fact are precisely the kind of money-based characteristics that most domestic writers cast as external to identity—both Beecher and Tuthill emphasize an internal dimension to such accommodation. In Beecher's view it is women's *desires* that expand and contract—what they actually want, not just what they get. Tuthill's call for "indifference" similarly suggests that women are to alter their attitudes and values, as well as their physical appearance, in response to economic status. Tracing the origins of a nineteenth-century feminine consumer ethic, Lori Merish identifies economic desire as a fundamental signifier of subjectivity in the writings of Scottish Enlightenment philosophers such as Adam Smith and David Hume, who influenced nineteenth-century American economic thought. Women's subjectivity in particular, she notes, was seen as constituted in faculties such as "taste," which govern the selection of commodities. Thus women's increasing consumer role,

Merish contends, not only enabled the advancement of trade and civilization, as the Scots argued, but also functioned as an expression of female subjectivity within American society (31, 18). Assuming economic desire, therefore, to be an important component of antebellum women's identities, we can see competing messages in the advice of domestic writers such as Beecher and Tuthill. Middle-class women are to maintain domestic stability by embodying unchanging interior qualities, but at the same time, their tastes and desires for material objects are to be infinitely adaptable to the vicissitudes of family income—valuing expensive, high-quality goods when their husbands or fathers can afford them, preferring modest furnishings when income drops.

The majority of panic novels come closest to acknowledging fears that character or identity might change with altered economic circumstances in their portrayals of the difficult adjustments made by middle-aged women. Characters like Lee's Jane Fulton and Mrs. Harcourt temporarily lose their self-possession when confronted with the need to tailor their tastes and expectations to reduced financial circumstances. For both women, the physical adjustments to smaller houses and plainer furniture are less disturbing than the psychological effects of no longer being a person who is allowed to take pleasure in the possession of a new "centre-table" or in entertaining guests with costly refreshments. Jane, in particular, seems lost without the material bearings of her former status. Her uncertain sense of self becomes most apparent in relating to others, alternately shrinking from the imagined shame of facing previous acquaintances and haughtily claiming the same women as her "friends" when her daughter criticizes them (*Elinor Fulton* 53). Far from embodying constancy, Jane clearly flounders in her attempts to come to terms with her altered status, revealing a fundamental uncertainty about "who" she is.

While panic texts allow voices such as Jane's to express embarrassment, fears of social ostracism, and even confusion about identity in the face of failure, they also recontain such expressions—usually pretty quickly—casting them as evidence of moral weakness resulting from corruption. Jane's depression is acknowledged but not validated. Such aberrations from domestic constancy are depicted as needing to be either quenched or reformed. Characters who do embody constancy serve as models for both weaker characters and readers to imitate. Thus while panic fiction may intimate some connection between feminine middle-class identity and economic status, it manages to disavow such a link by painting it as aberrant, as manifested only in the absence or deficiency of proper domestic character.

The dependence of domesticity itself upon economic level, however—and I refer here to the arrangements of the home and performance of familial duties—is not so easily dismissed in panic fiction. It is difficult to depict such arrangements and duties without reference to the material possessions that furnish the domestic space and that distinguish homes belonging to members of different classes. Even the most antimaterialistic of panic novels include some description of domestic objects in their portrayals of the model post-panic home. Merish argues that nineteenth-century domesticity was in fact rooted in beliefs that the possession and proper care of appropriate consumer goods were essential to a specifically middle-class identity. Ownership of goods that were unavailable or unusable to a working-class population, such as books, musical instruments, finely made furniture, and artifacts of aesthetic value, emphasized the comparative refinement of middle-class individuals, while preference for domestic objects that promoted the comfort and nurture of others over those designed to display wealth distinguished middle-class consumers from a wealthy elite.

Beyond merely identifying class status, however, Merish notes that domestic consumption was crucial to the development of qualities that the middle class appropriated as its own, such as sociality, benevolence, emotional engagement, and good manners. Even simple objects like sets of chairs or diversified table implements served a "civilizing" function by promoting social occasions and the practice of complex manners (92); the domestic ideal's emphasis on beauty and comfort, Merish claims, increased "social sensibility" by stimulating emotion and fostering interests beyond the body (122).[10] Mere possession of domestic objects was not enough, however. Sentimental attachment to and loving care of such objects were what made such possession beneficial, since such attitudes demonstrated corresponding qualities of character. Nevertheless, while Gillian Brown's inaugural notion of "sentimental possession" emphasizes the transformation of "commodities" into "possessions" through a sentimental valuation that "purifie[s them] of their market origins" (47), Merish's model shows middle-class women unapologetically defining their status through consumption.

Panic authors resist the overt consumerism that Merish describes, but they do rely at times on material objects to convey the status and identity of characters. Acknowledging that economic loss requires changes in possessions, for instance, their novels often convert retrenchment into an opportunity for demonstrating domestic simplicity, contrasting the superficial glitter of the expensive items that must be given up with simpler furnishings that convey the essence of domesticity. In *The Harcourts*, "useless" objects such as chandeliers and vases are approvingly exchanged for an armchair and an "old-fashioned chintz-covered sofa," both suggesting the comfort and use value that Merish and Brown associate with appropriate middle-class consumption. Other specific objects that are retained following failure, such as Elinor Fulton's piano, symbolize the education, culture, or taste of the middle-class home. Elinor's refinement is defined partially by her musical skill and attachment to her piano, while her domesticity is evinced in part by the piano's prominent place in the home. Similarly, in Elizabeth Oakes Smith's 1838 novel *Riches without Wings*, the Cleveland family's middle-class gentility is signaled as much by its claims to "taste and intelligence" as by its evidence of moral qualities. Attractively arranged flowers and a special room built to house their books indicate the Clevelands' cultural superiority over wealthier neighbors who do not understand the value of learning.

Lee's and Smith's use of such fairly expensive objects as a piano and a home library to sustain their characters' middle-class status and identity exposes their underlying consciousness that class status derives from economics despite efforts to disguise that link. Lee justifies the Fultons' determined retention of the piano—despite Mrs. Reed's clumsy attempt to purchase it for her own daughter—on the grounds that Elinor's income from giving lessons helps to provide for the family. In fact, Elinor's refusal to sell to Mrs. Reed—and our understanding that her musicianship makes her a far more appropriate owner of the instrument—confirm her cultural superiority over the would-be buyer and uphold her middle-class credentials in a moment of crisis. In short, the piano becomes a crucial marker of the Fultons' self-definition. Whether Elinor's character (and thus status) could remain constant even if economic circumstances had forced her to sell the piano is a question that Lee does not explore. Nevertheless, it is clear that Lee recognized a threat to middle-class identity in complete loss, and thus she limited the degree of her characters' falls. Although panic fiction is largely successful in conveying the constancy of domestic character as a basis for middle-class stability, the underlying power of economic status and the impossibility of constructing a social identity entirely independent of economics create telling gaps in these narratives of constancy.

Neither Rich Nor Poor: Reinforcing Class Distinctions

Given this impossibility of completely separating identity from economics, panic authors turned to other strategies for depicting middle-class stability in their novels. In particular, they focused on the relationships between the middle class and other strata of society, both higher and lower, reinforcing the social positions of their protagonists by emphasizing inherent and unbridgeable differences between classes and advocating interclass relations that maintain those distinctions. As already seen in Lee's disparaging portrayal of social climbers, 1830s panic authors appeared very hesitant to promote social mobility, representing advancement from one class to another only under limited circumstances and by closely regulated means.

While panic authors are understandably most concerned with the potential blurring of lines between the middle class and poor, they also frequently contrast an idealized middle class with those they label "rich." Many of the wealthy characters in panic novels, such as the Winwoods in Lee's *The Harcourts*, are characterized by a love of fashion, excessive spending, and a snobbish self-centeredness—qualities that help to accentuate the contrasting modesty, simplicity, and genuine benevolence of their more domestic middle-class counterparts. Catharine Sedgwick's 1836 novel *The Poor Rich Man, and the Rich Poor Man* provides a clear illustration of this strategy of contrast. In it, the positive characteristics of her protagonists Harry and Susan Aikin—economically poor but rich in spiritual blessings—are given greater emphasis by comparison with the selfishness and hypocrisy of the novel's "poor rich man," Morris Finley, and his unnamed wife. Harry and Morris have grown up together but have chosen very different paths as adults. While Morris, the son of an unscrupulous speculator, follows in his father's footsteps by pursuing wealth by sometimes shady means, Harry sacrifices financial success for a job as a cart driver that allows him to spend time with his family. Although Harry and Susan are labeled as "poor," and their respective occupations of carman and tailoress might mark them as working class, Sedgwick endows the Aikins with a very middle-class sensibility; they treasure their "independence," cultivate a private domesticity, are mindful of their duties as citizens, and are benevolent toward those in greater need. Thus when Sedgwick contrasts the Aikins' generosity—sharing their limited means and space with a young seamstress, a destitute old man, and the child of a drunken mother—with the Finleys' refusal to allow Mrs. Finley's destitute mother and sister to live in their expensively furnished and spacious mansion, the disparity marks not only dissimilar moral character but also class distinction. Harry and Susan Aikins' specifically domestic virtue is conspicuously linked with their modest financial circumstances through Sedgwick's opposing characterization of the wealthy Finleys.

Even among the rich, however, panic authors make telling distinctions, demonstrating that their quarrel was not with wealth itself but with a destabilizing social mobility. Significantly, they rarely attack—and often even defend and admire—an established wealthy elite, while focusing their critiques upon speculators and those of newly achieved fortunes who aspire to higher status. Sedgwick, for instance, is careful not to suggest that all wealthy families are like the Finleys. At one point, Harry seems to contradict the message of the novel by defending the rich as "some of the best men of the city" (111). One such man, a Mr. Beckwith, unselfishly uses his wealth to build decent housing for the poor, while his family lives almost as simply and unpretentiously as the Aikins. Sedgwick thus complicates her previous distinction between rich and poor, suggesting that her real concern is to defend a middle-class identity defined by cultural values and behavior against the social and economic fluidity that was making the middle class contested terrain. By labeling those who were claiming middle- or upper-class status on the basis of money alone as "rich," and then linking those "rich" with selfishness and lack of moral virtue, Sedgwick and other panic authors could maintain at least a fiction of a stable middle class rooted in republican virtue rather than in economic status.[11]

Distinguishing the middle class from the poor and working class was, however, clearly of greater concern to panic authors. As economic panic and failure threatened to obliterate distinctions such as income, assets, and living spaces—and even forced many middle-class women to engage in some form of paid labor, thus erasing that crucial distinction from the working class—panic authors hastened to reinforce biological and cultural differences that could not be erased by economic fluctuation. They were aided in this by prevalent nineteenth-century American attitudes toward poverty as the result of physical defect or moral failing on the part of the poor themselves.[12] Sedgwick reflects such an attitude early on in *Poor Rich Man* when the narrator comments, "in all our widespread country there is very little necessary poverty. In New-England *none* that is not the result of vice or disease" (22). While some panic authors mitigate this characterization by expressing an understanding of the way lack of education or opportunity perpetuates poverty, and Sedgwick herself frequently champions those who are poor because of misfortune, most depict the poor as primarily responsible for their own condition. None represents poverty as the result of an economic system that exploits workers. All appear to be invested in marking the poor and working class as identifiably different—physically, morally, and intellectually—from the middle class.

The most obvious difference depicted is that of ethnicity or race. Unlike novels of the same time period by Southern writers such as Caroline Gilman or Maria McIntosh that treat the relations between blacks and whites within slavery, Northern panic novels only rarely refer explicitly to African American characters. There are some hints, however, that some domestic servants are of African descent; Sedgwick mentions a "coloured" cook in *Live and Let Live*, while the Harcourt family in Lee's *The Harcourts* hires a woman named Dinah, who wears a head kerchief and is said to have been "raised at old master Southwoods" (90). More prevalent are the Irish maids. Christine Stansell's claim that between 1820 and 1860, New York City's working class became dominated by European immigrants, particularly the Irish (44), is borne out by the ethnic identification of domestic servants in panic novels. Sedgwick and Lee both specifically mention Irish servant girls, making an implicit link between ethnicity and socioeconomic status.

Lee's *Rosanna, or Scenes in Boston*, published just two years after the Panic of 1837, illustrates how ethnicity and behavioral markers of poverty were often intertwined in public discourse, especially with regard to the Irish. Although Lee clearly seeks to create sympathy for the Irish poor in the novel, her stereotyped characters ultimately reinforce the notion that their plight results from a whole catalog of moral and psychological failings, including drunkenness, domestic filth, and lack of a work ethic. The title character, Rosanna McCarty, is fired from her position as a servant in the household of the upper-middle-class Mrs. Jones when she ignores the Jones's advice and marries a fellow Irishman without having saved any money. Predictably, her marriage goes bad, and soon Rosanna is on the road to ruin—broke, alone, and increasingly solaced by liquor. Down on the wharf one night, intending to drown herself, Rosanna is instead caught up in a crowd of rioters, gets arrested, and then sent to prison; found there by Mrs. Jones, she is released and gratefully accepts a second chance as chambermaid. Perhaps the greatest distinction between Rosanna and her middle-class employer is her lack of self-control, both fiscal and sexual, so essential to a middle-class ethic. Rosanna's haste to marry before having acquired the financial means with which to set up a household implies that she desired marriage for physical rather than for domestic reasons. Lee represents a similar lack of emotional control in her depiction of Rosanna's friend Catty, whose husband had died en route to America. Unlike the idealized genteel mourner, typified by self-restraint or sentimental weeping, Catty expresses her grief by howling in Gaelic until she is threatened by the ship's captain. By inviting her readers not to take Catty's grief seriously, Lee marks Catty as affectively different from her female middle-class readership. Even the virtuous Dora McCree, the one Irish character in the novel who does epitomize middle-class virtues and with whom the audience *is* clearly intended to identify, owes her poverty to the moral failings of her Irish husband, who is in prison for having burned a barn. Mr. McCree's criminality, along with the drunken rioting that lands Rosanna in jail, signal an undercurrent of social disorder that is perhaps Lee's most damning signifier of the poor and working class and the one that triggers the most anxiety for her.

Lest these moral and behavioral shortcomings be read solely as markers of ethnicity rather than of class, however, it is important to note that other panic novels attribute nearly identical characteristics to poor and working-class characters not explicitly marked as Irish. A character in Sedgwick's *Poor Rich Man* named Paulina Clark, for instance, is almost a direct parallel to the destitute women of *Rosanna*. At one time a schoolmate of the main characters, Paulina is discovered by the Aikins to be living in squalor, her poverty a result of drunkenness combined with an implied sexual lascivity. Despite common origins and presumably a common ethnicity with the novel's middle-class characters, Paulina's moral weakness signifies a difference that explains her poverty.

Still other poor and working-class characters in panic fiction are marked as unbridgeably distinct from the middle class in their lack of certain qualities essential to middle-class identity, including industry, ambition, and education. Even as members of the middle class, as Stuart Blumin notes, were separating themselves physically and rhetorically from manual labor, their discourse of class tended to appropriate the moral value of labor for their own class (125). Despite the obvious fact that members of the working class worked, middle-class discussions of social and economic differences associated the moral superiority of industriousness with those whose labor resulted in greater prosperity. In Lee's *Elinor Fulton*, for example, a young architect rises in status by virtue of his industry and ambition, while a poor laborer of unspecified occupation is depicted as improvident, having too many children, squandering his wages on transient gratifications, and apparently having no determination to rise in status.

On occasion, panic fiction's characterizations of rich and poor overlap, emphasizing the distance of both from an idealized genteel middle class. Rudeness, or a lack of manners, for instance, is emblematic of both those whose poverty has prevented them from acquiring education and those whose drive for wealth dominates their character at the expense of developing refinement. Social climbers are particularly seen as deficient in manners, having often jumped from poor to rich without pausing to assimilate middle-class standards of conduct. A desire for luxury, often represented by a female character's love of fashionable dress or "finery," also links the rich and poor in opposition to a middle class identified by republican simplicity and domesticity. In the wealthy, fashion signifies a greater regard for money than for home and family, while in the poor, wearing finery calls attention both to the wearer's false sense of her social position and to the falsity of the values inscribed in the garments. For both the wealthy and poor, the superficial, external nature of fashionable dress contrasts with the middle-class emphasis on internal character. Further, when finery is worn by poor characters such as Paulina Clark in Sedgwick's *Poor Rich Man*, it is almost always associated with degradation, as suggested by Paulina's "filthy lace cap" and "soiled silk gown" (130). Contrasted with the "substantial, neat, warm, and lasting garments" worn by the Aikin women, Paulina's dirty finery serves not only to mark her as deficient in the physical and moral qualities that set the middle class apart but also to define her aspirations for material possession as insubstantial and impure (126). The very idea of finery is thus stained by its association with degraded poverty, further tainting its possession and use by the wealthy as well.

Panic authors thus help to create and reinforce a stable social identity for middle-class women by defining their position against extremes of wealth and poverty, attempting to mitigate the effects of economic flux by imagining fixed social positions. By linking "rich" and "poor" with specific moral failings, as well as the absence of moral qualities such as benevolence or industry, panic fiction identifies a middle ground for its middle-class subjects that is defined as much in moral as in economic terms, thus preserving a stable identity in times of loss. Further, by frequently linking the poor and working class, in particular, with the inherited and often visible identifiers of ethnicity and race, panic authors suggest that distinctions between classes are natural, easy to identify, and difficult to dissolve.

Benevolent Hierarchy: Advocating Paternalistic Class Relations

Maintaining the stability promised by such fixed social positions, panic authors suggest, requires that appropriate relationships between classes be established. Relations between middle-class and wealthy characters in panic fiction are usually fairly indirect. Middle-class women like the Fultons or the Harcourts in Lee's novels often start out admiring and wishing to associate with members of fashionable society, then either transfer their admiration to less flashy wealthy families or learn to treasure their own moral superiority while conceding a less valuable social preeminence to the rich. In either case, panic authors perform something of a balancing act, maintaining their middle-class characters' carefully cultivated moral distance from the selfish rich, while minimizing social distance by imagining possibilities for social intercourse.

Relationships between the middle class and the poor and working class in panic fiction usually take one of two forms, charity or domestic employment—both of which maintain distance between the classes and place the middle class in positions of power and authority.

Charity, or benevolence, figures large in panic fiction for a number of reasons other than defining class relationships. Economic crisis resulted in unemployment and starvation for many, and thus the panic produced a pressing need for charity in a time before any institutionalized welfare system. The middle-class authors of panic fiction, while not quite candidates for charity themselves, would almost certainly have been aware of the needs around them, informing their portrayal of middle-class characters who reach out to the poor. In addition, benevolence provided a sanctioned outlet for women's economic participation, both in the home and on the national scene, a purpose that will be discussed more fully in the next chapter. But the manner in which acts of charity are depicted in panic novels does emphasize a relationship between giver and receiver that is simultaneously benevolent and hierarchical. Middle-class characters render aid to the poor out of genuine loving concern for their welfare, but the inequity of the socioeconomic positions between the needy and grateful recipients and their gracious benefactors reinforces class distinctions. As both Lori Ginzberg and Deborah Carlin have argued, antebellum benevolence was a specifically middle-class activity, and although it theoretically was employed to elevate the poor, middle-class reformers' emphasis on teaching domestic values rather than addressing the economic origins of poverty tended to keep class differences intact (Carlin 211). Panic fiction's particular interest in philanthropy as a mode of economic agency for women further emphasized the hierarchical nature of the relationship by focusing attention on how charity empowers the giver. Those who receive charity in panic novels often serve as little more than opportunities for the moral and economic development of middle-class philanthropists.

In Lee's *Elinor Fulton*, for example, a chapter entitled simply "Charity," about the destitute Bemis family, serves largely as an opportunity for the author to compare and evaluate different modes of aiding the poor. The first person to attempt to help the Bemis family is a woman named Mrs. Smith, who is "full of kind feeling" but inexperienced and unwise in matters of philanthropy. She draws up a "petition" detailing the family's woes and circulates it among some wealthy women in order to obtain their "subscriptions" or pledges of money. But as her own signature is unknown to those she solicits, and her "pathetic appeals" regarding the family's situation are found by some who inquire to be misleading, Mrs. Smith's first effort is unsuccessful. Next she proposes "getting up a fair" at which articles such as needle-books and pincushions would be sold to benefit a number of poor families. This suggestion is shot down by a Mrs. Watson, clearly voicing the author's opinion, who opposes any form of charity in which the giver receives a tangible benefit—in this case, a purchased product—for her contribution. Philanthropy should not be conducted "through traffic and barter," Mrs. Watson argues, but for spiritual blessing alone (26). Finally it is Elinor herself who successfully aids the Bemis family, further evidence of her competence. Enlisted by Mrs. Watson, she investigates the situation, makes out an "exact statement of the case," presents the appeal to a few well-chosen individuals, and "judicious aid was given" (31).

While all of the approaches to charity that Lee presents in this discussion could certainly be characterized as paternalistic—casting the poor as passive recipients of aid generated by the efforts of middle-class benefactors—that which she endorses most emphatically plays up both the helplessness of the recipients and the skillfulness of the philanthropist. Although Mr. and Mrs. Bemis must surely have been the source for Elinor's information, she is given all the credit for determining their needs and defending their worthiness to be helped:

> She had accurately made out her statement, had arranged the industrious earnings of the family opposite their necessary ex-

> penses for rent, clothes, food, light, and fuel, and fully proved, that, though their daily labor was sufficient to enable them to live from day to day in a state of health, when sickness came, nothing remained for such exigences.
>
> "It was evident," Elinor said, "they had not desire or habit of begging, and a little temporary assistance was all that was needed, to save them from much suffering." (30)

By removing Bemises' own voices in these exchanges, and noting several times Elinor's "accuracy" and "exactness" in stating their case, Lee makes Elinor's actions the focus of this scene. Following her successful appeal, readers learn only that "Mr. Bemis was put into a better way of earning a living; and in a short time the family were again going on well" (31).

Sedgwick promotes a model of philanthropy in *Poor Rich Man* that is in some ways even more paternalistic than Lee's, as it favors the bestowal of time and moral influence rather than money. When Harry Aikin encounters a poor old man in need of aid, he has difficulty finding anyone who is willing to help. The selfish Morris Finley excuses himself, saying that he "made it a rule never to give to strangers" (91); a second gentleman contributes five dollars but cannot spare the time to tend to the man's needs. Harry, by contrast, takes the man home with him, providing him with the comfort of a loving family as well as food and shelter. In similar instances throughout the novel, Harry and Susan give of themselves rather than money—their home, their time, their talents, and their moral wisdom.

While on one level, such an approach to charity is more leveling than that described by Lee—the Aikins and their beneficiaries share a standard of living and become a kind of family—it also reduces the physical and moral autonomy of those that the Aikins help. Whereas gifts of money can presumably be spent in any way the recipient chooses, the Aikins' kind of philanthropy is designed precisely to mold the very thoughts and characters of their recipients. Thus, while the physical and material distance between philanthropist and recipient is actually lessened rather than widened in Sedgwick's model, the middle-class philanthropist's ability to control the behavior of the poor and to impose his or her moral standards is increased.

Philanthropy of both types provides a model for relationships between the middle class and the poor that maintains the superior status of the middle class, either in terms of resources, intelligence, or moral direction. The poor remain dependent, while middle-class women (and in Sedgwick's novel, men as well) exercise economic agency and display moral virtue. Sedgwick even suggests that "inequality of condition" is divinely mandated in order to encourage the practice of benevolence: "If there were a perfect community of goods, where would be the opportunity for the exercise of the virtues, of justice and mercy, humility, fidelity, and gratitude?" (40). While in this formulation, the poor also benefit morally from philanthropy, the obvious implication that the middle-class givers exercise justice and mercy while the poor recipients express gratitude maintains a hierarchy of virtues.

Panic fiction's concern with regulating class relationships is most apparent in its discourse on domestic service, the most common situation in which middle-class women would have interacted with the working class on a regular basis. As middle-class female characters wrestle with the problems of reduced economic circumstances, one of their principal concerns regards domestic servants—whether they can afford to retain any and if so, how many; what are fair and appropriate terms of service, including work expectations, wages, and time off; and most important, what is the appropriate relationship between mistress and domestic, and how is that relationship achieved? Christine Stansell notes that growing social and cultural differences between middle-class ladies and their often immigrant servants, combined with a middle-class sense of mission to inculcate working-class domestics with genteel behavior and values, led to such widespread tensions between mistresses and domestics that "the servant problem" became a common topic of conversation among middle-class women in the 1840s (161). Mistresses complained that servants were not pliable enough or did not perform work satisfactorily, while domestics charged that their employers made unreasonable demands, particularly concerning personal matters such as leisure activities or company. In panic fiction, the class dynamics that underlie such tensions are exacerbated by financial insecurity, lending a greater urgency to panic authors' efforts to define appropriate relations between mistresses and domestics. Two novels in particular—Sedgwick's *Live and Let Live* and Lee's *Elinor Fulton*—devote considerable space to analyzing the servant problem and recommending solutions.

Given that the preponderance of casual middle-class discourse on "the servant problem" (as cited by Stansell) noted servants' shortcomings, it is perhaps surprising that 1830s panic fiction assigns the larger part of the blame for poor relations to mistresses. Writing specifically to a middle-class readership, many of whom may have employed domestic help, panic authors invite their readers to compare their own behavior with that depicted and rebuke those who oppress their servants with inadequate pay, overwork, or capricious expectations. *Live and Let Live* is particularly concerned with exposing such abuses of power and admonishing readers who might see themselves reflected in the novel's parade of bad mistresses. The novel's young protagonist, Lucy Lee, enters domestic service when her alcoholic father can no longer support her, and she immediately encounters every possible type of ill-treatment. One employer overworks Lucy, then refuses to pay her when she leaves before the month is up, while another expects perfection without giving any instruction; still others treat her rudely, offer inadequate wages, or promise a position to one girl but hire another.

Possibly the only panic novel written from a servant's perspective, *Live and Let Live* most completely acknowledges the very real hardships faced by those women who performed domestic labor. Sedgwick's novel is also the most explicit about a fear that remains beneath the surface of most panic fiction—the fear that economic failure could reduce middle-class women to the status of domestic servants. Mr. Lee's occupation as a lawyer prior to his alcoholic self-destruction signifies the family's original middle-class status, and Lucy's value system remains consistently middle class despite her circumstances. Sedgwick's advocacy of the humane treatment of servants is thus based not only on an abstract code of ethics but also, by implication, on a very concrete application of the Golden Rule—that mistresses should treat servants as they would want to be treated, since economic misfortune could place them in that position someday.

Lee does not entertain this possibility for her young heroines but joins Sedgwick in condemning tyrannical relations between mistresses and servants. In *Elinor Fulton*, for example, Lee depicts the logical extreme of such relations through her satiric portrayal of the social-climbing Mrs. Reed, who horrifies her friends by wishing "it was the fashion to have slaves" (63). Hastening to erase the racial import of her statement—"saying she did not mean *black slaves*, but *white ones*"—Mrs. Reed nevertheless sketches out a mistress-servant relationship that mimics slavery in its language of exploitation and violence. Wages should be lowered when other prices rise, she argues, and servants' deference enforced by employers uniting to "put down their insolence" and grind them "to powder" (65). Mrs. Reed's desire for complete mastery over her servants is emblematic, Lee suggests, both of an allegiance to that economic system of values that warps domestic values and human relationships and of her own insecurity and desire to be considered of high social status.

At the same time, however, panic authors also reject overly permissive models of mistress-servant relations, which would posit servants as equals, able to govern themselves and direct their own labor. The absence of a clearly defined hierarchy between employer and employee in their texts uniformly results in anarchy and in poorly and inefficiently run households. Sedgwick expresses a concern for racial as well as class distinctions in a telling anecdote early on in *Live and Let Live*. Musing on the improprieties of various households, the narrator relates with a sort of amused horror an instance in which a cook had asked to borrow her employer's dress cap as a pattern. Even worse, the narrator continues, was a case in which another woman had herself borrowed a cap from her cook—"a *coloured* woman" (28). Such promiscuous sharing of clothing styles between mistress and servant clearly struck Sedgwick as an inappropriate blurring of lines between racial and class positions.

The middle ground between these two extremes of tyranny and permissiveness lies in a paternalistic model of employer-employee relationships, one in which mistresses can maintain order without oppressing. Paternalism enables panic authors to delineate clear distinctions between middle-class employers and their working-class employees but promises to bind the classes together in love rather than separating them with antagonism. One reason for focusing so much on the appropriate role of the domestic employer is to establish her paternalistic authority. She is responsible for establishing appropriate relations with her servants just as a parent is responsible for her relations with a child or a teacher with a student. Servants are less criticized in these novels than mistresses because they are depicted as dependents, needing to be trained, guided, and supervised in order to fulfill their roles properly. Panic fiction thus creates a stable hierarchy between middle-class employer and working-class employee by envisioning the mistress-domestic relationship as quasi-familial, with the servant as apprentice or perpetual junior family member.

Sedgwick's *Live and Let Live* most clearly presents domestic service as an apprenticeship role. We first see Lucy as a young girl and a daughter, striving to be dutiful to her parents. Within a few pages, that relationship is explicitly transferred to her employer. In helping her to find a position, Lucy's mother seeks an employer who will be in loco parentis—a place "where the weaknesses of childhood would be considered; where its faults would be patiently borne with, forgiven, and corrected; where its ignorance would be instructed; where the employer would feel the responsibility, and the privilege, we may add of training a young creature in virtue and religion, of converting a domestic to a friend" (18–19). While Sedgwick registers numerous complaints about Lucy's various employers, among the most emphasized are that too many mistresses abandon their responsibility to train their domestics—either for their duties or in a moral sense—and that they thus wield little moral influence over their servants' lives and behavior. The novel's exception is the extraordinary Mrs. Hyde, whose only difficulty in retaining good servants is that she trains them so well in housekeeping skills and moral responsibility that they tend to leave her service to set up homes of their own. Rather than creating great distance between herself and her servants, Mrs. Hyde acts like a parent to the young girls she hires, teaching by example and making them "comfortable members of a little family community, regulated upon principles of reciprocal affection and confidence" (91).

While Lucy's youth makes such an apprenticeship model plausible—and she does eventually marry and apply her acquired housekeeping skills in her own home—other panic novels employ elements of the same rhetoric to mistress-domestic relationships regardless of servants' ages and without reference to future independence. In *Elinor Fulton*, for example, Lee stresses the role of love in binding mistresses and domestics together in a familial relationship, even when a servant's depth of experience makes the issue of training irrelevant. The principal servant figure in the novel, Lucinda, originally propounds a view of domestic service as an economic contract. Speaking with a group of her peers, Lucinda explains very simply, "they hire us because they want help, and we live with them, and put up with a great deal because we want their money, and that is the long and the short of the matter" (73). Another domestic, Sally, counters this view with a competing model of service—the one clearly advocated by the author—in which domestic labor is performed out of love for a mistress who serves as a surrogate mother. In order to win such loyalty and encourage a sense of familial responsibility in their servants, Lee admonishes her readers, mistresses need to show sympathy, care, and affection—to bind "them to *our* interest, by respecting *their* interests" (82). Lucinda finally comes to understand this model of the mistress-servant relationship when she goes to work for the Fultons, who show her respect, demand nothing unreasonable, and practice the same simple lifestyle they expect of her. In response, Lucinda willingly subordinates her desires for independence—that is, she asks permission before going out—and "soon felt like one of the family," referring to "*our* children" and "*our* young lady" (92).

Gradual Ascension: Regulating Social Mobility

Panic authors' advocacy of paternalistic class relations captures their profound ambivalence toward the social mobility of the antebellum period. On the one hand, an apprenticeship model might imply acceptance of future social and economic advancement, even as it established clear class distinctions for the present. After all, apprenticeship assumed at least in theory that apprentices would eventually become masters of their trade, entitled to equal status with their former employers. The role of child even more explicitly assumes a process of growth and maturation into the responsibilities of adulthood. Panic authors' use of such analogues to delineate appropriate relations between working-class domestic servants and their middle-class mistresses might suggest, therefore, that they considered servant status to be temporary—a stage in which employees developed sufficient knowledge, financial means, and appropriate values to enter the ranks of the middle class.

In some panic fiction, this is just what happens. Catharine Sedgwick's novels, in particular, portray class lines as permeable; poor characters are able to raise their own status through hard work and education. In *Live and Let Live*, once again, Lucy's "apprenticeship" as a domestic servant is genuinely geared toward training her for future independence. The household work she learns to do prepares her to run her own home as a wife and, presumably, to employ and supervise her own servants someday. The domestic values and spiritual training she receives from her final employer, the wise and generous Mrs. Hyde, ensure that Lucy's home will be harmonious. Thoroughly trained in all respects by the end of the novel, and financially equipped by the judicious investment of her earnings, Lucy prepares to marry her childhood friend Charles Lovett—the son of a baker and thus both a worker and business owner—and commence her life as a mistress in her own right.[13]

But while Sedgwick's paternalism toward the working class employs an apprenticeship model that genuinely leads toward independence and higher social status, Lee's seems instead to mask the portrayal of a permanent working class. Her domestic servant characters remain fixed within their dependent roles even as she pays lip service to American ideals of egalitarianism. In *Elinor Fulton* and *Rosanna*, for instance, the servant girls Lucinda and Rosanna both learn from their experiences and develop morally throughout the course of their respective novels, but they are not depicted as prepared—or even preparing—for any role beyond that of domestic servant. In Rosanna's case, race or ethnicity clearly plays a part in the author's inability or unwillingness to imagine the character's social mobility. None of the Irish women in the novel rise from poverty, including the model of domestic virtue, Dora; Rosanna's ultimate reinstatement as Mrs. Jones's chambermaid represents a high point in a career that had included drunkenness and jail time. Although the novel implicitly pleads for tolerance toward Irish Catholics, Lee's own expectations for them apparently rises no higher than respectable servitude.

Lee's treatment of Lucinda is similar, even though the girl's ethnicity remains indeterminate, and the narrator of *Elinor Fulton* characterizes domestic servants as descended from the "honest independent yeomanry of our country" (80). Lee's extended discourse on the claims to liberty by "all classes" of Americans appears intended not to remind readers that domestic servants are free and equal citizens but to advise them on how to tame those who "breath[e] the spirit" of liberty into docile servanthood. Without "unrequited labor" or "hereditary bondage" in New England—clearly a slap at Southern slavery—Lee's solution to the maintenance of social order is what she calls "the subordination of the free and willing mind" (81–82). Domestics are to be coaxed into voluntary subordination through affection, sympathy, and guidance—that is, through paternalism. But the familial treatment that tames Lucinda's initial rebelliousness disguises her fundamentally unequal relation to the Fulton family. Encouraged to identify as a member of the family, Lucinda is nevertheless not one, a fact made apparent at the end of the novel. As Elinor and her younger sister Julia look forward to impending marriages, Lucinda's most cherished goal is to accompany Elinor as her maid (143). Paternalism, for Lee, thus functions less as a means for upward social mobility than as a way to keep those of lesser status content in their fixed positions.

A further condition that nearly all panic authors propose is that social mobility occur in small increments, advocating what Ann Fabian calls a gradual ascent up the socioeconomic ladder, in order to ensure that those with money would also have acquired the manners, values, and identifications appropriate to their positions.[14] Those who rise quickly from relative poverty to great wealth—the social climbers that are so prevalent in panic novels—usually serve as negative examples. They have money at their disposal before they have learned how to spend it appropriately, and thus they waste it on fashion and luxury rather than on benevolence. Their sudden wealth gives them social power before they have acquired the manners or education necessary to exercise it on behalf of preserving middle-class culture. In Sedgwick's *Live and Let Live*, for instance, Lucy's very first employer, a woman named Mrs. Broadson, is described as "the wife of a man who had, by speculating, suddenly gained a fortune, and, like too many who thus emerge into a new element in our country, she required (but had not) a new organization to fit her for it" (44). Still used to the mind-set of poverty, Mrs. Broadson exploits her employees in order to save money. By contrast, Lucy's own rise is gradual, allowing her to learn the skills and values she will need as a middle-class woman. Even at the end of the novel, Lucy's marriage to a baker's son means that her step up from domestic service is a small one, while the couple's ambitions for their own business suggest a continued gradual ascent.

In her saga of the Fulton family, Lee shows appropriate upward social mobility taking place over at least two generations. The elder Fultons, Frank and Jane, rise too quickly from their humble beginnings when Frank abandons his medical practice to pursue his speculations full-time. Although Jane has genteel manners, she is too inexperienced with money or society to resist the temptations of extravagance offered by their association with wealthy merchants. Following their inevitable failure, the Fultons are able to start over and advance more gradually. While Frank pays off his debts and regains a modest prosperity, the women slowly reestablish a modified social position. With the Fulton daughters' marriages at the end of the novel, Lee hedges her bets as to the appropriate speed of social advancement: the younger daughter, Julia, becomes engaged to the son of the city's wealthiest family, while the elder Elinor chooses a promising young architect who is more slowly working his way up into an emerging professional class.[15]

Given their caution regarding social mobility, it is not surprising that panic authors do not support worker-led initiatives for changing the economic circumstances of the poor and working class. During the half-decade leading up to the Panic of 1837, journeymen and other wage laborers, including female workers, were actively organizing trade unions and other cooperative groups in the cities of the Northeast. Thousands of urban workers protested wage cuts through union actions such as strikes in the mid-1830s and struggled for greater worker control over the manufacturing process. After the panic had decimated manufacturing jobs and destroyed the unions, starving workers took to more direct collective actions, such as food riots.[16]

Panic authors' overriding concern about the effects of panic on the middle class may explain their relative silence about such working-class activism, but the strikes and riots clearly form a subtext of the class-based anxieties expressed in their novels. Fears of working-class violence or even of working-class collective power can be discerned in brief passages such as when Lucy's mother in Sedgwick's *Live and Let Live* warns her against having a "combination against your employer"—that is, against attempting to resolve problems with employers by joining together with other domestic workers to request change or force concessions (41). "Combination" was a word frequently used in reference to trade unions, with a pejorative connotation similar to conspiracy. Worker violence becomes explicit only in the riot scene in Lee's *Rosanna*, and even there it remains unexplained, a seemingly causeless and frightening manifestation of social disorder among the poor. While any urban riot depicted in an 1839 novel must have been understood as related to panic-produced unemployment and poverty—perhaps a flour riot in which warehouses of stored foodstuffs were looted and trashed—Lee does not attribute the riot in which Rosanna is swept up to any specific cause, nor does she express sympathy for the desperation of the rioters. Along with the reported imprisonment of Dora McCree's husband for property destruction, the riot seems to reflect a generalized fear of social disorder resulting from actions taken by the poor on their own behalf.

One mode of social and economic advancement for the poor and working class that panic fiction does advocate is western settlement, a solution that will be discussed in greater detail in chapter 5. Echoing a solution to urban poverty and economic inequality proposed by groups as disparate as elitist politicians and radical land reformers, panic authors suggest that in the West, easterners of working-class origins can become landowners and business proprietors without disturbing normative class relationships. In Sedgwick's *Live and Let Live*, for example, the bake shop that Lucy and her prospective husband plan to start will not be in New York or Boston—possible models for the nameless northeastern city in which Lucy's domestic service takes place—but in Ohio, where Charles's father owns some land that was "promising to become very valuable" (141). Thus despite panic authors' disapproval of land speculation, they also acknowledge that rising prices on the frontier promised opportunities for upward mobility that did not exist in the east and that did not threaten social upheaval. By imagining Lucy and Charles's success taking place at a future time in a distant territory, Sedgwick does not have to confront the social adjustments required by changing social positions within a society, nor does she have to portray Lucy interacting on an equal footing with her former employers.[17]

Whether imagining the opportunities of an idealized West or seeking to regulate an orderly course for socioeconomic advancement in the major urban centers of the Northeast, panic authors ultimately promote a doctrine of the "harmony of interests" between social classes.[18] Such a doctrine contended that the interests of the middle and working classes were not oppositional, that prosperity for each depended on prosperity for all. In practice, this usually meant that the working class was advised not to attack the class privileges of those better off but to support opportunities for individual gain that were theoretically open to all. Panic fiction of the 1830s is particularly explicit and insistent in its preaching of class cooperation. "We are all members of one body," Lee's narrator proclaims in *Elinor Fulton*, quoting Scripture to urge that employers and employees see themselves as mutually dependent on each other and equally vital to the functioning of society (85). In Lee's formulation, such a doctrine seems to foreclose possibilities for upward social mobility, at least for members of the working class, by counseling acceptance of a benevolent hierarchy. Rather than striving for equality with employers, the novel suggests, domestic servants should seek their happiness in willing subordination, while employers ought to ensure that such subordination is voluntarily offered by returning respect and affection. Moderate ambition is appropriate for middle-class individuals—males, in particular—as long as it is harnessed by industry and aimed at public welfare rather than social advancement for its own sake. This advocacy of the harmony of interests thus serves to preserve middle-class status by protecting it from the leveling forces of working-class frustration and desire, while maintaining the possibility of continued economic expansion.

The panic fiction of the late 1830s was clearly a genre that came into being as a response to crisis, a means by which authors like Lee and Sedgwick and others could attempt to assuage readers'—and perhaps their own—fears about economic instability by telling stories in which women like them maintained their social identities and recovered from failure. But these narratives were not simply reactionary. Panic was frightening, but it also offered an opportunity for female authors to enter the economic debates of their time with stories that addressed broader policy questions as well as how to survive imminent loss. The optimal degree and pace of economic growth in a nation of seemingly unlimited possibility and how to maintain relative social stability in the face of a constantly fluctuating marketplace were clearly two of these broader questions that panic authors of this era grappled with and offered solutions for in their novels. Both of these questions were intimately connected with panic, their need for some kind of resolution made more urgent by the disruption and suffering panic produced.

Another question that occupied the minds of panic authors at this time was what role women could and should play in helping to either prevent or remedy panic. The importance these authors placed on "domestic constancy" as a way to counteract the socially destabilizing effects of panic signals how closely interconnected gender and class definitions were for them, but their interest in women's economic roles went beyond the concerns of class formation. A parallel purpose in the rhetoric of 1830s panic fiction was to combat the particular vulnerability faced by middle-class women in times of panic by imagining expanded economic agency within traditional domestic roles. In the next chapter we turn to this question, examining disparate strategies panic authors employed to argue for women's greater economic power.

three

Female "Economists"

Expanding Women's Financial Agency

So far I have been discussing responses to and analyses of panic that are remarkable more for their placement of economic discourse within domestic settings than for any major differences in content from the responses of male writers. Both men and women condemned greed, expressed fears about the excessive extension of credit, and blamed panics on overtrading. Many male writers of the 1830s also expressed similar anxieties about class instability, often evidenced by disapproval of those they felt were attempting to become wealthy without the gradual process of hard work. But for women authors, unlike most of their male counterparts, the gender definitions that were integral to class identity emerge as a central concern in their narratives of panic. The movement toward industrialization in the Northeast during the 1820s and 1830s had repercussions on conceptions of gender just as it did on relations between emerging socioeconomic classes. This was in part because class formation utilized distinct class-bound definitions of women but also in part because industrialization changed traditional work practices, moving production out of the home and thereby altering women's roles in family and national economies. The 1830s were thus a critical decade in the creation of women's domestic identity, and a time in which gender definitions—and their relation to economics—were in a process of change.

As a result, the anxieties about gain and loss so apparent in women's panic fiction of this time are not only attributable to changes in social hierarchies but also to a mounting sense of middle-class women's economic powerlessness in both an industrial and a speculative economy. Diminishing access to the means of making money or even of being economically self-sufficient increased women's economic vulnerability in times of panic. A distinct, though interwoven, strand of this fiction's rhetorical purpose, then, was to combat emerging definitions of middle-class women as occupying a wholly noneconomic sphere by making visible the ways that women exercised economic agency within their domestic roles and proposing expansions to that agency. These novels repeatedly place the key to social and economic stability in the hands of middle-class women, not through their own passivity or withdrawal from economic activity but through strengthening the economic power of the domestic realm. This is where women's panic fiction differs most sharply from male-authored responses to panic. Because its authors recognized the potential dangers of women's economic dependence, they highlighted both the necessity for middle-class women to retain some measure of economic control and their ability to act in economically beneficial ways for the family and for the nation.

We can see this difference clearly in the contrast between Hannah Farnham Sawyer Lee's novels and a male-authored imitation that appeared shortly after her *Three Experiments of Living*, titled *Living on Other People's Means, or the History of Simon Silver*.[1] The title character of the novel, Simon Silver, rejects his family's agricultural life as too arduous and goes to the city to make his fortune through speculation. Picking up the pieces of his uncle's failed mercantile house, Simon soon constructs an empire of his own based entirely on credit or "other people's means." Despite the fact that he does not actually engage in trade, he is able to stay in business by skillfully shifting his debts from one creditor to another and by attracting funds from others wishing him to invest for them. Each time financial pressures threaten to topple his house of cards, Simon devises a new scheme for staying afloat. As executor of a friend's will, he steals money left in trust for a widow and her children. He creates a dummy corporation—the Drumstick Manufacturing Company—on credit, then sells out his shares for cash. Somewhat later, he applies for and receives a bank charter capitalized at five hundred thousand dollars. In the end, Simon is killed by a runaway horse, and his actual state of insolvency is discovered, bringing ruin upon his many investors.

While the novel's obvious condemnation of greed and fraud echoes some of the moral and economic messages of women's panic fiction, its setting, tone, and outcome reveal a very different agenda. To begin with, Simon Silver's world is almost wholly male. His economic irresponsibility takes place in the masculine sphere of banks and corporations and even his victims, except for the cheated widow, are male participants of that world—bankers, merchants, and stockholders. The novel gives little sense of how such a credit-based economy affects women or domestic life and even less consideration to women as agents of economic recovery. Simon does have a virtuous sister back home, named Lucy, who might be seen as representing a domestic alternative to Simon's financial world, but unlike Lee's strong and effectual heroines, Lucy is blind and utterly helpless—emblematic, presumably, of the inadequacy of domestic virtue to restrain rampant economic self-interest or to provide either moral or economic guidance to the marketplace.

In addition, the novel's satiric tone and catastrophic ending run completely counter to the serious purposefulness of women's panic fiction, inviting readers merely to laugh at the excesses and point the finger of blame at the extreme perpetrator of fraud. While *Living on Other People's Means* clearly critiques the abuses of a speculative system, it provides no models for recovery, no suggestions for reform, and no role for women other than victim.

It seems likely that *Living on Other People's Means* was intended as a deliberate rebuttal to Lee's hopeful and female-oriented proposals for economic recovery, mocking her optimism about reforming financial behavior while denying women's potential to effect such reform. But the novel's implicit dismissal of women's relevance to the tumultuous world of finance is common to a number of other panic novels written by male authors. In general, male-authored panic fiction pays little attention to the domestic ramifications of economic crisis, focusing instead on the masculine spaces of the street and the countinghouse. Charles F. Briggs's *Adventures of Harry Franco: A Tale of the Great Panic* (1839), for instance, treats panic as a kind of man's game or as simply one of a series of adventures experienced by its hero, a single young man adrift from home and family. Like going to sea, negotiating the promises and pitfalls of speculation offers Harry challenge and excitement; even when he loses a promising position due to his employer's business failure, readers understand that Harry's potential for future success is only temporarily derailed. Female characters are peripheral to the action, having no effect on Harry's successes or failures and no opportunities for successes or failures of their own. T. S. Arthur's *Debtor and Creditor* (1847), another novel by a popular male author, takes the consequences of panic much more seriously but still subordinates domestic concerns to the effects of panic and failure on business. Although the failed Mr. Coleman has a wife and daughter who suffer the same social and material diminishment as the female characters in Lee's novels, their trials are clearly secondary to the negotiations between Mr. Coleman and his creditors, which take up most of the narrative. More significantly, Mrs. Coleman and Marion are almost entirely passive, submitting patiently to Mr. Coleman's directives rather than guiding the family's retrenchment themselves as Lee's heroines do. Such novels echo the discourse on panic found in many nonfictional accounts of the time as well, which similarly treat women and the home as peripheral to the central economic problems of overtrading and failure. Newspaper coverage of antebellum crises, for instance, mentions women occasionally as objects of pity, thus stirring readers' outrage against banks and speculators, but never as potential sources for economic solutions.

Women's panic novels thus provided a new and distinct way of thinking about panic, offering solutions to economic crisis that were outside of male financial institutions. They depicted panic and failure as breakdowns in a masculine economic system that called for a new approach and opened up opportunities for women to contribute their expertise and values to the creation of a better system. Some authors were optimistic about the possibilities for women's economic participation to protect the home from loss, to strengthen women's own influence in American society, and even to have a positive impact on national economic policies. This chapter will examine in detail a text by one such author, Eliza Follen, whose 1838 novel *Sketches of Married Life* portrays a woman acting economically within the home as a domestic manager, philanthropist, and economic adviser to male relatives. Such a portrayal performs a dual function. First, it asserts a legitimate economic role for middle-class women, thus refusing to bow to an ideology of mutually exclusive domestic and economic spheres. In addition, it models a domesticated economics centered on thrift, trust, and benevolence that could be applied to the broader economic scene.

Other authors offered similar analysis of the failures of male-identified speculative economics and also contended for middle-class women's economic competence and understanding but differed on the actual possibilities for women to wield any economic power. This chapter will also look at Anna Warner's semi-autobiographical novel *Dollars and Cents*, which repeatedly illustrates the positive impact women *could* have on family and national economies, if their good sense and capabilities were respected and put to use, but which also depicts female characters silenced and their competence rendered irrelevant by an arrangement in which men hold all the power and women uncomplainingly acquiesce. These radically different assessments of the potential for women's economic agency reflect both real-life disagreement over the form and content of women's domestic roles during these decades and disparate strategies for persuading readers of the need for women to wield more economic power. Differences between the novels also perhaps signify changes of perception between the late 1830s and the early 1850s. Warner, writing in 1852, offers some retrospective on the panic from a decade in which women's domestic identity had become more rigid and less open to the kinds of economic agency earlier authors imagined.

As in the panic novels that focus on stabilizing class identity, the novels discussed in this chapter use sentimentality very sparingly and in strategic ways. Once again, a calm narrative tone and self-restrained protagonists help to highlight women's competence and independence and thus reinforce the novelists' implicit argument for their economic participation. Those authors most hopeful in their visions of reform tend to admit the least sentiment, seemingly striving for reader response that is actively prepared to assume the mantle of responsibility that the texts model. Less optimistic texts such as Warner's do invite readers' sympathy for both the losses and the powerlessness of their heroines, but that sympathy tends to be tempered by those heroines' ironic awareness of the causes for their plight, pushing reader response toward either indignation or good-humored resignation rather than tears. Both ends of the spectrum eschew overt sentimentality or melodrama that might make women seem like victims and thus reinforce the very powerlessness panic authors were attempting to combat.

From Producer to Consumer: Antebellum Women's Changing Economic Role

During the colonial era and the first several decades of the early republic, nearly all but the wealthiest American women contributed to the national economy as producers as well as consumers. Since a majority of the nation's population were farmers and small artisans, the home and workplace were often one, with women working alongside men to supply the needs of their families. In addition to tending gardens and livestock and preparing food, women produced items such as cloth, soap, and candles for home consumption. Surplus produce could be sold locally for cash or exchanged for other needed goods. Women also routinely helped their husbands, and sometimes fathers, in their occupations, whether farming or small businesses.[2] The historian Claudia Goldin notes that Philadelphia city directories for the 1790s list thousands of female heads of households who occupied positions as tallow chandlers, shoemakers, coopers, glass engravers, and pewterers, among other occupations. Most of these women appear to have been widows who inherited their husbands' businesses, but Goldin speculates that they had probably already been engaged in the work during marriage, suggesting that many other women were similarly occupied without there being any record of their work (47–49). During the Revolutionary War, women were particularly encouraged to participate in economic activities, especially the home manufacture of goods no longer available from England. After the war, as the first American factories appeared on the scene and their required labor force exceeded the number of available male workers, young women were invited to join the ranks of mill workers (Kessler-Harris 21).

This picture of economically productive women does not, of course, mean that women and men possessed equal opportunities. One route to economic independence was land ownership, a privilege largely denied to women. Some colonies had permitted women to own land in the seventeenth century in order to promote settlement, but Alice Kessler-Harris notes that "colonies soon began to recognize that giving land to women undermined their dependent role" (11). Single women could often inherit land from their fathers, and widows from their husbands, but married women's property nearly always passed into their husbands' control.[3]

Similarly, the customary route to independence through a trade—an artisanal apprenticeship—was also usually closed to women. Although many learned aspects of their husbands' or fathers' trades, only a minority ever achieved ownership of their own shops (Kessler-Harris 13). For those women who worked for pay, earnings lagged far behind those of men. According to Goldin, the gender gap was greatest in agricultural and domestic work, with women earning only about a quarter of men's wages in 1815. This ratio improved slightly with industrialization, bringing women's manufacturing wages to just under half of men's in the northeastern states in 1850 (Goldin 63).

Despite the evidence of women's subordinate economic position, their role in America's premarket economy was substantial—a circumstance that many historians claim changed dramatically, especially for married women, between 1820 and 1850. The growth of manufacturing and the subsequent development of a genuine market economy during these decades, especially in the northeastern United States, created several circumstances that converged to reduce women's productive economic role in the home and in the nation. The rise of factories and less expensive methods of distribution eventually led to a sharp decrease in women's home production of goods, although many women continued to perform home manufacturing in the form of "given-out" or "putting-out" work. Childbearing and other household labor made work within the factories an unlikely option for married women. At the same time, men's work—again, particularly in the cities of the Northeast—was shifting from the traditional crafts performed in a home workshop to more centralized industrial labor, removing for married women the opportunity to engage in those trades while carrying out domestic duties. As home and workplace became progressively separated in the early nineteenth century, then, married women's opportunities to engage in economically productive labor decreased (Kessler-Harris 25–28; Goldin 11).

The historian Jeanne Boydston has contended that the "disappearance" of women from productive economic roles in the early nineteenth century was as much (or more) discursive as actual. She argues that, in fact, large numbers of women continued to produce commercial goods or labor for wages but that their visibility as producers began to threaten a growing ideological link, forged by the rhetoric of republicanism and European Enlightenment, between economic independence and maleness. The familiar domestic ideology that posited women as nonproducers thus emerged to counter the reality of working women and to discursively redefine the marketplace as exclusively male. Female producers and wage laborers were increasingly marginalized in representations of the marketplace, while "femaleness" was defined by "absence from the work place" or domesticity (Boydston 39–40).

Whether women's decreasing economic participation was a material reality or primarily rhetorical, the familiar nineteenth-century image of the domestic woman engaged in emotional and spiritual rather than economic labor was a construct bounded by race and class, serving to sharpen distinctions between black and white and between working-class and middle-class women.[4] Those who needed to support themselves or their families, or to supplement family income, continued to work for wages—in the factories, performing "putting-out" work in their own homes, as domestic servants, or, less commonly, as teachers or writers. Although historians' figures vary considerably, perhaps as many as 10 percent of American women worked outside the home in 1840, with many more doing home manufacturing of various kinds.[5] Women who could afford to perform the developing domestic role of noneconomic emotional nurturance, on the other hand, signified their families' relative affluence. A nonworking wife thus became a symbol of a man's economic success. As the market economy created increased wealth for a growing middle class and produced an ever-growing range of consumer goods to spend that wealth on, middle-class women's principal economic role changed, as Julie Matthaei writes, from that of "a home producer of goods to a purchaser of commodities, a consumer" (164). By midcentury, the dominant image of the Northern middle-class woman was not as a creator of wealth but as one charged with the dependent role of spending and displaying the wealth produced by husbands and fathers. Even those middle-class women who continued to perform income-producing labor would have experienced a lessening of economic agency by virtue of having their labor rendered invisible by this ideal, and thus their public influence on economic matters diminished by the erasure of their economic identity.

Investing Domesticity with Economic Agency: The Domestic Manager, Philanthropist, and Economic Adviser

Critics of nineteenth-century domestic fiction have long noted its authors' complicity with the development of a domestic ideal stripped of economic agency for women. Seeing moral influence as a potent source of cultural power, domestic authors such as Susan Warner, Mary Jane Holmes, and Augusta Evans Wilson reinforced the ideal by portraying women finding fulfillment in home and family, while men, contaminated by the soil of politics and the marketplace, look to them for comfort and spiritual strength.[6] Female characters who, conversely, understand and are savvy about financial matters are often depicted as literally and figuratively "calculating"—that is, greedy, self-centered, and motivated by the (masculine) head rather than by the (feminine) heart. From Rebecca Rush's scheming Mrs. Hammond, who counts every lavishly spent penny in her quest for wealthy sons-in-law in *Kelroy*, to the numerous literary and actual con women described by Kathleen De Grave in *Swindler, Spy, Rebel: The Confidence Woman in Nineteenth-Century America*, the woman who transgresses gender norms by speaking the language of finance is characterized as selfishly seeking financial advantage and is thus marginalized as unnatural.[7]

Panic fiction, as a subgenre of domestic fiction, participates in this idealization of the domestic role for women but with deep ambivalence. For the ideal of the nonworking, consuming middle-class wife depended on a healthy, expanding economy—a requirement that did not exist in times of panic and widespread economic failure. Thus, even though panic fiction posits domesticity as a stabilizing force amid economic fluctuations, it reveals, to a far greater degree than other domestic novels, the domestic realm's vulnerability to panic when women have little economic agency. An extreme example of this is Frances Draper's complete dispossession as a result of her husband's speculation in Lee's *Rich Enough*, discussed in chapter 1. Although Frances ironically suffers from James's successes rather than from his ultimate failure at the end of the novel (an event which coincides with her death), it is her lack of economic power in a society ruled by money that makes her so vulnerable. Supposedly the mistress of the family's home and of the farm bought expressly for her by James, Frances has no voice in his business decisions and thus cannot stop him from selling off the house for profitable development or from turning the farm into an industrial complex, ruining its value for her and hastening her illness. In sharp contrast, Frances's sister-in-law Charlotte, depicted as a co-owner of her family's land and true economic partner with her husband in the work of farming, blooms with health and maintains the only stable household in the novel. With this comparison, Lee underscores the impossibility of preserving the sanctity of women's domestic domain if women themselves have no economic authority or control over that domain. A speculative economy, Lee argues, by removing economic activity from the home and making it inaccessible to women, threatens women's ability to maintain their homes and thus threatens the domestic ideal itself, whether the speculation is successful or ruinous. To counteract this danger, 1830s panic authors such as Lee advocate women's control of family finances and, on a national scale, push for recognition of women's economic rationality and morality as an antidote to the madness and greed of masculine speculative economics.

Thus panic fiction resists the equation of true womanliness with financial helplessness, but it does so without challenging domestic ideals of women's selflessness and natural urge to nurture. Panic fiction heroines calculate prices and income not for personal advantage but in order to protect the family and preserve the home. Faced with a choice between embracing a domestic role stripped of economic agency or endorsing routes to economic power that are motivated by self-interest, panic authors chose a third alternative: reinvesting traditional feminine roles with an economic dimension not found in other domestic writing. In so doing, they may also have represented middle-class women's actual relationship to money more realistically than domestic fiction that strove to disguise the economic underpinnings of domestic life.

The most prominent economic role proposed for middle-class women in panic fiction—the domestic manager—is an extension of the socially sanctioned roles of housekeeper and consumer. Panic authors resist the economic dependence implicit in middle-class female consumerism by transforming it into a position of real authority and responsibility. The domestic manager does not just spend the money that her husband or father brings home; she makes decisions about how much to spend and what to spend it on, supervising the purchase and use of household goods. She exercises economic power by controlling the domestic budget.[8] Panic novels further grant economic importance to women's consumerism by illustrating its far-reaching economic consequences. Rather than simply reflecting male economic status, the ideal domestic manager's expenditures themselves help to determine such status, as well as affecting the economic well-being of her suppliers, employees, and the recipients of her benevolence.

While the middle-class matron supervising her household was not an invention of panic fiction nor a sudden nineteenth-century development, the importance of the domestic manager as a fictional character arose largely in response to both the economic turbulence of the early nineteenth century and, somewhat paradoxically, to the increasing availability of consumer goods. The sudden poverty experienced by many in the wake of economic panics gave increased importance to the control of household expenditure. When male unemployment or loss of property made income uncertain, families' survival often depended upon women's ability to spend wisely and stretch available resources. Antebellum domestic advice manuals such as Lydia Maria Child's *The American Frugal Housewife* (1831) and Catherine Beecher's *A Treatise on Domestic Economy* (1841) emphasized the need for middle-class women to be prepared for financial reverses that would require them not only to perform their own domestic labor but also to be knowledgeable about the most economical methods for managing their households. Child's manual, which contains such hints as how to choose the cheapest cuts of meat and how to get more than one meal out of a single piece, advises in a separate section titled "Hints to Persons of Moderate Fortune" that daughters have a thorough domestic education; Beecher's *Treatise*, while acknowledging that men usually control the purse strings, urges women to keep detailed household accounts.[9]

Crucially, as we have seen in chapter 2, the most capable domestic managers in panic fiction are often daughters or young wives rather than older women, making it seem that the role is a new one, a break from past dependence. Young female characters like Lee's Elinor Fulton and Sophia Harcourt respond to economic loss by assuming responsibility for reducing household expenditure and thriftily managing remaining resources. In contrast, Sophia's mother, converted only reluctantly and by necessity from conspicuous consumption to a simpler life, symbolizes the danger of restricting women's economic role to the display of male wealth. She is not only helpless in the face of failure but also partially responsible for the family's subsequent poverty.

The domestic manager's economic power rests equally in regulating consumer desire as in economizing. The growing abundance of consumer goods during the 1830s, combined with an increasing number of people made wealthy through commerce and manufacturing, made conspicuous consumption possible for the first time in America for more than just an elite few. Novels of the era reflect this expansion of opportunity, abounding in minute descriptions of furniture, carpeting, and cashmere shawls. But desire for such objects signifies acquiescence to the speculative economics and financial system of values that panic fiction resists. The domestic manager must negotiate between "legitimate" and "illegitimate" consumer desires—deciding which consumer goods appropriately reflect domestic values and which constitute ostentatious display. Two of the criteria used to make such distinctions, as both Gillian Brown and Lori Merish have noted, were use and comfort. Stressing the use value of household furnishings, Brown argues, allowed writers—Harriet Beecher Stowe is her example—to "de-commodify" such objects or distance them from marketplace valuations (45). Comfort, according to Merish, signified "a middle ground between monastic asceticism and material indulgence" and thus was conducive to interests beyond the body, such as domestic qualities of benevolence and emotional engagement (122).

The demarcation in panic fiction between goods that are useful, legitimately adding to a home's comfort and therefore to its ability to nurture, and those that represent excessive expense is clearly a fluid one, varying from author to author and even from text to text. Nevertheless, it is the act of such discrimination that gives the domestic manager power. By exercising restraint and emphasizing utility, she makes her choices as a consumer, rather than her husband's or father's income level, the determinant of her family's material lifestyle. Sophia Harcourt's sacrifice of the blancmange moulds and the chandeliers is thus not only a means of cutting expenses and raising extra cash but also a rejection of consumption for the sole purpose of displaying wealth. By portraying the ideal female consumer as able to make judicious decisions about what she purchases and to reject goods that do not reflect appropriate values, panic fiction gives her power *over* consumption rather than making her subject *to* it.

As the conception of women as domestic managers took hold in the 1830s and 1840s, and as separate spheres ideology became more pervasive, domestic fiction as a whole frequently began to portray household management as a profession parallel to men's work in business and industry. Although the home was usually depicted as a haven from the competitive marketplace, it also mimicked some of the concerns and relationships of the commercial world. Panic fiction, in particular, emphasizes the financial aspects of the domestic "profession." The fictional domestic manager is, in effect, the boss of a fairly complex operation, overseeing the diverse labors of domestic employees as well as handling household finances. She is responsible for hiring and firing servants, settling labor disputes, supervising the purchase and use of household goods, and seeing that all domestic affairs are run smoothly and efficiently.[10]

Closely tied to the role of domestic manager is that of philanthropist. Middle-class women's increasing association in the early nineteenth century with moral virtue and nurture gave them implicit responsibility for the care of the sick and poor within their communities, as well as for the nurture of family members within the home. Historians have argued that many of the reform movements of the 1840s—including temperance, moral reform, work with immigrants, and even abolition—extended women's domestic role into the public sphere, seeking to bring a similar order and harmony to the wider community.[11]

In panic fiction, as we have seen, charity often functions as a way to make clear distinctions between classes and thus to shore up the social identity of the middle-class characters who practice it. While part of that identity involves the philanthropist's moral character, it also relies on her ability to be an economic agent. Thus charity is very much an economic act in panic fiction, not simply a moral one. Just as the domestic manager makes decisions about household expenditures, she also allocates money or other resources to promote the well-being of those in need outside her home. In *Three Experiments of Living*, Lee juxtaposes charitable giving and spending on household goods as competing budget items, marking failure to give as a sign of a poor domestic manager. The wealthy Mrs. Hart, for instance, cannot come up with five dollars for a charity subscription, just minutes after buying a three-hundred-dollar shawl for herself (31). Pleading an empty purse, she asks Jane Fulton to advance the contribution for her. The moral contrast between the two claims on Mrs. Hart's purse is obvious, but Lee is equally interested in exposing that lady's financial mismanagement. Wasting money on frivolous luxuries prevents her expenditure on more worthy objects and encourages her to incur debts for the expenses she cannot meet. Mrs. Hart's failure to appropriately manage her household funds plays up by contrast Jane's competence in balancing charitable and household expenses. As Jane's husband later comments, if "you would have a pelisse as costly as Mrs. Hart's, then you would be as poor as she was to-day, and could not afford to give any thing away, instead of becoming her creditor" (32). Even with a small income, Jane is able to direct the family's resources to where it is needed most.

Panic fiction's emphasis on the financial aspects of charity apparently reflects the reality of antebellum benevolent activities. Lori D. Ginzberg contends that despite persistent rhetoric that characterized benevolence as a "peculiarly female 'impulse from the heart,' removed from crass economic considerations," most charity work—women's as well as men's—revolved around money. Women raised and invested funds, distributed grants, disbursed pay to employees, and occasionally even received wages for supposedly voluntary work (42). Many antebellum benevolent organizations operated like businesses, Ginzberg notes, seeking and receiving incorporation. Corporate status allowed married women to control funds in the name of the corporation, despite their legal inability to direct their own individual financial affairs (50). Although female philanthropists in panic fiction are often motivated by pity or sympathy, their attention to budgeting and distributing funds reflects this conception of benevolence as a form of economic agency.

As a philanthropist, a female character's decisions about who to help and by what means also articulate an economic philosophy about how to deal with poverty. While some panic fiction protagonists merely supply food or money for basic needs, others, like Mrs. Jones in Lee's *Rosanna* or Susan Aikin in Catharine Sedgwick's *The Poor Rich Man, and the Rich Poor Man*, attempt to prevent future poverty by educating the children of the poor and training a young woman to support herself as a seamstress, respectively. While neither of these modes of philanthropy attacks competitive market economics as a root cause of poverty, the latter approach clearly sees poverty as a condition that can be altered through education and employment, while the former merely treats the visible symptoms. Through their charitable projects, then, these characters give voice to theories about the nature of economic inequality as well as the most effective means of relieving poverty.

While the roles of domestic manager and philanthropist give middle-class women the power to direct household finances, panic fiction also advocates a role that gives women influence over the marketplace without having to leave the home—that of economic adviser. Refuting conventional beliefs that women did not "have heads for business," or were not as capable as men of either understanding financial transactions or making tough business decisions, panic authors portray women as competent and knowledgeable in advising husbands, fathers, and male friends on economic matters. In her 1844 novel *The Log-Cabin, or the World before You*, Hannah Farnham Sawyer Lee reverses traditional gender roles. Her young male narrator, Henry, naïve in his trust of strangers, turns for financial advice to his childhood friend Ellen, depicted as practical and worldly wise. Her ability to read character and her distrust of speculative schemes enable Ellen to save Henry from being swindled by a fellow apprentice—later proved a criminal—who has promised to pay him 10 percent interest on a hundred-dollar loan.

When women are excluded from the role of economic adviser, panic fiction suggests, misguided financial practices lead to crises and failure. In novels in which female characters are kept informed of their male relatives' business affairs and their advice is heeded, characters prosper, while those in which wives and daughters are kept isolated from or powerless to influence economic decisions, they suffer failure and loss. In Lee's *Three Experiments of Living*, one of the signs of Frank Fulton's impending downfall is that he has "ceased his communication" with Jane about business matters (123). Earlier in their marriage, he had consulted with her on all decisions, considering that she was "his dearest friend, and there was a straight forward good sense in her mind . . . of which he fully felt the value" (92). When Frank begins to speculate, however, he considers such ventures to be his own "affair" and thus stops consulting Jane and excludes her from his investment decisions. Even the scant economic role left to her at that point—consuming for display—is compromised by her ignorance of her husband's true economic position. Panic authors do not necessarily suggest that women are smarter about economics than men or could conduct business more profitably—although that is clearly sometimes the case. Rather, they contend that partnership between men and women in decision making ensures that women's knowledge, whether of finance or of human nature, is utilized. Jane Fulton's exclusion from Frank's decisions divides them as a couple, removes the restraints on spending that they might have provided for each other, and encourages Frank to engage in riskier investments than he might have if he had been confiding in his wife. Throughout 1830s panic fiction, women's understanding of and participation in their husbands' business affairs are seen as vital to the family's economic health, and by extension, to the economic health of the nation.

All of these proposed roles—domestic manager, philanthropist, and economic adviser—cast middle-class women as particularly suited to making economic decisions based on two attributes: their reason and their moral virtue. The first of these is clearly the most radical. Contending that women's economic agency is warranted by their rationality contradicts centuries-old characterizations of women as guided by emotion rather than reason and inferior to men in logical thinking. Panic authors reverse this hierarchy by pointing to the irrationality of man-made speculative economics and depicting the male speculator as the embodiment of irrational economic behavior. Women, more grounded in the reality of domestic concerns, exhibit a greater capacity for rational economic understanding and action. In times of economic crisis brought on by speculation, the rational woman of panic fiction is the one who—unblinded by illusion or unwarranted optimism—most clearly understands the family's economic position. Guided by that understanding, her domestic management and economic advice bring order and harmony to a chaotic male economy.

Claiming moral virtue as a province of women accords much more with nineteenth-century gender ascriptions, but panic fiction makes middle-class women's supposed moral and spiritual understanding a further basis for economic agency. Rather than conforming to a current trend toward removing moral considerations from economic decisions and making women's moral sensitivity a barrier to their economic participation, panic authors insist that wise economic decisions must have a moral foundation. How this applies to domestic management and philanthropy is easy to see, as both are geared toward care for others. Female characters in panic fiction make decisions about domestic and philanthropic spending according to principles of unselfishness, rejecting ostentatious spending on luxuries because it fosters vanity and greed. Panic authors also claim, however, that women's moral understanding underlies and supports their fitness to give economic advice that affects the commercial world. In *The Contrast* (1837), for instance, Lee defends knowledge of scripture as an appropriate qualification for dispensing advice about commercial employment. Ralph Colman, the young son of a religious mother, insists upon consulting her before deciding whether or not to take a particular job. The superintendent considers this to be folly: "Women know nothing of business. All they can do is to consult others. Here you have an offer of twenty dollars a month; and you lose the opportunity of relieving your mother from the burden of your support, for the idle ceremony of consulting her. If it was a father, of course, I should expect you to refer the matter to him" (95–96).

Nevertheless, Ralph persists and takes the superintendent to visit his mother, who succeeds in persuading him that the Bible is the best guide to action as well as to devotion. Rather than being an "idle ceremony," Lee suggests, consulting women about business matters ensures that business will be conducted upon moral principles.

In emphasizing this combination of reason and moral virtue, panic authors create for middle-class women an implied avenue of economic influence that goes beyond the immediate confines of home and community. Female characters' ability to bring financial order to households disrupted by speculative failure and their compassionate and effective aid to the poor of their communities suggest at least a potential capacity for women to bring a similar order and harmony to the nation's economic chaos. Women's rationality and compassion are seen, in other words, as having the power to counteract the masculine frenzy of greed that had produced the panic and also as providing a blueprint for a more cautious and humane national prosperity. Benevolence thus becomes key to panic novels' visions of economic restoration. Scenes of charity not only reinforce middle-class women's social position and economic agency but also model economic relationships that are mutually beneficial rather than competitive and individualistic. Incorporating benevolence as an integral element of the national economy, these novels suggest, would help to restrain the unbridled pursuit of self-interest that causes financial instability in the first place, while also promoting concern for public welfare during times of hardship. While both the specific features of a national policy of benevolence and women's precise role in implementing such a policy are left largely undefined, women's traditional association with benevolence makes their participation and influence seem natural and perhaps even essential. An economy centered on benevolence thus has the combined benefit of alleviating economic hardship in ways that put women's nature and experience to good use.

A final economic role that panic fiction proposes for middle-class women, but only with deep ambivalence and numerous qualifications, is paid labor. Despite their defense of women's rational and moral fitness for economics, despite the financial need posed by panic and failure, and despite the fact that many women did in fact work for their livings in the antebellum era, panic authors clearly find it problematic to portray middle-class women as wage earners. Those who do portray women as producers—of either commodities or income—as well as consumers, tend to either cling to older models of female labor in the face of changing circumstances or feel compelled to characterize their female heroines' labor as exceptional, not as a model for women's economic participation.

Most of the middle-class female characters who do earn money in these novels, for instance, are young unmarried women, temporarily helping to supplement family income following a financial failure, while their fathers are absent or otherwise unable to support the family completely. Lee's Elinor Fulton and Emma Embury's Constance Latimer, for example, give piano lessons. Teaching music was an occupation that could be pursued in the home rather than in a place of business—factory work is not even mentioned as a possibility—and that made use of a skill considered appropriate for young women. Even so, the narrators of the respective novels feel compelled to justify such work, characterizing the girls as self-sacrificing and interested only in their families' welfare. Their labor, while economically productive, is clearly not undertaken for personal achievement of wealth or status.

Most of the domestic servants depicted in panic novels are, of course, female, and panic authors seem to take wage labor among women of the poorer classes for granted. Only Catharine Sedgwick's *Live and Let Live* treats paid domestic labor as a legitimate occupation for middle-class girls, arguing that, in the event of financial loss, honest labor for money is less degrading than taking charity. The wage-earning aspect of main character Lucy Lee's labor is muted, however, by the book's focus on her domestic service as training for middle-class wifehood: "In a well-ordered family," her mother says, "a girl is fitting herself for the duties that belong to her sex. She is learning to fill honourably the station of a wife, mistress, and mother of a family" (17). In addition, Lucy's poverty at the beginning of the novel and the fact that she marries a laborer rather than a professional or merchant all place her in a fairly low middle-class position, suggesting that Sedgwick may not have been prepared to recommend paid domestic service as training for all middle-class girls. Nevertheless, *Live and Let Live* does defend the respectability of paid labor for unmarried middle-class women who are without male support and takes domestic labor seriously as an economically productive occupation, perhaps reflecting nostalgia for the home production of the late eighteenth century.

Panic fiction rarely portrays married women as engaging in paid labor, with Sedgwick again providing one of the few exceptions in *The Poor Rich Man, and the Rich Poor Man*. As in *Live and Let Live*, the laboring woman of *Poor Rich Man*, Susan Aikin, is on the margins of the middle class. Both Susan's husband and the novel itself apparently take for granted the fact that she continues to sew for money after she marries. While Susan's contribution to the family economy is substantial, it is also, like the work undertaken by unmarried female characters cited above, homebound and tied to women's traditional domestic duties. Susan stitches fancy garments for customers while teaching her children and supervising the rest of the household work. Susan's work is, in effect, a type of home manufacture—still a significant part of the national economy in the 1830s but becoming less common. The only other significant example of a married woman performing wealth-producing labor in panic fiction is also a representative of pre-capitalist home production—the farm wife Charlotte Draper in Lee's *Rich Enough*. Charlotte's partnership with her husband in the business of farming—raising grain and livestock, as well as making cheese and butter for market—is one of the most substantial economic roles for women in panic fiction, but it represents a nostalgic look back to an earlier economic system rather than imagining a substantial role for women within the developing market economy.

Not until 1860 does a panic novel—Alice B. Haven's *Loss and Gain; or, Margaret's Home*—portray a woman working for money outside of a domestic setting, and even then it is not in a very positive context. The Margaret of the title works as a shopgirl in a department store, spending twelve-hour days lifting heavy bolts of fabric and waiting on rude customers. Far from celebrating her heroine's participation in the labor force, Haven clearly deplores such employment for a woman, showing it to be Margaret's only alternative for supporting herself and her family. Paid labor for middle-class women is portrayed by panic fiction largely as an unfortunate necessity in times of economic crisis—at best a valuable contribution to the family economy but rarely a source of economic power. Growing ideological strictures against middle-class female employment combined with the harsh realities of nineteenth-century working conditions hinder panic authors from imagining direct engagement in marketplace activities as providing economic agency for women.

In depicting meaningful economic roles for women, panic authors do not propose radical departures from those already accepted in society. They do not envision women taking over the stock exchanges or heading up newly forming corporations. They do not even suggest that women's labor outside the home be valued equally with men's or equally with domestic duties. Panic authors' proposals, for the most part, keep women in the home, managing their households, caring for those in need, and supporting family members. But far from seeing these domestic roles as isolating women from the economic world or making the home a haven from financial concerns, they portray such roles as inherently economic. Strongly resisting tendencies to make the domestic sphere and the marketplace into binary opposites, panic authors instead blur the lines between home and market, imagining them as ideally coextensive in philosophy even if spatially separated. Economic activities in the forms of production, budgeting, expenditure decisions, and discussion of investments take place within the home, while marketplace decisions about employment and investment are (or should be) made according to criteria of domestic stability, moral rightness, and the welfare of others. The degree to which domestic roles could actually serve as bases of economic power for women, however, is a question that panic authors answered very differently. Whether an ideal of a domesticated economics could rival the power of speculation and whether the marketplace could be made receptive to women's contributions were matters of some debate.

Economic Partnership: Eliza Follen's *Sketches of Married Life*

Of all the panic novels of the 1830s, Eliza Follen's *Sketches of Married Life* probably best captures the optimism and enthusiasm about the nation's economic potential that characterized the explosive growth of the Jacksonian era. The novel treats the panic not as a catastrophe that threatens the nation's economic future but as simply one of the costs of being a rising commercial and industrial power. In fact, Follen defends American commerce and industry against an implied argument that the United States should return to an earlier, more agrarian economic basis. One of the principal questions that Follen addresses, though, is whether women might wield any of the new economic power being created in this more urban, affluent American society, and if so, what kind.

Follen herself, born in Boston in 1787, came from a long-established commercial family. Her father, Samuel Cabot, was a merchant engaged in foreign trade and her mother, Sally (Barrett) Cabot, was the granddaughter of a tea merchant. Follen was well educated for her time and served as a Sunday school teacher in William E. Channing's Unitarian Church in Boston. At the age of forty-one she married Charles Follen, a German émigré who became the first professor of German at Harvard and later a Unitarian minister. They had one son. The Follens' deep involvement in antislavery activities caused Charles to lose more than one position, plunging the family into financial difficulties in the mid-1830s. To earn money both during her marriage and after her husband's early death in 1840, Eliza wrote children's stories, novels, abolitionist tracts, and a biography of Charles and edited materials for Christian teachers. She also served on the executive committees of both the Massachusetts and the American antislavery societies. She died in Brookline, Massachusetts, in 1860.[12]

Sketches of Married Life, which Follen dedicated to her husband, delineates the most ambitious economic role for women in panic fiction to that date. In effect, she imagines women and men as economic partners, with the home and marketplace brought together through the unity of equal marriage. Although the novel has generally been characterized as a portrait of ideal marriage, its thematic focus is distinctly economic. Published just a year after the Panic of 1837, the novel depicts not one but two financial failures. It opens with the sudden bankruptcy of Edward Selmar, a young merchant and the future husband of the novel's female protagonist, Amy Weston. While Edward is in China repairing his fortune, Amy's father, a very wealthy man and pillar of the community, also loses his money. Through Amy's responses to this double failure and her assumption of economic responsibilities, first in her father's household and then in partnership with Edward, Follen presents a model for how women might exercise considerable economic power within a domestic context.

Despite the centrality of financial failure to its plot, *Sketches of Married Life* is far more affirming of the nation's rapidly expanding economy than most other panic fiction. Unlike authors such as Lee and Embury, Follen embraces the opportunities for gaining wealth that commerce presented, as long as that wealth is achieved with integrity and employed for the general welfare of all. She represents Edward's risky venture to China and his eventual financial recovery—accomplished through "some very successful speculations"—as neither irrational nor indicative of an unhealthy desire for wealth but rather as admirable acts that restored economic stability and provided abundance (176).

Most significantly, Follen does not portray speculative economics as a threat to women or to domestic values because she envisions women as fully engaged partners with men in economic decision making. At a time when an ideology of separate domestic and economic spheres was still emerging, Follen resists rigid barriers between the two by depicting a society in which market values are consonant with domestic values. Amy can rejoice at Edward's regained wealth because both are dedicated to using that money for benevolent ends. Thus, despite the author's own experiences of financial insecurity, Follen's novel exhibits little of the anxiety of other panic fiction, emphasizing instead the possibilities for women, men, and the nation to profit—morally as well as economically—from a healthy market economy.

The novel's dual themes of a benevolent economy and women's capacity for economic judgment and action are established almost immediately in Amy's actions. When Edward loses his money, she demonstrates a commitment to love over wealth by insisting that they proceed with their engagement despite the sudden disparity in their financial positions. More significantly, while Edward is absent, Amy becomes a philanthropist, establishing a school where poor children can be cared for while their mothers work. Both her engagement and her charity work are carried out against her father's opposition, reinforcing Amy's ability to make independent financial decisions. When Mr. Weston refuses to contribute to Amy's project, she funds the school through money she has inherited from her mother and by canvassing acquaintances for contributions. Follen signals the importance of Amy's specific form of benevolence—and of a worldview that embraces benevolent changes in society—in a debate between Amy and her father over the value of her work. Mr. Weston objects to charity from the perspective of a wealthy man who wishes to maintain the economic inequalities that permit his privileged life: aiding the poor makes them "discontented," he asserts, and merely perpetuates poverty that would "die out, of itself, but for the mistaken efforts of benevolent enthusiasts" (77). Citing the Bible, he declares that "Jesus was careful never to meddle with any of the existing relations of society," even slavery, a view his daughter deems a "perversion" of Christianity (78). For Amy—and hers is clearly the privileged voice in this debate—charity is beneficial to both the giver and receiver. The children in her school receive care and instruction, their mothers are enabled to work in order to support themselves and their families, and Amy herself gains discipline and a strengthened religious faith, as well as financial and managerial experience. Despite Mr. Weston's fears, altering the "existing relations of society" by aiding the poor promises a better society for all its members.

When Mr. Weston loses his fortune nearly midway through the novel, Amy assumes the dual role of domestic manager and her father's economic adviser—or as Follen terms it, she becomes an "economist" (117). While her independence and economic views have already been established in the novel prior to Mr. Weston's failure, her father's loss of economic power and status—as in other panic novels—permits Amy to assume the greater economic responsibilities that fit her for later partnership with her husband. The Westons' previous wealth had made decisions about consumption moot, since they could afford to buy everything they wanted. Now, Amy has to make choices, determining what they need and what can be sacrificed in order to save money. Like Lee's heroines, she supervises their move to a smaller house and discharges the domestic servants.

Throughout this process, Follen emphasizes the reversal of roles between Amy and her father. Amy becomes the one with both power and responsibility, while the formerly imperious Mr. Weston is depicted as helpless and dependent upon Amy for all his needs: "In all their arrangements, she took care that her father's comfort should be especially consulted. All the sacrifices she managed should, as far as possible, fall upon herself; all the indulgences that she thought they could allow themselves were for his comfort. Her father had gradually acquired the habit, from seeing Amy so efficient, of consulting her about every thing. All his affairs were now known to her" (117–18).

The bases for Amy's new role as manager, decision maker, and adviser are both rational and moral. She is, as her father notes, "efficient"—that is, she understands what needs to be done and does it. At the same time, her concern is for her father's welfare above her own; her household economic decisions reflect an ethic of love and benevolence rather than one of personal gain.

Thus far, Amy is clearly an independent and financially knowledgeable heroine, again very similar to Lee's young protagonists. Where Follen surpasses other panic authors of the time, however, is in her portrayal of Amy's economic role as a married woman. Developed in response to her father's loss of power and wealth, Amy's economic agency does not diminish when she marries Edward, but it expands into an active participation in her husband's business affairs. Although she does not literally join Edward in his countinghouse, she continues in her role as adviser, most notably in their joint decision to pay Edward's creditors in full. Unable to pay his debts completely at the time of his bankruptcy, Edward had settled with his creditors for seventy-five cents on the dollar and was thus legally released from the remainder of what he owed. Once he had remade his fortune, however, his conscience begins to bother him and he turns to Amy for advice. The couple decides that they have a moral obligation to repay the entire debt that supersedes the legal remedy of a partial settlement. Amy's duties of preparing the household for the effects of further retrenchment and of informing her father—who considers such scruples to be romantic nonsense and detrimental to the continued conduct of business—are seen as equal to Edward's task of making the actual payments.

In effect, Follen acquiesces—somewhat reluctantly—to the emerging nineteenth-century middle-class convention that men produce wealth while women spend it, but she elevates expenditure to a position of equal economic importance.[13] In fact, Follen ultimately suggests that, assuming wealth is gained honestly, how one spends it is more important than how one earns it because using money reveals and expresses one's values. Amy's responsibility for the expenditure of the money her husband earns includes the judicious consumption of household goods. It also extends her economic participation beyond the home through her payment of servants' wages. In making decisions about how much to pay her domestics, Amy not only exercises control over the living standard of her own employees' families but also takes part on a small scale in debates about appropriate remuneration for workers. In contrast to a neighbor, Mrs. Lovell, who pays low wages "on principle" and instead rewards good servants with presents in order to make them deferent, Amy expresses her conviction that fair wages are a servant's right in exchange for her or his labor.

The most important form of domestic expenditure in *Sketches of Married Life*, though, is clearly philanthropy, since Follen presents Edward and Amy's "works of beneficence" as the ultimate end of their business enterprises. Although they practice charity regardless of their economic circumstances, their ultimate goal is to acquire wealth in order to "do good" with it. Defending Edward's profession of merchant against his own self-doubts, Amy emphasizes the opportunities it provides for righteousness—both in the resistance of temptation to extravagance and in the practice of charity. "When I think of your profession," she muses, "it gives me pleasure to notice that merchants in general, as they acquire property more easily, are more disposed to spend it liberally." Agreeing, Edward observes that "the greater proportion of our public benefactors have been merchants" because greater wealth permits more lavish giving (191).

By the end of the novel, the Selmars resolve to turn financial success, and the benevolence it makes possible, into their mission. The narrator tells us that "Edward returned to his business with a new zeal for the accumulation of wealth, that he might be enabled to enjoy the luxury of changing tears of sorrow to tears of joy. . . . All of his earnings beyond a certain sum, which he set aside for the support and real good of his family, he solemnly dedicated to works of beneficence; not to a useless and enervating almsgiving, but to intelligent, thoughtful, consistent methods to alleviate the sufferings of the poor, by enabling them to raise themselves to a dignified independence" (290).

He also, we are told, worked for "the great cause of human freedom"—an allusion to Follen's and her husband's dedication to the abolition of slavery (291). Thus, Follen defines benevolence, or "works of beneficence," fairly broadly—as implicitly including political action that aims at improving the lives of others, as well as more direct modes of relief.

Given the novel's overall insistence on gender equality, it is perhaps curious that this passage is so exclusively devoted to Edward's philosophy of charity. Although the paragraph in its entirety concludes with the sentence "In all these duties and pleasures, Amy was his intimate adviser and efficient helpmate, his equal partner, his best friend," Edward's own commitment to benevolence is clearly the focus. Such masculine benevolence seems to serve as a strategy of authorization for Follen's proposal of a benevolent economy—an attempt, perhaps, to sidestep the kind of criticism voiced by Mr. Weston's complaint that "the wise and the experienced people of the world must sit still and listen, while boys teach them morals and women instruct them in political economy" (205). By giving Edward the principal role here, Follen avoids the simple opposition between feminine morality and masculine business sense that Mr. Weston posits, thus deflecting potential criticism of women's effect on the economy if allowed to put moral concerns into practice.

Elsewhere in the novel, however, Follen grants to women an important role in making the economy more benevolent by putting a human face on the consequences of financial decisions. In her argument with her father over charity, Amy responds to his disapproval with repeated "appeal[s] to [his] heart" (78). She attempts to make the poor real to him, to describe the mothers and the children whom she desires to help in order to make him see them as human beings for whom he has a responsibility. A bit later in the novel, Amy's cousin Fanny humorously contrasts her husband's interest in "rail-roads, and silk-worms, coal-mines, and sugar-beets, Swedish turnips and steam-boats" with the women's efforts on behalf of the "dirty, crying children," suggesting that women are more concerned with "the individual good of human beings," while men aim for a more abstract "public improvement" (87). Aiding the poor functions thus as a humanizing complement or corrective to commercial and industrial development, as well as an appropriate means for spending the money that such development produces.[14] Follen herself participates in exposing the human side of economic decisions by showing how Edward and Amy's repayment of their creditors changed the lives of two affected families. Edward is personally able to witness the joy and gratitude of one boy who could now afford to go to college, while Amy receives an account of a girl reprieved at the last minute from going to Georgia as a governess to help her family's finances (207). Understanding how mercantile failures affect individuals such as these becomes something that Follen the author, as well as her female characters, can contribute to economic discourse. Follen's main concern, however, is not to pit masculine and feminine interests or modes of benevolence against each other but to show how men and women could work together in partnership to reform the American economic system for the benefit of all.

Follen's emphasis on Amy's philanthropic partnership with Edward signals her purpose throughout the novel of advocating equality between men and women in marriage. Near the beginning of *Sketches of Married Life*, a conversation between Amy and Fanny provides the opportunity to contrast two views of the marital bond: Fanny declares that a woman loses her very self by marrying because the relationship requires her complete submission, while Amy counters with her conception of marriage as an equal partnership of like minds guided by morality. Both agree that laws prohibiting married women from owning property are unjust and infantilize women (31). Fanny's subsequent marriage to the wealthy William Roberts stands in contrast throughout the novel to the partnership of Amy and Edward. While the latter couple cements their relationship through mutual decision making, Fanny and William grow further and further apart because they fail to trust each other and do not communicate about their needs and expectations for each other. Uninvolved in her husband's business affairs, Fanny drifts aimlessly into fashionable amusements and spends money recklessly. At the point of permanent separation, they are brought back together only by a complete sharing of all that each had kept hidden and a commitment to future partnership.

The story of Fanny and William's troubled marriage is crucial to the economic message of the novel as well. Serving not only as a contrast with the Selmars' happy partnership, the Roberts' unhappy bond also illustrates the parallels between marriage and economics. In a letter to Amy, Fanny describes her relations with William in financial terms, saying that if she had married Edward instead, "we should not have had any long accounts on hand, but have paid off every charge as we went along. Now, my husband has terrible arrears against me; and, ah! if he ever calls upon me for a just settlement, what a poor bankrupt I shall be! Bankrupt, alas! in that only wealth that can never be recovered when once lost—happiness!" (152–53).

By figuring Fanny's complaint to Amy in economic language of charges, arrears, and bankruptcy, Follen suggests that a commercial economy and an economy of love function in similar ways. Both require mutual trust and a principle of equal exchange in order to operate to the advantage of all. Neither love nor business can thrive when partners withhold information or give and take unequally. Not explicit in this passage, but suggested by the narrative as a whole, both also require steady growth—of capital and affection, respectively—rather than the excess inherent in speculation and romantic passion.

While Fanny suggests here that her own behavior within the marriage relationship ought to have been modeled on economic principles of paying debts and settling accounts, Follen is clearly making the reverse argument as well—that the economy should operate according to the same moral principles of honesty, trust, and mutuality that govern healthy domestic relationships. Amy and Edward provide a model for both marriage and economic behavior by applying the same principles to both. In this way, Follen resists the separation of home and marketplace, advocating a philosophy that sees the two as vitally connected.

The novel ends on a pastoral note, as Edward and Amy visit the Roberts family, who now live in the country as benefactors of a lovely little factory village. Although Follen has primarily addressed the opportunities for a benevolent economy within the commercial world, here she suggests that the manufacturing and agricultural sectors of the economy could be equally dedicated to cooperation and mutual support. Nevertheless, she has Edward and Amy reject this world in favor of returning to their lives as an urban merchant and his wife. Given a choice between agrarian-industrial and commercial models of virtue, Amy and Edward ultimately embrace the latter.

By having her virtuous protagonists choose to engage in commerce and endeavor to be successful at it in order to benefit their community and nation as well as themselves, Follen implicitly endorses the nation's economic expansiveness. At the same time, by emphasizing benevolence as the ultimate aim of becoming wealthy and portraying the Selmars as partners in everything, including economic endeavors, Follen demonstrates her participation in panic fiction's project of imagining women's rightful inclusion in that expansion.

Anna Bartlett Warner's *Dollars and Cents*

While most panic fiction of the 1830s focuses either on the frantic and ill-fated speculative ventures that lead to failure or on the systematic process of restoring prosperity following failure, Anna Bartlett Warner's 1852 novel *Dollars and Cents*, a retrospective account of the Panic of 1837, centers on the experience of failure itself. More than any other novel of the era, *Dollars and Cents* details the actual physical and psychological effects of failure on middle-class women. Anna and her more famous older sister, Susan Bogert Warner—popular midcentury authors who, between them, wrote and published approximately seventy-five books—knew the hardships of financial failure firsthand. Their father, a prominent New York lawyer, lost his money in the Panic of 1837, forcing the family to retreat to their country property on an island in the Hudson River. In the face of repeated financial setbacks, Susan and Anna began writing in order to support themselves, their father, and their aunt.[15] Several of the sisters' novels, including Susan's best-selling *The Wide, Wide World* (1851) and *Queechy* (1852), feature young female protagonists who experience financial loss and must struggle for survival and fulfillment. Both Ellen Montgomery of *The Wide, Wide World* and Fleda Ringgan of *Queechy* embody some of the psychological as well as physical difficulties that the Warners themselves faced with the loss of social position and material comforts. But it is the semiautobiographical *Dollars and Cents* that most compellingly relates the consequences of failure for women and, in the process, challenges the assumptions and optimism of earlier panic novels about the possibilities for women's economic empowerment and their opportunities to influence or reform a speculative economic system. Although *Dollars and Cents* confirms the interrelatedness of home and marketplace, creating one of the most powerful illustrations of the economic nature of the domestic space, Warner exposes the downside of this interrelatedness, depicting women's inability to protect the home from loss despite domestic and financial competence. Less didactic, and thus less idealistic, than much other panic fiction, Warner's novel displays a tension between an ideology of domestic constancy and empowerment and the actual lived experience of uncertainty, loss, and accommodation.

Dollars and Cents tells the story of the Howards, a once wealthy Philadelphia family that has to sell their richly furnished city house and move to the country following a sudden economic failure. The family comprises two sisters—Kate, who is in her teens as the novel begins, and Grace, a few years younger, who narrates the novel—as well as their father and stepmother. Mr. Howard purchases the country property Glen Luna as a speculation as well as a residence, hoping to double his purchase price. He has many plans for the property, including the building of cottages and a sawmill and the introduction of model farming methods. The successive failure of these plans forms the downward trajectory of the narrative, as the Howards sink ever more deeply into debt. A series of lawsuits filed against Mr. Howard by neighbors combines with misfortune and poor investment decisions to bring the family to the point of complete ruin, signified by the forced removal and sale of their furniture. But just when things are at their worst, Mr. Howard is offered a position teaching Greek at a new college nearby, promising a regular income, and Kate marries a local farmer turned minister.

One biographer of the Warner sisters claims that, except for its conclusion, *Dollars and Cents* is remarkably faithful to the Warners' actual experience following the Panic of 1837. Details are changed—Aunt Fanny is transformed into the stepmother Mrs. Howard, Constitution Island becomes Glen Luna, legal battles over a dam are made to concern a mill instead—but the basic story recounts the hardships that Anna and Susan actually faced (Foster 78). However, instead of recording the fact that the sisters continued to live on the edge of poverty for the rest of their lives, supporting themselves with the income from their writing, Warner chooses to end the novel more conventionally, with the older sister's marriage and the father's financial recuperation. Ultimately, the power of Warner's representation of failure lies not in her replication of real-life events but in her ability to convey the complicated role adjustments and changes in self-definition that accompanied women's experience of loss.

A motif of powerlessness pervades Warner's representations of failure from the beginning. By giving the narrative perspective to the youngest daughter, the origins of the family's difficulties are left plausibly vague, without any clear cause or sense of possible remedy. Grace simply notes that "I was but a young thing . . . when there came a change in our outward circumstances" (5). First came "years of speculation" in which money seemed "inexhaustible," followed by some undefined event made known to Grace only by her stepmother's purchase of lesser-quality handkerchiefs—an act clearly signifying to readers a need to economize but inexplicable to the child. Later on, Grace begins to attribute the Howard family's deepening debt and straitened circumstances to her father's repeated unwise speculations. Her descriptions of his plans for cottages he cannot finish and purchases of cattle he cannot afford to feed evince a developing understanding of the family's financial problems but not the ability to solve them.

To some degree, Mr. Howard himself is depicted as a victim of misfortune and injustice rather than an agent of his own failure. Most of his ventures are well-intended efforts to benefit his family and community, failing more as a result of inexperience and misplaced enthusiasm than of either greed or overt recklessness. Already shaken by several losses, he is dealt a further blow when his brand-new sawmill is burned down, apparently by a competing mill owner. Subsequent legal proceedings, including multiple countersuits regarding various property claims, always seem to go against the Howards, causing Grace to label it "the war of poor rights against rich injustice" (144). Later, when the family's furniture is being removed to settle a claim—their lowest economic point—Mr. Howard expresses a sense of powerlessness. Reacting to a workman's claim of his employer's "rights," he exclaims, "His rights! . . . Well—it don't signify—he has the power at any rate, which answers as well,—I suppose the law will protect him as it has done many another oppressor" (383). Thus at least a portion of the Howards' economic loss is attributed to unjust acts that even Mr. Howard is powerless to influence.

In other places, Warner uses natural images to suggest a more complex relationship between agency and circumstance. Mrs. Howard at one point describes the speculation mania as a wild horse that cannot be controlled by its rider and may carry him by force over the brink of a precipice (39). On another occasion, Grace likens herself and her sister to butterflies, blissfully unaware of coming hardships, while depicting her father as "the busiest of bees." "But he made one grand mistake," she notes, "instead of filling his cells as fast as they were finished, he went on adding comb to comb while not one contained any honey" (57). These seemingly dissimilar images both suggest an ignorance or perversion of the laws of nature. Mr. Howard fails, Warner implies, because his economic decisions are not governed by the way the economy "naturally" operates. He attempts to "ride" or master a speculative mania that is both irrational and more powerful than the individual investor. Similarly, he comes up empty-handed because he expends his energies and money on new projects without waiting for earlier ones to become profitable.[16]

Still other images used to describe the Howards' failure emphasize the frightening realization of loss and the sense of futility experienced by the rest of the family. Glen Luna is like "a great tree that we thought would sustain us—finding too late that its top spread further than its roots," while the family's long, slow process of descent is "like a child slipping down hill,—afraid to let ourselves go, and catching at every bush to stop our progress" (7). In these images of finding temporary respites but gradually and inexorably slipping yet further down the slope of poverty, Warner captures a sense of helplessness and spectatorship. Her perspective is that of those whose presence on the slope is of others' making and who can only watch and feel their own downward progress without being able to stop it.

Because Warner's primary focus in the novel is the consequences of failure on the women of the family, we see their domestic space and their activities within that space in explicitly economic terms. Mr. Howard's successive losses have very direct effects on the material, social, and emotional facets of the Howards' domestic arrangements—how their home is furnished and taken care of, what the women do within the home to meet physical and emotional needs, how family members relate to each other and to others outside the home, and how the women perceive themselves and their domestic roles. In particular, Warner emblematizes the family's economic decline in their diminishing access to the material goods of middle-class domesticity. Prior to her father's initial failure, Grace's principal memories of city life are of buying as much candy as she liked and shopping often for fine dress materials—"muslins and silks" (7). The "lesser-quality" handkerchiefs that serve as Grace's benchmark for determining the family's change of condition presage a long sequence of similar substitutions. Once established at Glen Luna, the family's domestic life is documented primarily through Mrs. Howard's efforts to economize. Faced with little money, the women at first sacrifice their silk dresses for calico and wear hoods instead of more stylish bonnets. As Mr. Howard's debt increases, it is the household and the women who absorb the losses. While he continues to spend money on the "improvements" that created the debt in the first place, his wife and daughters attempt to alleviate their financial situation by doing without household linens, new shoes, or new dresses of any material. They pawn the company tea set to pay one creditor and sell the silver to satisfy another.

These material deprivations, in addition to changing the physical appearance of the household and causing discomfort and inconvenience to family members, also affect the social and emotional aspects of domesticity. One consequence, for example, is a dramatic change in the Howard women's social relationships. Without proper dishes they cannot entertain visitors; without a carriage or appropriate clothes, they cannot visit others. Former friends begin to treat them with condescension or abandon them altogether. The resulting social isolation demonstrates a direct correlation between economic status and the social element of women's domestic function. The social rituals of visiting and entertaining that create and sustain middle-class society are seen to be dependent on the possession of particular household and personal goods that are, in turn, dependent on monetary income. Another consequence of the Howards' household economizing is its impact on the very way the women define domesticity and themselves. Grace comments that while "our neighbors thought our [reduced] style of living both comfortable and pretty," their own contentment was "shadowed by the preliminary 'ought we?' or 'can we have it?'" (206). Having to create domestic beauty and comfort on a limited budget results in a heightened consciousness of the "dollars and cents" of daily life, a frame of mind that puts a price on every element of middle-class domesticity. Thus the women begin thinking about the home and their role in it in specifically economic terms. Even their own identities seem challenged by these changes, an uncertainty signaled again by the substitution of cheaper handkerchiefs. Decorative as well as functional, and principally associated with sentimental acts of weeping, the handkerchief serves as a symbol for middle-class gentility and thus for the women's class-based domestic identity.

Having to make do with coarser material suggests that economic loss affects even the most private or interior facets of domesticity.

In the second half of the novel, this portrayal of a distinctly "economized" domestic realm reaches a climax, as Mr. Howard's losses force the confiscation of most of the family's household possessions. Repeated scenes in which their furniture is appraised, catalogued, and finally removed to satisfy a creditor's legal claim underscore the economic underpinnings of domesticity. The first such scene occurs just before the end of volume one, when Grace returns from a visit to Philadelphia to find that her father has been made liable for someone's debt and that the creditor has obtained a judgment against him and an execution upon the family's furniture (207). Sometime later, appraisers come to the house to identify items of value. Then follows a period in which, while Mr. Howard is away from home, the women blockade themselves into the house to keep out the sheriff and the creditor's hired men. They stand guard at the door and nail down the windows to protect their belongings, making them feel like prisoners in their own home. Once more the appraisers return, this time making a detailed inventory of each piece of furniture, noting which are to be taken and which left behind, since, as Grace notes, essential household items and the women's personal property could not be seized for debt. Finally, the furniture is removed. Throughout the appraisal scenes, Grace's own inventory of the family's departing possessions—her fond and lingering descriptions of black walnut and satinwood chairs, maple chairs, an ebony cabinet, silver, dressing cases, Kate's harp—functions much as the litany of sacrificed luxuries did in the first half of the novel, keeping the reader's attention focused on the material constituents of domesticity. The women's anxiety about potential loss and their efforts to prevent confiscation reinforce not only the importance of material goods to their way of life but also their emotional investment in the household objects that define their existence. Because this sequence of events takes up much of the last half of the novel, Warner successfully conveys the thorough and devastating impact, both material and emotional, of financial loss on the domestic realm and the lives of women.

As a result of this focus on loss, the economic dimensions of women's domestic roles are perhaps even more evident in *Dollars and Cents* than in the panic fiction of the 1830s. Mrs. Howard's substitutions and decisions about which household goods the family can do without parallel the judicious consumption noted earlier in Lee's heroines, but Warner places an even greater emphasis on the financial necessity of such choices and accentuates a heightened consciousness of how much each sacrifice is worth. When Kate suggests they give up sugar, for instance, Mrs. Howard acknowledges the symbolic value of such a sacrifice but notes that it will not save enough money to make much difference (192). Since one of her principal measures of economy is to dismiss the domestic servants, we see yet a further impact of financial loss on the domestic sphere in the women's changing relationship to physical labor. Whereas at first, day laborers and domestic servants perform most of the work at Glen Luna—and Kate, the most sensitive to class distinctions, is dismayed when their father toils along with his hired men in the field—gradually the girls take on domestic tasks to help out and to occupy their time. When Mrs. Howard decides that they will do without servants altogether, she and the girls begin to perform all the housework themselves. In Grace's description of that labor, Warner makes explicit the disproportionate share of economic hardship borne by women:

> Nevertheless the want of servants fell much more heavily upon us than upon him. The work Mr. Howard had to do, was good, wholesome exercise in the open air—not more than his health required; and the chars once done, the rest of the day and night was his own. His meals too were better cooked than when we had Caddie, his bed sloped with a nicer grading,—his linen might have been the envy of the neighbourhood; and the weariness of hand that sometimes accomplished the one and the other, was quite beyond a strong man's imagination. The endless routine of meals and dishes, sweeping, dusting, bread and bed making,—the toil of mind to contrive and arrange it all,—the want of a pail of water when the clothes were to sprinkle, of *good* wood when they were to iron, of kindling when the fire went out,—the cold rooms and mornings when and where we came down to get breakfast—it took women to understand or to get through it. (378)

Written at a time when middle-class ideals of domesticity downplayed the physical labor of housekeeping, and most domestic novels portrayed the mistress's role as largely emotional in nature, Warner's description here of difficult and exhausting work is unusual and demonstrates the degree to which economic circumstances determined the character of women's domestic role. While Mr. Howard's work remains largely the same, that of Mrs. Howard and the girls shifts dramatically from social and supervisory roles to the immediate and physical work of providing meals and making the home clean and comfortable. Although Mrs. Howard and her stepdaughters are not paid for their household labor, their performance of it for the explicit purpose of reducing expenditure on servants' wages underscores their labor's economic value, while also emphasizing their role in managing the household budget. Kate and Grace further extend their labors into wage-earning endeavors by copying maps and legal papers at home for a local lawyer, an occupation that, like Elinor Fulton's piano lessons, brings in money while retaining feminine propriety.

More important even than what the Howard women do, however, is what they are clearly capable of doing. Warner emphasizes throughout the novel Mrs. Howard's far greater understanding of the family's true financial situation than that of her husband and her superior rationality when it comes to economic judgments. In addition to economizing while he continues to spend, and making the hard choices about what to give up, Mrs. Howard repeatedly cautions her husband about his rash schemes, gently questioning their advisability. When Mr. Howard first decides to purchase Glen Luna, for example, she presses him for an explanation of his decision, representing what Warner calls the "woman's desire to know the *what for*—even of a speculation" (9). When he presents his ambitious plans for the property—symbolically elaborate on paper, a "lithographer's fancy"—she asks about costs and expresses concerns about the plans' profitability that are later borne out by continual losses (38). Every time Mr. Howard announces another "sure way" to invest money or a project that can't "help paying for [itself]," she demonstrates her practical understanding of economics with questions and objections. Grace's narration of the story gradually takes on a similar skepticism about her father's financial affairs, suggesting that even a young girl has sounder judgment than a man in the throes of speculation. At one point she remarks that her father "never went out without a bag of dollars to put somewhere"; on another occasion, her consciousness of the irony of Mr. Howard's question, "Shall I bring you some silk dresses?," denotes not only an awareness of the family's situation but also knowledge of her father's inability to face the realities of his failing projects.

But theirs is knowledge without power. Unlike Lee's heroines, who, faced with failure, seize the opportunity to set the household economy on a rational course, or Follen's Amy Selmar, whose partnership with her husband extends to financial decisions, Mrs. Howard is prevented from implementing her financial wisdom by her subordinate role in the household and her husband's assumption of her financial ignorance. When she voices her objections to the cost of some new construction, for example, Mr. Howard simply laughs at her fears and declares his intent to have the stone quarried immediately. When she continues to express concerns, he coerces even her mental submission:

> "Pshaw my dear . . . you don't know anything about the matter—
> won't that content you?"

> "It would if I could think so."
> "Well think so," he said smiling and taking her hand. (39)

Mrs. Howard responds to such disregard of her opinions with resignation—a smile that is "half a sigh" (9)—and acquiescence to her position of powerlessness. When Kate asks her why she does not confront their father more assertively, she replies, "it does little good to speak when the thing is done; and besides I don't know that I ought. Your father must know his own affairs, one would think" (70).

Hindered both by her husband's actions and by her own acceptance of conventional gender roles, Mrs. Howard is unable to assume the guiding role promoted for middle-class women by earlier panic fiction. Although she capably performs the economic role of managing the household's resources, she recognizes that without the power to influence business expenditures, her efforts will be insufficient to reverse the family's financial failure. Real recovery will have to come from a change in the economic arena occupied by her husband—either an upturn in his investments or a change in his financial philosophy. This understanding of women's relation to economic agency is reflected in Mrs. Howard's advice to Kate that "there are few principles more important to a woman, my dear child, than that of patient submission to circumstances. They are very seldom brought about by her own agency,—her work is not to build, but beautify; and that may be done in a log cabin" (68), a sentiment echoed later in the novel by Mr. Howard's declaration that "every true woman" can adapt herself like india rubber to "any niche where she may be placed" (428). While Warner thus, on the one hand, implies that women might have much to teach men about economics if men would only listen, on the other hand, she overtly reinforces the subordination that makes women's increased economic agency unlikely. Readers are clearly meant to sympathize with Mrs. Howard's powerlessness to influence her husband, but they are given only acquiescence and adaptation as possible responses. This suggests that while Warner may have shared other panic authors' ideals of a domesticated economics, she was not optimistic about the prospects for displacing the individualist, competitive masculine model.

Ironically, it is in Warner's very lack of cheerleading for women's domestic empowerment that we can see most clearly the links between Northern panic fiction's two principal rhetorical purposes—advocating a greater economic role for middle-class women and shoring up middle-class social stability. When middle-class women like Mrs. Howard are unable to exercise their economic competence or control their family finances, they are also unable to preserve either their domestic realms or the social identity that is dependent on domestic constancy.

Warner echoes other panic authors in her construction of a middle-class identity for the Howards that is based on domestic skills and values, but because her depiction of domesticity is so rooted in the material—the fabric, the china, the sloping of a bed—it cannot provide a stable identity independent of economic circumstances. For example, although the Howard girls' ironing and baking skills serve to distinguish them both from an idle wealthy neighbor and from the household chaos of a poor acquaintance, thus reinforcing their middle-class identity through domestic competence, the always-present fact that they learned to do housework specifically because their father has lost money imbues that quality with an economic basis. Similarly, the repeated scenes in which their furniture is appraised seem at first to strengthen the Howards' middle-class identity because the process reveals them as the ones best able to place correct value upon their possessions. Unlike the uneducated men with "unkempt heads" who have been hired to count and move the furniture, the Howards embody Gillian Brown's concept of "sentimental possession": they know what each item is, what it is made of, and how it should be cared for and used. Grace repeatedly differentiates the family from the workmen according to their respective familiarity with the trappings of a middle-class household. She notes with amusement the appraiser who mistakes a bust of Hebe for Martha Washington, and when one of them says the Howards will not need the fish knives because he only has fish about once a year, Grace thinks to herself, "I wonder what your table has to do with ours!" (396). Ultimately, however, having defined her family's status and identity through their departing material possessions, Grace finds that when those possessions are taken away, that basis for identity is lost. When all the furniture is gone, Grace reveals, "we almost wondered whether we were not some family of Smiths, just waked up!" (404). Her response conveys not just uncertain identity but identity reduced to the lowest common denominator, to the level of anonymous poverty and nondistinction.

In portraying this dimension of the Howards' loss, Warner thus reveals the seams in domestic ideology that other panic authors ignore or strive to hide. Domesticity and identity based in domesticity are not, Warner suggests, independent of economic status or material possession and cannot therefore provide the stability in the midst of economic fluctuation that some domestic fiction contends. *Dollars and Cents* demonstrates that, in fact, middle-class domesticity and the identity it confers are linked very closely with the number and quality of household objects possessed, as well as with who does the labor connected with the household, both of which are dependent upon economic status. And because women have virtually no control over the financial decisions that determine economic status, they are also powerless to use their financial and domestic competence either to maintain domestic stability or to achieve economic recuperation. Like Frances

Draper, whose complete dispossession of home and health is chronicled in Lee's *Rich Enough*, Warner's female characters can only watch and, as Mrs. Howard says, "see how little we can cost," as a male-controlled speculative economy strips them of possessions, control over the home, and, potentially, their very identities.

Unlike Frances Draper, however, the Howard women are rescued from their descent into poverty before they hit the bottom. Warner avoids spelling out the long-term implications of women's helplessness in the face of loss by providing financial recuperation in the form of Kate's marriage to a rising young professional and Mr. Howard's offer of professorial employment. In appending such a conventionally happy ending—rather than having Kate and Grace face the same prospects of deprivation and life-long wage labor that the Warner sisters themselves faced—she restores the economic basis for the Howards' threatened social status and reaffirms middle-class domesticity through the creation of a new family. Significantly, this restoration is not achieved by the women's economic role in the home, as happens in so many other panic novels, but by masculine exertion and ambition. It is Kate's fiancé, Mr. Collingwood, who achieves the greatest gain in economic agency in the novel, rising from the lowly status of a farmer's son to the professional ranks of the ministry by means of his access to education. One implication of this solution is that economic recuperation, if it is to be achieved at all, will come from a turn away from financial speculation and toward the greater stability of advancement through education and entry into the professions—an avenue just as unavailable to women in the 1850s as speculation.

Whether Warner's portrayal of the Howard women's inability to wield control over their own domestic economy signals resignation to such economic disempowerment and advocacy of the kind of solution to failure that her novel's ending provides or whether it was intended as a covert "call to arms," aimed at inspiring reforms that would give women greater power, is difficult to determine. The fact that the novel is both autobiographical and retrospective could suggest an element of resignation, with Mrs. Howard's powerlessness meant to represent the reality that Warner and her sister were unable to reverse the effects of their father's financial losses with their writing income. The conventional ending might then be seen more as a fantasy of rescue than as advocacy of any particular method of economic recovery. Written so much later than the panic novels of the 1830s, *Dollars and Cents* might also be seen as a deliberate counter to the optimism of authors such as Lee and Follen, coming from the perspective of a decade in which women's domestic roles had become much more clearly defined in noneconomic terms and the discursive erasure of women's economic participation that Jeanne Boydston describes had been largely accomplished. On the other hand, Warner clearly did not subscribe to typical 1850s representations of domestic isolation from the marketplace or of women's confinement to moral influence and emotional support. Mrs. Howard's financial understanding and her evident frustration with being unable to make use of it is in tension with the smiling acquiescence that readers see her perform. The fact that she clearly *could* solve her family's financial problems if given the chance poses women's competence as a potential solution to be considered even if the novel shows her as powerless to exercise it.

Ultimately, the answer rests in the response from readers that *Dollars and Cents* seems to have been intended to evoke. Is it simply sympathy for the women's losses and powerlessness to stop those losses? Is it resigned agreement with Mr. and Mrs. Howard's advice to Kate about adaptation to circumstances? Or is it indignation at men's refusal to take women's opinions seriously and frustration at their rejection of women's advice? While a twenty-first-century reading cannot reproduce the experience of an 1850s audience, it seems probable that all of these responses would have been evoked in some combination. By tempering a sympathetic response with both irony and frustration, Warner avoids the sentimentality that would have rendered her female characters simply victims and creates an opening for readers to see alternative solutions. Thus, whether we see Warner as participating in panic fiction's aim of advocating greater female agency or simply mourning the impossibility of such agency, it is clear that she joins authors like Lee and Follen in promoting middle-class women's economic competence and connecting speculative instability with women's lack of power to demonstrate that competence.

Joining the issue of women's decreasing economic power to that of social instability in a speculative economy, Northern 1830s panic fiction focused on the middle-class domestic woman as central to solving the nation's economic crises. Most panic authors envisioned economic roles for women within the home that would not only protect the home from loss and help restore prosperity but also provide models for rational and benevolent economic practices at the national level. Eliza Follen's depiction of economic and benevolent partnership within marriage is one formulation of this project to construct an economically empowered domesticity, thus connecting home and marketplace in a single system operated according to a shared system of values. Anna Warner's far less optimistic vision of middle-class women's economic role following panic demonstrates the dire consequences for both women themselves and the economy when women are economically dependent on men and unable to exercise financial agency.

What both facets of this debate over the possibilities for women's economic role share is a distinctly middle-class perspective and an economic analysis that locates the causes for failure squarely within the characters' own societies and points to potential solutions for failure within their homes. Although Follen's fictive world is that of the urban merchant and Warner's that of a rural landowner, both authors respond to the excesses of the 1830s Northern economy by imagining a stable prosperity brought about by a controlled embrace of opportunity. In the next chapter, we turn to Southern panic fiction, the narratives of which reflect a very different perspective and economic analysis. For Southern writers of the 1840s and 1850s, panic was integrally linked with sectional economic disparities and strife over slavery, and thus panic was seen as largely the fault of hostile Northern interests. As a result, solutions to failure are often removed from the home to arenas of more direct conflict.

four

Threats from Outside
Defending the Southern Economy

Toward the end of her 1852 novel *Marcus Warland; or the Long Moss Spring*, the Southern author Caroline Lee Hentz depicts the financial failure of a wealthy Georgia planter named Bellamy. Mr. Bellamy had not speculated or been extravagant; in fact, he is a model landowner and slaveholder—benevolent, just, and (usually) prudent. His failure comes as the result of massive debts incurred by a friend and neighbor, Mr. Arnold, for whom Mr. Bellamy had generously promised security on a loan. It is Arnold who has speculated irresponsibly, as the reader immediately recognizes from his plea to Bellamy: "I have an opportunity of making a splendid speculation, and it would be madness to slight it. In a few years I shall double all my property. The plantation and negroes I am now going to purchase belong to an estate contiguous to my own. If I do not buy immediately I shall be forestalled" (167).

Trusting his friend, who is "considered a wealthy man," Bellamy complies only to find himself liable for the debt and thus "ruined" when Arnold is unable to pay the notes he has signed and flees to Texas with all of his slaves (his only liquid property). Mrs. Bellamy reassures her husband that their new creditors are all "honourable men" who will grant them time to raise the money owed through proceeds of the next few years' harvests. She also counsels increased measures of economy, noting that "household discipline will do us good" (171).

But the Bellamys do not have to wait quite that long for recompense. Their young protégé, Marcus Warland—whose education and romance forms the main narrative of the novel—leaps into action on their behalf, pursuing Arnold all the way to Texas to bring him to justice and return with the slaves. With only a local sheriff to aid him, and hampered by a wounded arm, Marcus wages an epic battle against four men until he is stabbed in the back by Arnold's stepson and then rescued in the nick of time by reinforcements from home. Although Arnold is not brought back for prosecution, Bellamy's friends are ultimately successful in recovering the slaves, who are "taken by virtue of the warrant" and conducted "home" (202). Whose ownership that "home" signifies is not specified, but the novel suggests that the slaves' financial value will be used to cover Bellamy's debt and return him to his original state of prosperity.

While only a small portion of *Marcus Warland* fits the definition of panic narrative, and Bellamy's failure seems designed more as a dramatic episode to showcase its hero's courage and loyalty than an opportunity for economic commentary, Hentz's treatment of the crisis and of its resolution illustrates many of the specific features, as well as the overall rhetorical agenda, of Southern panic fiction from the 1840s and 1850s. As discussed in chapter 1, these novels share with their Northern counterparts an overwhelming condemnation of speculation on both moral and economic grounds. Mr. Arnold's misplaced confidence in a venture that promises the unlikely return of double his investment, his rash haste to take advantage of the opportunity, and the obsessiveness signaled by his ironic declaration that "it would be madness to slight it," all denote the irrationality and single-minded pursuit of wealth that both Northern and Southern panic authors attribute to speculation and the speculator. Whether Arnold intended to defraud Bellamy from the beginning is unclear, but his precipitous flight from financial consequences and his removal of the slaves—property that could have mitigated Bellamy's debt if they had been left behind—not to mention his name, which resonates as "traitor" to Americans even now, certainly indict Arnold as a man of no integrity, willing to betray a friend for his own financial interest. In addition, the novel's comment that Arnold was "*considered* a wealthy man" rather than "*was* wealthy" echoes earlier panic fiction's representation of speculation as illusion; Arnold is able to get credit on the basis of his reputation, not his actual worth, a distinction that proves costly to all those who trust that reputation when it turns out to be false.

Beyond this depiction of speculation, however, Hentz's brief story of failure and recovery diverges from Northern narrations in a number of significant ways that are typical of Southern panic fiction. First, and perhaps most obviously, the class and occupational perspective has shifted from that of the middle- or upper-middle-class "merchant" of Northern panic novels to that of the Southern elite—the plantation owner. One significance of this shift is simply the recognition of regional differences between the economies of the North and South; planter protagonists signify the centrality of agriculture to the Southern economy in contrast to the commercial and industrial world pictured in Northern novels. Bankers and traders crop up occasionally in these novels, but their marginality suggests that Southern panic authors saw land, crops, and slaves as the economic arenas in which panic and a speculative economy took their most visible toll. But because the planter and slave owner are at the pinnacle of Southern society, the socioeconomic perspective of Southern panic fiction changes as well. The principal characters in these novels tend to be already wealthy as the story begins, and thus they do not display the "anxiety of gain," or concern about the method by which they might achieve financial advancement, found in Northern novels. And because their social position is secure and preeminent relative to those around them, we do not see the same attention paid to issues of interclass relationships.

Instead, the source of tension and of financial threat in Southern panic novels tends to be external—not from the protagonist's own speculation or extravagant spending as in most Northern panic fiction, or from within his immediate family and social circles, or even from dependents such as employees or slaves, but from an outsider whose speculation or other financial misdeeds bring ruin upon the main characters. In *Marcus Warland*, that person is a neighbor and fellow planter, but in many other Southern panic novels, the threat is more clearly differentiated—a stranger whose origin is unknown, for example, or even a Northerner. Novels in which the Southern male protagonist is complicit in his own financial failure usually cast him as either a victim to this stranger or outsider or seduced by an economic system alien to the Southern economy, such as the Southerner who moves to the North and finds failure in Wall Street speculations. In all of these variations, failure is not a danger inherent within the main characters' own regional economic milieu, as in most Northern panic fiction, but it is either visited upon them from the outside or the result of venturing outside a zone of safety and stability.

Another significant difference to note in *Marcus Warland* is that the agent of Mr. Bellamy's economic restoration is male rather than female. Although Mrs. Bellamy is given voice at a critical moment in the novel immediately following the discovery of financial disaster and, in fact, her counsel of thrift, steady industry, and gradual repayment of debt echoes the course of recovery guided by numerous panic heroines of the 1830s, it is Marcus's heroic battle against Arnold's men and his reclaiming of Arnold's slave property that are given credit for restoring the Bellamy's financial position. While female characters in Southern panic novels often (but not always) demonstrate some degree of financial competence, the economic roles available to women—for example, managing household expenses, providing a modest income, and advising financial restraint—are not the solutions to failure generally proposed in these novels. Rather than restraint and retrenchment, Southern panic novels tend to advocate some more proactive means of economic restoration or development. The physical exertion and even violence required for recovery in *Marcus Warland* are clearly exaggerations of economic action, but they serve to suggest the need for vigorous and decisive conduct of economic affairs that Southern panic authors envision. Thus, the agents of recovery are most often male characters who restore financial status and stability by means not open to women—physical strength, recourse to law, or the creation of new wealth through professional opportunities.

Given this emphasis on action, it is not surprising that Southern panic novels differ somewhat in style and generic conventions as well, manifesting a number of sentimental and melodramatic elements that are markedly subdued in their Northern counterparts. The violent conflict, dramatic rescues, and tender scenes of the hero being nursed back to health that are seen in *Marcus Warland* appear in other Southern novels as well, providing a rather different reading experience for the audience. Whereas Northern panic fiction of the 1830s seems designed to assuage the financial anxieties of readers and encourage imitation of its unflappable young heroines, Southern panic novels a decade or so later appear instead meant to excite and even alarm readers—to heighten their anxiety with melodramatic crises—and then to comfort them with highly emotional scenes of rescue and restored harmony.

All of these differences from the panic fiction of the 1830s—the plantation settings, the "outside" threat, the male agent of recovery, and the tendency toward melodramatic resolutions—point to a rhetorical agenda that is focused on defending an elite planter society and an economy based on slave labor from political attack and perceived economic domination of the North. Portraying the threat of financial ruin as coming from an external source not only echoes Southern anxiety about abolitionist rhetoric from the North but also reflects beliefs that panic was a creature of Northern commercial and banking interests, afflicting the South with financial hardship not of its own making. While such outside threats need to be repelled, the weaknesses that allow an "outside" financial crisis to devastate the South also have to be addressed. Thus, Southern authors' emphasis on masculine action and dramatic solutions to failure reflect their assessment of the South's particular need to actively develop its industrial and commercial resources in order to cease being vulnerable to Northern economic hegemony. At the same time, male agency and melodrama both serve to reinforce the hierarchies upon which Southern society rests. White male authority and dominance are legitimized by the actions of white male characters to resolve crises and protect their families, property, and communities, while melodramatic situations in which women or slaves need to be rescued underscore their rightful status of dependence. The relief (for readers) attendant upon the successful resolution of an abduction or a threatened foreclosure encourages acceptance of the hierarchical relations established or restored by that resolution. Thus, Southern panic fiction links its economic discourse on the causes and effects of panic to the prevalent political discourse about slavery and sectional power struggles. Panic and financial failure serve in these novels as symbols for a much broader threat to elite Southern society, comprising not only the specter of abolition but of Southern economic and political subjugation to Northern dominance.

Southern Economic Discourse: Contrasting Views on Strength and Vulnerability

Although it is difficult to assess the comparative effects of panic on different parts of the country, most historians agree that the South was hit hard by the Panics of 1837 and 1857. While a relatively small industrial base precluded the kind of mass unemployment seen in the urban areas of the Northeast, commerce was similarly disrupted in both regions and falling prices of export crops like cotton devastated Southern agriculture. In his listing of cities where banks suspended payment of specie in the spring of 1837, R. C. McGrane reports that Baltimore banks suspended payment on May 11, just one day after New York, while Mobile and New Orleans followed suit on May 12, Charleston on May 17, and Louisville and Augusta on May 19. The contraction of credit that accompanied these bank closings affected Southern speculators in much the same way it affected those in the North: investors who had borrowed in order to take advantage of rising land and slave prices in the booming Southwest (Alabama, Mississippi, and Texas) suffered great losses and many went bankrupt. Agricultural losses in the South, like those in the West, took perhaps the longest to recover from. Long after banks had reopened and manufacturing resumed, prices for land, crops, and slaves remained depressed. One factor that contributed to the South's rate of loss and hindered rapid recovery was the region's lack of economic diversification—in particular, its dependence upon the production of cotton. Thus, until cotton prices finally rose again in the 1850s, the whole Southern economy continued to feel the effects of the lingering depression.

Southern discourse about the causes of panic varied a good deal, as it did in the North, with speculators and banks usually sharing the blame. A typical article in the *New Orleans Picayune*, for example, in the May 20, 1837 issue, condemned bank suspensions as contrary to the interests of the community and called for a thorough investigation of banking corruption. The Southern economist Jacob Cardozo, on the other hand, largely exonerated the banks and pinned the blame on inevitable "business cycles," arguing that the low prices of the 1820s (following the previous panic in 1819) stimulated speculation, which in turn caused uncontrolled expansion of credit, rather than the other way around.[1] By the 1850s, however, many Southern commentators placed the blame either directly or indirectly on the North, arguing that Northern financial interests were ultimately responsible for both the speculation and the banking practices that created the crisis. The historian James Huston reports, for example, that those he terms "Southern fire-eaters" (outspoken defenders of slavery) blamed the Panic of 1857 entirely on New York bankers, while Kenneth Stampp concurs that Southerners felt "at the mercy of reckless Northern bankers and . . . rapacious Northern merchants" (230). Even in the 1830s, there was already a degree of suspicion and resentment toward the North in relation to the effects of panic. Another article from the *New Orleans Picayune*, this one written May 7, 1837, in anticipation of the general failure that would occur in the next few days, speculates on the anarchy and disorder the author expects to see in New York City as a result of unemployed thousands incited by "men who are too indolent to work and gain a competency for themselves, and who begrudge the possession of wealth by others." Although the target of this invective is Northern labor and land reformers rather than Northern money interests, the vivid image of thousands rioting in the streets of New York conveys Southern contempt for the North's industrial sector and a degree of fear of the social disorder imagined to be the natural consequence of free labor.

Blaming the North for the panic and its effects was, of course, part of a much larger pattern of Southern resentment of perceived Northern economic dominance in the 1840s and 1850s. Much has been written about antebellum economic strife between the North and South and the economic factors that helped precipitate the Civil War, including conflict over tariffs and animosity between proponents of free-labor and slave-labor systems. In relation to panic fiction, the important aspects of this larger debate are the questions of whether the South's economy was more stable as a result of its concentration in the agricultural sector and its use of slave labor or, in fact, more vulnerable to economic crisis because of that concentration and thus whether the distress resulting from antebellum panics could be blamed wholly on destabilizing Northern policies or whether it signaled Southern economic weakness. And if the latter were true, would economic diversification, including industrial development, strengthen the South's economic position relative to the North? These are the questions that Southern panic fiction addresses, directly or indirectly, in its treatment of the causes and effects of financial loss on the elite Southern home.

One prominent strand of Southern economic discourse during the 1850s was a fervent defense of Southern agriculture and the plantation system as not only more stable than Northern commerce and industry but also the preeminent source of the nation's wealth. In this view—a version of Jeffersonian agrarian philosophy prominent in the South since the eighteenth century—Southern wealth, rooted in the land and its produce, was seen as "permanent and real," while Northern wealth, manifested in the less tangible forms of stock certificates and other financial papers, was characterized as "fugitive and fictitious" (Van Vleck 88). Regardless of losses sustained in panics—and ignoring, apparently, the speculation through which the most profitable Southern land was trading hands—adherents of this view argued that the inherent value of Southern land-based wealth remained more stable than that of Northern factories and financial institutions. Proponents of Southern economic strength also pointed to the central role that slave-picked Southern cotton played in creating and sustaining the success of northeastern textile mills and shipping concerns in order to demonstrate Northern (and national) economic dependence on the South and on slave labor. Without such labor, they contended, there would be no cheap cotton to supply to subsequently profitable Northern mills or to provide the mainstay of American trade with Europe.

At the same time, ironically, many Southern defenders of plantation economics rejected purely capitalistic measures of economic strength and value, sometimes even adopting socialist language to condemn the exploitive nature of Northern industry, in particular. In promoting slavery as a superior labor system to Northern free-wage labor, they did not tout its profitability or efficiency as evidence of superiority but rather downplayed the economic aspects of the plantation altogether, locating "stable value" not in a competitive rate of growth but in a fixed hierarchical social order that was immune to the turmoil of class conflict.[2] One of the most prominent proponents of this view was George Fitzhugh, a Virginia lawyer, journalist, and author of two influential treatises on slavery, *Sociology for the South* (1854) and *Cannibals All! or, Slaves without Masters* (1857). Fitzhugh defends slavery largely by attacking the evils of "free society"—defined by the practices of economic competition (free trade) and the payment of wages to workers free to move from job to job (free labor). Grounded in an individualist philosophy, he argues, free society ignores man's social nature, his need to function wholly within the norms of his society and to be directed by it for society's greater good. Free society's individualist emphasis on competition pits men against each other, he notes, promoting antagonism rather than association, ultimately "array[ing] capital against labor" (*Sociology* 56). Those who are wealthy and talented thrive in competition but at the expense of those who cannot keep up—"the unemployed poor, the weak in mind or body, the simple and unsuspicious, the prodigal, the dissipated, the improvident and the vicious" (49–50).

Conscious of the similarities between his own criticisms of laissez-faire capitalism and those of socialists and other reformers, who had a much different agenda, Fitzhugh casts socialism as merely an inferior form of slavery. Socialists, he claims, were trying to protect the poor by essentially re-enslaving them (and everyone else) to the state or to some collective "master"; what Fitzhugh calls the "domestic slavery" practiced in the South is far superior, he contends, because individual human masters are more benevolent than collective masters (68). Essentially, it was this supposed benevolence that made slavery a better system of labor than free labor. Defenders of slavery routinely claimed that slaves were protected from the anxiety and poverty endured by wage laborers, wholly supported year-round by their owners, and cared for in sickness and old age when they could no longer work. Fitzhugh attributes this benevolence to the properties of ownership. In contrast with the competition seen between employer and employee, the interests of owner and slave were uniquely joined. Because slaves were his property, it was in the interests of the owner to protect and provide for them rather than gain advantage at their expense. In addition, ownership apparently engendered a kind of familial affection between slave and owner: "A man loves not only his horses and his cattle, which are useful to him, but he loves his dog, which is of no use. He loves them because they are his. What a wise and beneficent provision of Heaven, that makes the selfishness of man's nature a protecting aegis to shield and defend wife and children, slaves and even dumb animals" (*Sociology* 70).

Whether or not this ownership of slaves was actually of economic value to the slave owner is a matter of some inconsistency in Fitzhugh's writing. In his zeal to differentiate Southern slave labor from the well-known sufferings of industrial workers, Fitzhugh several times implies in *Sociology for the South* that slavery entails an overall cost to the slave owner and that the real economic value in slavery is the value of financial support *to* the slave: "Infant negroes, sick helpless, aged and infirm negroes, are simply a charge to their master; he has no property in them in the common sense of the term, for they are of no value for the time, but they have the most invaluable property in him. He is bound to support them, to supply all their wants, and relieve them of all care for the present or future. And well, and feelingly and faithfully does he discharge his duty" (82).

Thus he suggests that plantations are not operated for profit but as a kind of welfare institution for "negro" laborers who do not have the capacity to support themselves. However, in *Cannibals All!*, Fitzhugh acknowledges the plantation as a capitalist enterprise, if only to paint it as a less exploitive one than Northern industry: "The profits, made from free labor, are the amount of the products of such labor, which the employer, by means of the command which capital or skill gives him, takes away, exacts or 'exploitates' from the free laborer. The profits of slave labor are that portion of the products of such labor which the power of the master enables him to appropriate. These profits are less, because the master allows the slaves to retain a larger share of the results of his own labor, than do the employers of free labor" (111).

While Fitzhugh himself did not directly address the question of who or what was to blame for economic panic, nor whether the South's use of slave labor made it more or less vulnerable to the effects of panic, many of those Southerners who did blame the North employed rhetoric very similar to Fitzhugh's in their arguments. The same competitive drive, released by the North's individualist free-trade philosophy, was responsible, in their view, for both the exploitation of industrial workers and the reckless excesses of speculation that produced panic. The disorder wrought by labor conflicts between the northeastern working class and their employers seemed all of a piece with the chaos surrounding commercial bankruptcies, bank closings, and mass unemployment following panic. Conveniently ignoring the facts that speculation was also rampant in the Southern land-based economy and that periodic slave insurrections contradicted Southern claims of harmony and "identified interests" between slave and slave owner, some defenders of slave labor thus depicted the Southern plantation economy as an oasis of orderly prosperity, standing in stark contrast to Northern working-class poverty and discontentment. Losses sustained by plantations or Southern businesses due to panic were entirely unwarranted in this view, perpetrated against them by either deliberate Northern fraud or the unfortunate ripple effect of irresponsible Northern commercial practices.[3]

Not all Southerners held this view, however, even among the supporters of slavery. A second distinct strand of Southern economic discourse in the 1850s held that the South's economy was vulnerable, both to panic and to Northern domination, because of its unbalanced concentration in agriculture and failure to develop manufacturing capabilities. Even many who believed that the production of export crops was the South's principal strength feared the consequences of being too dependent on the North or on Europe for basic goods—that is, of not having the capacity for self-sufficiency should the political need arise. One proponent of this view was Maria McIntosh, one of the novelists whose panic fiction is discussed at some length below. McIntosh, a native of Georgia, who lived and wrote for many years in New York but never abandoned her Southern sympathies or identification, also wrote a nonfiction work titled *Woman in America: Her Work and Her Reward*, in which she challenged American women to raise American social life to the standards set by the nation's political ideals. In this work, she chastises Southerners, in particular, for valuing inherited wealth and status more than the education, labor, and useful trades that are necessary to establish an American meritocracy. She writes that "contempt for labor," especially that performed for money, is very common in the South—gentlemen are not supposed to need remuneration and thus avoid looking like they do. In response, she exclaims, "work! Though it be only to improve your own land; and if you work successfully, the world has become so much richer by your labors. Especially in a country professedly republican, can no wise or conscientious man remain an idler" (122). McIntosh's concerns here are clearly regional as well as national. She goes on to express her fears that Southern manufacturing, mines, and railroads will fall into the hands of "strangers" if Southerners continue their contempt for labor (123). And although she defends slavery as a benefit to both slaves and slave owners and to Southern culture in general, she also worries that slavery can discourage Southern self-reliance and thus reinforce a tendency toward economic stagnation (114). In contrast, she sees the North as a place of bustling enterprise that values labor but that needs to be calmed and channeled because its energies are focused on risk, gain, and attempts to achieve distinction (129). Interestingly, she sees the North as most representative of America itself, implying that the South needs to emulate the North in some respects if it is to maintain its political and economic viability. It must actively and energetically promote economic development in all sectors in order to remain independent of outside control and remain distinctively American.

Voicing a variation of this stance was the Southern economist Jacob Cardozo. Cardozo's complex view was that Southern economic health was dependent on revenue-producing export crops like cotton, and therefore the continued existence of slavery was essential to the South, but slavery could only be preserved if the South maintained political and economic strength equal to that of the North. And that, he argued, could only be achieved through regional self-sufficiency, which required industrial development (Leiman 177). While the South did, of course, have an industrial sector—and some historians argue that it was greater than usually believed—many in the South had resisted the diversion of resources from agriculture to manufacturing for a variety of reasons.[4] According to the historian Melvin Leiman, some worried that industrial development would divide Southern interests and produce a pro-tariff faction; others were concerned that Southern competitiveness in manufacturing (especially if slave labor were used) might stir greater abolitionist sentiment in the North; many simply feared that slaves and poor whites working in factories might develop class consciousness that could lead to insurrections (179–80). Cardozo rejected these arguments (without always addressing them directly) and contended forcefully for the development of a strong manufacturing sector, using slaves as a major component of the labor force. He saw the use of slave labor in manufacturing as a solution not only to Southern self-sufficiency but also to the problem of surplus slaves in the Old South (including his native South Carolina) and to the pressing need for renewed economic vitality in the coastal states being outstripped in agricultural production by the western interior. Noting the already diminished agricultural capacity of the Carolinas, Virginia, and Maryland, Cardozo foresaw a need for economic diversification if the entire region of the South were to remain an economic power. While Cardozo's concern for a more balanced economic development in the South was more directly aimed at protecting the institution of slavery than at protecting the South from the effects of panic—and he tended to see panics as largely unavoidable elements of natural business cycles—he did see steady economic growth as the best defense against crisis and warned against the destabilizing effects of the economic stagnation he saw in the more established Southern states.

What these two dominant strains of Southern economic discourse—that which boasted of superior Southern stability and that which warned of vulnerability—shared was a sense of the South as a distinct economic entity, less responsible than the North for the periodic upheavals of antebellum panic. Although historians note now that the financial practices most closely associated with panic—speculation, banking, monetary policies, foreign trade—operated much the same in the South as in the North, Southern discourse of the 1850s focused much more on the factors that differentiated the regions, including the extent of industrial development and respective modes of labor.[5] Southern economic fiction by women, not surprisingly, parallels the course of other economic discourse, both in its divisions and in its common central concerns. Some novels of the era that focus on demonstrating Southern economic strength follow George Fitzhugh's path of denying the capitalist nature of the plantation to such an extent that they can hardly be called panic fiction; fears of loss are deeply buried beneath strenuous claims of invincibility. Other examples focus much more directly on the potential for loss, advocating changes in Southern economic practices in order to better protect a society susceptible to attack or disintegration. But all the novels discussed below find ways to defend, rhetorically, the Southern plantation system from perceived outside economic threats.

Touched by Loss: Caroline Gilman and Caroline Hentz

Many of the most popular female authors of the antebellum South had personal experience of financial loss, with several directly affected by panic. Caroline Gilman, one of the earliest Southern fiction writers and already a successful novelist by the mid-1830s, suffered a dramatic drop in royalties when book buying decreased following the Panic of 1837. This placed a strain on the Gilman family finances, since Caroline's writing supplemented her husband's small salary as a clergyman. Both Caroline Hentz and Maria McIntosh turned to writing as a means of support following financial losses. McIntosh, a native Georgian from a wealthy planter family, lost all of her inherited fortune in the Panic of 1837 and began writing a few years later to reduce her dependence upon relatives. Hentz began writing in the early 1850s, ostensibly to rebut Harriet Beecher Stowe's characterization of Southern slavery in *Uncle Tom's Cabin* but also to ease financial strains caused by debt and her husband's long-term illness. Augusta Evans, the youngest of this group and perhaps the most successful, with best sellers *Beulah* and *St. Elmo* in the late 1850s and 1860s, experienced the financial reverses of panic as a child. Over a period of several years in the late 1830s and early 1840s, a combination of commercial panic and natural disasters bankrupted Evans's father and plunged the family into a state of poverty that lasted until Evans's own publishing successes. According to the critic Elizabeth Moss, financial loss and anxiety played a large role in the lives and careers of all of these authors, providing incentive for their publishing endeavors and shaping their views of society.[6]

And yet, one does not find in Southern fiction anything like the outpouring of responses to panic that occurred in the North during the same period. In fact, with the exception of McIntosh, panic and failure play very little direct role in the novels of these authors. One principal reason for this is that the most overt target of their social and political commentary is the issue of slavery rather than the consequences of a speculative economy. Even before the 1852 publication of *Uncle Tom's Cabin*, an increasingly radicalized abolition movement in the North—galvanized in part by Nat Turner's rebellion in 1831 and given organizational weight by the formation in 1833 of the American Anti-Slavery Society and publications like William Lloyd Garrison's *Liberator*—spurred Southern slave owners and their supporters to articulate ever-warmer defenses of slavery. Following the appearance of Stowe's novel, a number of Southern novelists jumped into the fray, penning direct responses to her claims of rampant cruelty and abuses of power and countering with idyllic depictions of contented, loyal slaves and benevolent masters. The degree to which these novels incorporated *economic* analysis of the merits of slavery versus Northern free labor, or depicted either system as vulnerable to financial loss, varied widely.

At one end of the spectrum, Gilman's fiction of the 1830s contains very little overt economic discourse at all. Her best-known works, *Recollections of a Housekeeper* (1834) and *Recollections of a Southern Matron* (1838), chronicle domestic life in the two worlds that Gilman knew—her native Massachusetts and the plantations of South Carolina, where she raised her family and lived for more than sixty years.[7] The two novels provide a fascinating contrast of Northern and Southern societies, subtly suggesting a greater degree of social harmony in Southern customs and structure. While the "matrons" of both texts cope with numerous domestic difficulties and demonstrate the vital importance of the woman's role in the home, the tone of each is quite different. The domain of Clarissa Packard, the New England "housekeeper," is barely contained chaos. Constant interruptions, problems with servants, and imperfectly learned responsibilities humorously characterize the Packard home as a place that has not yet achieved the peace and harmony of the developing domestic ideal. One of the chief sources of humor in the novel is the clash between Northern democratic ideals and actual social differences; two separate episodes feature rustic, uneducated servants in the Packard household attempting to converse with cultured guests on an equal basis to comic effect. While the Wilton household in *Southern Matron* displays a few similar moments, for the most part it represents, as Elizabeth Moss has noted, a "stable, ordered world" (67). Mrs. Wilton runs her domestic realm smoothly, labor is performed by slaves who understand and are contented with their places in the plantation hierarchy, and the poor, rural whites who correspond in education and manners to the servants in *New England Housekeeper* "voluntarily" refrain from mingling in "society unsuited to their unsophisticated habits" (*Southern Matron* 153). While Gilman does not explicitly favor one region or societal structure over the other, nor does she offer a socioeconomic analysis of respective labor systems, one can see in a juxtaposition of the two novels a fairly early illustration of the Southern claim to greater order and benevolence within the South's hierarchical slave society, in contrast with the chaos and inefficiency of Northern free labor.[8]

Nearly two decades later, Caroline Hentz makes the same claims, but much more explicitly and with a clear economic agenda, in her best-known novel *The Planter's Northern Bride* (1854).[9] As Eulalia Moreland, the bride of the title, overcomes her Northern prejudice against slavery on her husband's Georgia plantation, readers are privy to the tenets of her Southern education: that relationships between slaves and their owners are life-long ties of love and mutual benefit rather than fetters of exploitation; that in exchange for the economic benefit of their labor, slaves receive fair and kind treatment and are cared for when they are old or sick and can no longer work; and that slavery is a divinely sanctioned condition, with both slaves and owners born to their respective roles and thus obligated to perform their corresponding duties—obediently, in the case of the slaves, and benevolently, on the part of the owners.

Robert Hunt has argued persuasively that Hentz constructs slavery as an institution that is in direct opposition to market capitalism by erasing all signs of the plantation as an economic enterprise in her fiction and transforming it into a model domestic arena of mutual benevolence. Hentz's black slaves and white owners take care of each other, exemplifying relations of family rather than marketplace and thus refuting charges of economic exploitation. In addition, what we see of plantation life is centered around the house rather than the fields, and the only signs of labor visible are not connected to the commercial production of cotton but instead are the carpentry tools and spinning wheels used to produce domestic goods for the slaves. Nevertheless, a close reading of *The Planter's Northern Bride* shows that Hentz's erasure is not complete; traces of the economic basis of slavery can be found throughout the novel. One such trace is seen as Eulalia makes her first survey of her new surroundings and begins to realize the extent of her husband's holdings: "All around, far as the eye could reach, rich, rolling fields of cotton, bearing the downy wealth of the South, stretched out a boundless ocean of green, spotted with white, like the foam of the wave. Long rows of white-washed cabins, extending back of the central building, whose superior style of architecture distinguished it as the master's mansion, exhibited some black sign at every door, to show the colour of the occupants" (32).

The visual continuity between the long rolling fields of white cotton, specifically identified as "wealth," and the long rows of similarly white slave dwellings suggests these emblems of the plantation's human property as an equivalent component of Eulalia's dawning consciousness of her husband's social and financial position. Both images convey immensity, even near infinitude, and together they produce awe in Eulalia and the reader. Despite Hentz's efforts to downplay the economic dimensions of slavery, here the slaves (represented by their cabins) serve as both sign and source of Moreland's almost immeasurable wealth. This role of slaves in both creating and signifying the wealth of their owners has already been made apparent in an earlier scene, in which, on their journey to the plantation, Moreland and Eulalia stay overnight with a poor but honest white Southerner. Observing the man's efforts as a new landowner, Moreland predicts his future success, declaring, "this man, energetic and intelligent, is breaking in, as they say, a new portion of the country, and by and by the wild places will show the beauty of cultivation. He has already made money enough to purchase some negroes, who assist him in the field, he being chief workman, as well as overseer. His children, I doubt not, will be rich, and be associated with the magnates of the land" (29).

It is clear from this passage that the ownership of slaves is seen as a necessary step on the path of social and economic advancement in this society. The man's newly acquired "negroes" are both the tools with which he will break the land to create his plantation and the possessions that mark his children for Moreland as future "magnates."

But it is the climax of the novel—in which Moreland confronts and averts a slave insurrection that has been incited by a Northern abolitionist—that most clearly exposes the underlying economic agenda of Hentz's narrative. Having persuaded his slaves to stand down with a heart-felt appeal to destiny and mutual duty, Moreland expounds an explicitly economic vision of what would happen to the South and to the nation if such insurrections were successful:

> "Supposing, for one moment, the full triumph of fanaticism, how fearful would be the result! The emancipation of brute force; the reign of animal passion and power; the wisdom of eighteen centuries buried under waves of barbarism, rolling back upon the world; the beautiful cotton-fields of the South left neglected and overgrown with weeds; the looms of the North idle for want of the downy fleece, and England, in all her pride and might, bleeding from the wound her own hands had inflicted. . . . Suppose the triumph of fanaticism, agriculture would inevitably languish and die; the negro, as well as the white man, would not only sink into an abyss of poverty and ruin, but the withered energies, the decaying commerce, and expiring manufactures of the North would show the interests of the two different sections of our common country to be connected by as vital a ligament as that which united the twin-born brothers of Siam. Let the death-stroke pierce the bosom of one, the other must soon become a livid and putrifying corpse." (213–14)

In this apocalyptic vision of a new Dark Ages for America should slavery be destroyed, we can see that Hentz shares with panic authors a deep fear of national economic crisis, but she imagines it as arising from abolition rather than bank panic. The picture of slavery painted here is no longer a benign image of mutual love and voluntary obedience but rather one of enforced labor that produces wealth only under the enforcement of law and the sanctioned power of ownership. Beneath Moreland's racist language of animal passion and barbarism, his vision of slavery is essentially economic: it is slave labor that enables profitable mass production of cotton, which enriches Southern planters, provides labor for Northern and English textile mill workers, and supports Northern trade and industry. Without that enforced labor, cotton production would cease, bringing ruin to commerce and industry as well as to agriculture. By thus demonstrating the economic interdependence of North and South, and the dependence of both on the slave labor of Southern agriculture, Hentz positions the Southern economy as central to that of the nation and its preservation as crucial to protecting the nation from financial downfall.

In this light, we can see that Hentz's erasure of economics from her fictional plantation is actually part of an explicitly economic agenda, echoing the philosophy voiced by George Fitzhugh and others, that Southern slave labor was a more beneficial economic system than Northern free labor, protecting the worker from the abuses of a competitive system while providing a stable social structure for workers and masters alike. Hentz exhibits this view in numerous places in the novel, perhaps most explicitly in the example of Nancy, an impoverished former household servant whom Moreland meets while visiting in Massachusetts. Ill and starving, Nancy has been left to fend for herself since she is no longer strong enough to work. The narrator takes pains to explain that Nancy's former employer is not a cruel man but that customary employment relations in the North provide workers with support—wages—only for labor performed: "She had no claim on the affection of the man in whose service she had been employed. She had lived with him in the capacity of a hireling, and he, satisfied that he paid her the utmost farthing which justice required, dismissed her, without incurring the censure of unkindness or injustice" (26). Contrasting this attitude with the supposed lifelong care for old and infirm slaves, Hentz joins with Fitzhugh in disparaging labor arrangements based on economic exchange. Free labor, she suggests, is merely a monetary relationship between employer and employee, not an affectional one. Her assumption seems to be that only ownership can engender relationships of affection and obligation beyond the material, while independence is necessarily accompanied by detachment and lack of emotional bonds.

Hentz further develops these complicated links between relationships of dependence and emotional ties, on the one hand, and between economic independence and an isolating individualism, on the other hand, in her characterizations of women in the novel, both white and black. Specifically, these characterizations emphasize the role economic independence plays in destroying the mutually beneficial social hierarchy of the plantation. Moreland's first wife, Claudia, whom he has divorced, was an unsuitable wife precisely because she was independent from him, both emotionally and financially. Able to finance with her own money the entertainments she held for friends in defiance of Moreland's disapproval, Claudia's unwillingness to subordinate her own will to Moreland's is seen as inextricably linked with her financial independence. Having the means to finance her own desires enabled her to *have* desires distinct from her husband's and thus fostered cold individualism rather than the loving unity of marriage. Claudia's fate is, of course, tragic: she dies in semi-repentant agony, alone, still defiant, but with recognition of the happy life she could have had. Eulalia, Moreland's second wife, is Claudia's opposite. "Serene" rather than passionate, submissive to her husband's every desire, Eulalia's inexperience with money is made evident when Moreland pours the contents of his purse into her hands in order to use the purse for another purpose: "'What shall I do with this?' said Eulalia, blushingly clasping her fingers over the dripping money" (45). While he claims that everything he owns is hers to command, his trust in her—and the narrator's approval—depends on her implicit refusal to assume that command and her contented acceptance of her dependent role.

Clearly, those who acquiesce to the dependent roles prescribed for them find mutual love and unity of purpose in their surrender, while those who should be dependent but insist on controlling their own lives find only misery and isolation. This is most clearly illustrated in the story of Crissy, one of Moreland's slaves, who has the eccentric habit of hoarding gifts. Unlike the rest of the slaves, who, "certain of a future supply," immediately wear gifts of clothes and prodigally spend any money they get, Crissy keeps beautiful dresses in a chest, taking them out periodically to admire and air them, but she does not wear them. She also differs from the other slaves in being "wakeful"—not a napper or a deep sleeper—a quality that the narrator attributes to "her unusual prudence and forethought, anxious watchers by the bed of the white man, but strangers to the couch of the African" (224). Far from putting her on an equal footing with her white owners, however, these unusual qualities are seen as weaknesses for Crissy, making her vulnerable to the arguments of abolitionists who promise great riches to slaves who run away. When she does escape, Crissy finds only exploitation and poverty in Cincinnati, and ultimately she returns to the Morelands in penitence. The apparently intended message of this story is that Crissy's desire for financial gain caused her to sever the emotional ties between slave and owner, giving up the certain sufficiency of life lived in dependent relationship for the uncertain gains of individualist efforts. One can also see, though, that the quality of financial prudence, for which white heroines were admired in Northern panic novels, is depicted here as a shortcoming in Crissy because it implies independence of thought, an ability to plan and take control of one's own future rather than submission to the plans and control of an owner. Hentz finds both Crissy and Claudia to be inappropriate models of behavior, disrupting the fixed lines of hierarchy that allow the Southern slave system to function and to create wealth.

In emphasizing the familial nature of slave-owner bonds on the plantation, Hentz employs the conventions of 1850s domestic fiction to advance a Southern economic agenda. By (almost) erasing signs of the plantation as an economic enterprise and focusing on its domestic aspects, she presents the plantation as a version of the "haven" from the tumultuous marketplace depicted in numerous domestic novels of the era. But her location of that marketplace solely in the North and her heightened focus on the hierarchical nature of domestic relationships signal her specifically sectional purposes: to distance the plantation from critiques of exploitive and destabilizing economic practices, and to protect it from threats of social disorder. Hentz's sentimental style and portrayal of the plantation as held together by strong affectional bonds creates a vision for readers of a Southern idyll—protected from the vicissitudes of an unstable market by its noneconomic character and vulnerable to loss only if the protective armor of hierarchy is breached by individualist greed or the abolitionist outsider. A very different vision of how to protect the Southern economy emerges in the fiction of Maria McIntosh, who put the threat of loss front and center. At the opposite end of the spectrum from Caroline Gilman, McIntosh confronted issues of panic and failure directly in her novels, incorporating analysis of the South's financial situation into plots of gambling and bankruptcy and proposing solutions to the economic weaknesses she perceived.

A Panic Survivor: Maria McIntosh

As noted earlier, Maria McIntosh was born and raised in Georgia, in a small town south of Savannah. Her father, a lawyer and former military officer, was descended from Scottish immigrants who settled in Georgia in the early eighteenth century. At least one of her ancestors fought in the Revolutionary War. By the time she was twenty, in 1823, both of McIntosh's parents had died, leaving her to manage the family's property. She apparently remained in Georgia until 1835, at which time she sold the family estate and moved to New York City, living with a half-brother and investing her inheritance in bank stock. Just two years later, much of her money was lost in the panic and she turned to writing for income. Her first published works were children's fiction, published under the pseudonym "Aunt Kitty." She went on to write eight novels between 1843 and 1863, several of them quite popular and the most successful of which, *Charms and Counter-Charms* (1848), sold one hundred thousand copies. McIntosh did eventually achieve financial independence, never married, and died in 1878 at the age of seventy-five.[10] Whether because of her experience managing her own property for several years or from research related to her investment losses, McIntosh wove into her fiction the most detailed and knowledgeable descriptions of financial matters of virtually any antebellum writer. Her novels display a sophisticated grasp of such varied matters as marriage contracts, trusts, note discounting, and even the intricacies of the "post-obit"—a particular form of debt that falls due upon the event of inheritance. Thus, even though most of her fiction reaches far beyond the narrow focus of a typical panic narrative, it is permeated with a financial consciousness that makes issues of loss and gain central, regardless of actual plot.

McIntosh's first novel for adults published after her financial losses was *Woman an Enigma* (1843). Set in France just before and during the French Revolution, the novel follows the fortunes of a young woman, Louise de la Valliere, who is the daughter of a duke but has been raised in a convent so that her selfish parents might have more resources for their own pleasures. She is betrothed to a wealthy landowner, Henri de Montrevel, who pities her situation, but the two are separated by the machinations of Louise's cousin, who seeks the fortune that de Montrevel has settled on Louise. Accused of playing de Montrevel for his money, Louise ends the engagement, although she really loves him. When the French Revolution begins, de Montrevel joins the army to fight for the monarchy, while Louise and her now dependent mother flee to England. There they live in near poverty, surviving on the little money Louise can make doing embroidery for wealthy customers, since she refuses out of principle to touch the betrothal settlement from de Montrevel. During a lull in the war, alerted by a kindly banker to Louise's whereabouts and condition, de Montrevel comes to England, finds Louise, and falls in love with her. They are reconciled, marry, and use his ancestral diamonds to buy a simple cottage in England, the remainder of his estate having been confiscated in the revolution.

While the setting of *Woman an Enigma* certainly seems remote in time and place from the American economic crisis of the 1830s and 1840s, there are elements of the novel that suggest that McIntosh may have seen parallels between eighteenth-century French society and the antebellum South and between Louise's plight and her own. Many in the South certainly saw the elite planter society as a sort of American aristocracy, controlling small empires not unlike those of Europe's feudal landowners, and aspiring to a similar level of culture produced by wealth. Thus when de Montrevel returns to his neglected estate after many years away, and pledges to be a more dutiful landowner, responsive to the needs of "his" peasants, one senses a similar admonition aimed at landowners of McIntosh's own time. But to what end? Was she simply critiquing poor management of Southern estates? Was de Montrevel's removal of a tyrant overseer a remonstrance against oppressive aspects of slavery? Or was his determination to provide more "fatherly care" for his laborers an endorsement of slavery as a benevolent hierarchy à la Fitzhugh? The novel is rather ambiguous on the subject of the egalitarianism that was such a crucial aspect of the French Revolution: de Montrevel is clearly an aristocrat, motivated by notions of noblesse oblige, but when faced with confiscation, he happily leaves his estate in the hands of Jacques Brissot, a commoner whose democratic leanings are made clear throughout the novel.

The relevance to McIntosh's own experience of Louise's sudden poverty is much more evident. Left penniless by a combination of virtual orphanhood, war, and manipulation by villains who want control of a fortune intended for her, Louise is the epitome of the innocent victim who must undergo a financial education and expend great effort to take control of her own circumstances. McIntosh details Louise's transformation from an economic naïf who signs her marriage contract without comprehension and is repeatedly cheated of money by her father and cousin, to a much savvier young woman who finally refuses to sign a consent form—"I cannot, sir, till I know what it is"—and takes control of her financial arrangements (142). Like McIntosh with her writing, Louise also determinedly makes her own living in exile, refusing the alternative of dependence on others. The fact that she is rescued from this life of hardship by the arrival of de Montrevel, and her story ends with a fairy-tale marriage and life in a cottage, suggests an element of fantasy in McIntosh's depiction of loss and recovery. This first apparent attempt to treat the subjects of panic and financial loss in fiction seems very personal, focused as it is on the physical and emotional struggles of a young woman to cope with her own losses and conflicting feelings about dependence. But while *Woman an Enigma* lacks the broader economic scope found in a number of subsequent novels, it displays a melodramatic narrative and tone and an attribution of loss to outside causes that are picked up in McIntosh's later fiction.

Another novel from early in McIntosh's career, *Two Lives; or, To Seem and to Be* (1846), is more explicitly centered on issues of economic loss, although similarly removed for most of the narrative from a Southern setting. Two orphaned cousins, Grace Elliot and Isabel Douglass, are sent from the idyllic Georgia plantation where they were raised to an uncle's home in New York City. The first two-thirds of the novel follows the girls' romantic fortunes and moral development: Grace, pretty and spoiled, becomes engaged to an upright young soldier, but when he jilts her for taking part in a private theatrical production against his wishes, she marries a French nobleman and moves to Europe. Isabel, also lovely but less worldly and more principled, pines for the young minister whom she loves but has refused because she thought Grace loved him. Throughout this part of the novel, the moral contrast between the two heroines is underscored by their attitude toward, and use of, money. While Isabel dresses simply and spends her monthly allowance on charity, Grace responds enthusiastically to their aunt Elliot's worldly urban lifestyle, spending extravagantly for herself while forgetting her pledge to a local woman in need.

In its last third, the novel becomes a panic narrative, describing the course of two financial failures, and showing how the two young heroines respond to their respective losses of fortune. Showered at first with material abundance by her French husband, Grace becomes a gambler, wasting her fortune in an emotionally empty life of careless pleasure and a quest for "excitement." After her husband's death, however, with his entire property going to pay creditors, she lives out a nightmare of financial decline, gambling away her income, seeking to recoup her losses with money raised on her future income, and then losing that as well. Brought to her moral senses by a creditor who demands sexual favors as repayment, Grace returns home to die of consumption and shame.

Back in New York, Isabel also loses her fortune to the seductive lure of risk and the promise of gain, but she is not the one seduced. Uncle Elliot first loses his own money speculating on Wall Street, then, convinced that only a few hundred more would repair his fortune, he likewise speculates with and loses Isabel's money, which she has generously given to him when she discovers his failure. Following the pattern of earlier panic fiction, Uncle Elliot and Isabel auction off their unnecessary furnishings and move to a smaller home, while Isabel gives music lessons to supplement their meager remaining income. In stark contrast with Grace's frenzied efforts to restore her financial standing with ever greater risks, Isabel submits cheerfully to her uncle's losses and points to their mutual love as their real wealth. Eventually, her former lover returns, her true feelings for him are revealed, and they return to the South to live happily ever after.

In many ways, *Two Lives* parallels the concerns of Northern panic fiction. Like Hannah Farnham Sawyer Lee and other Northern writers, McIntosh blames financial failure on multiple and interwoven causes—extravagant spending, the excitement of potential gain through either gambling or speculation, and the role of easy credit in encouraging investors to risk what they cannot repay. If anything, McIntosh's understanding of the minutiae of a credit economy surpasses that of Lee and her Northern cohort, as she narrates the terms of Grace's sequence of loans and credit instruments in great detail. *Two Lives* also shares Northern panic novels' sense of anxiety about unstable value in a volatile economy. When Mr. Elliot, in declaring the scope of his failure, says, "I am a ruined man . . . I have raised money—all that they are worth, more than they would bring—on my place in the country, in my house in town, on my horses and carriage, on my furniture," the discrepancy he sees between what his property is "worth" and what it would "bring," or sell for, in the market posits a distinction between market value and "real" value (217). Concern about preserving "real" value—and being able to distinguish between the real and the merely "seeming"—is the novel's underlying theme, evidenced in both its subtitle, "To Seem and to Be," and in the motif of Grace's playacting.

For the most part, *Two Lives* develops this theme on a moral and relational, rather than financial, level. Grace's participation in a theatrical production is objectionable to her scrupulous fiancé Walter because her convincing portrayal of love for another man on stage—a rival for Grace's affections—calls into question both the sincerity of her declarations of love for Walter and the genuineness of her voiced repentance when he chides her for disregarding his wishes. When love can be feigned, how can one ever be certain of its reality? Anyone "skilled in artifice," as Walter describes Grace, becomes untrustworthy even when they are telling the truth. When the novel turns to the depiction of gambling and speculation, we see the financial subtext to this motif. Investment opportunities that "seem" to offer profit cannot be trusted. Credit produces the illusion of value but not its substance. Only when appearance and substance correspond exactly—a state epitomized by Isabel's complete sincerity and moral integrity—can value be trusted. It is no accident that McIntosh depicts the transparent Isabel as financially responsible, understanding what truly has value, while Grace, whose acting plays the same symbolic role as the imagery of vapor, bubbles, and gilding in 1830s panic novels—all emblems of insubstantial "seeming"—is the reckless gambler. In presenting this contrast between her two heroines and the relations to value that they represent, McIntosh echoes earlier panic authors' calls for complete transparency in financial practices and a true correspondence between investment and actual assets.

To a point, *Two Lives* also follows the narrative pattern of Northern panic fiction, as well as echoing its concerns. Extravagant spending, desire for quick gain, and the excitement of risky financial ventures build throughout the first two-thirds of the novel, reaching a climax with the alternating narratives of Grace's lavish wedding expenditures and her uncle's desperate attempts to retrieve his business losses through stock speculations. Mr. Elliot's failure is then followed by familiar scenes of domestic "downsizing," with the "carpets and tables, girandoles and chandeliers, couches, divans, and ottomans, splendid curtains, French china, and glittering plate"—the trappings of fashionable life—replaced with the "comfortable chintz-covered sofa" and simple muslin curtains that mark a household living within its means (251). Mr. Elliot repents of his financial folly and leaves behind the temptations of Wall Street.

McIntosh's narrative diverges from the 1830s model of Lee and other panic authors, however, in two significant ways. The first is that Isabel is not the agent of the family's economic recovery in the mode of Lee's Elinor Fulton or Eliza Follen's Amy Weston. She is not even a replica of the determinedly independent Louise Valliere in McIntosh's earlier *Woman an Enigma*. Although Isabel does supplement her uncle's income by giving music lessons, she remains dependent on his support and her principal role during the periods of loss and recovery is to provide unconditional comfort and sympathy. When she learns of her uncle's initial losses, for instance, she simply gives him five thousand dollars of her own money, which he promptly loses as well. When he confesses the extent of his losses, she assures him that "we will learn to endure all painful things cheerfully for each other's sake, dear uncle. Every smile I win from you will be worth more than a thousand dollars to me, and so you may soon bring me largely in your debt" (255). In short, Isabel's chief virtue is not her domestic competence or her thrift but rather the quality of caring so little for her money that she does not mind when her uncle loses it—that is, her generosity and self-sacrifice. It is also significant to note that Isabel does not direct the household retrenchment but follows her uncle's direction, receiving his "permission" to take what is needed from the old house to the new.

The second significant difference is Grace's transformation in the last section of the novel to that most shocking figure, the female gambler. While her extravagant spending earlier in the novel follows the well-worn path of positing excess consumerism as the feminine equivalent to masculine speculation, McIntosh places Grace beyond redemption when Grace becomes the speculator herself, attempting to both create and spend wealth rather than merely spending it. While McIntosh may have meant simply to draw upon the imagery of European decadence in contrast to American morality, Grace's actions also represent a violation of the ideal separation between women and monetary desire. She is not merely reckless in her spending but takes on the male role of actively pursuing gain. Although Grace, like her uncle, repents of her "madness" and returns home, she is not accorded the same chance to be rehabilitated and to reenter American society but is "punished" with consumption and death. McIntosh seems to suggest here a particular danger in feminine monetary desire, akin to Caroline Hentz's depiction of the rebellious and almost demonic Claudia Moreland, whose stubborn insistence on her own financial and emotional autonomy led her beyond the bounds of acceptability and to a similarly agonizing death. Both characters illustrate a perceived risk in women stepping beyond certain prescribed economic roles.

With Grace's sad, but apparently justified, death and Isabel's loving passivity in the face of failure, McIntosh preserves a patriarchal society in which women play only supporting roles or suffer tremendous consequences for taking economic actions on their own behalf. Both women and men are seen as capable of either responsible or irresponsible economic behavior, but panic and loss are not presented as opportunities for women to exercise a larger voice in reforming the marketplace or even their own family finances. Instead, McIntosh's principal agenda seems more aimed at blaming financial loss—and the moral corruption that produces such loss—on societal influences outside of the South. All of the main characters are transplanted Southerners who have left the innocent paradise of their upbringing only to be faced with the "soulless pleasures" of New York City and the temptations of Wall Street, as well as the even greater decadence of Europe. This Northern (and European) urban setting is seen to work differently on different characters; in the cases of Grace and both Aunt and Uncle Elliot, the ever-present temptations to extravagance, speculation, and gambling appear to nourish the growth of already existing characters flaws, while for Isabel, they are simply evils to be resisted and sources of undeserved suffering. One might speculate that McIntosh's own experience of suffering loss so soon after having moved to the North from Georgia and having transferred her property from Southern land to New York-based securities may have prompted this narrative of Northern corruption and catastrophe. In any case, the South remains a place of innocence and nostalgia in the novel, a place of return for those who have survived loss with moral integrity intact, while the North poses multiple dangers for the unwary.

The Lofty and the Lowly; or Good in All and None All-Good

Seven years after the publication of *Two Lives*, McIntosh wrote and published her most explicitly and completely panic-oriented novel, *The Lofty and the Lowly; or Good in All and None All-Good* (1853). Of all her work, this is the novel most centered on the issue of impending financial loss and treats in greatest detail the fear and anxiety associated with such loss. It also displays to the greatest degree the distinctive elements of a specifically Southern response to panic.

In the novel's preface, McIntosh announced that her intent—in this time of great tension between North and South—was to portray both Southern and Northern societies fairly and to "remove . . . prejudices" that readers from both regions had toward each other. To this end, the novel centers largely on three families: the Montroses, owners of a Georgia cotton plantation; the Brownes, a wealthy Boston merchant and his family; and the Grahames, proprietors of a New England textile factory. Colonel John Montrose is depicted as a typical Southern landowner, proud and imperious but also guided by honor and generous to his dependents. He and his wife have two nearly grown children, Donald and Isabelle, and also support his brother's widow, Mrs. Charles Montrose, and her two children, Charles and Alice. Mrs. Charles Montrose was originally from Boston, which is where her husband died as a result of anxiety following bankruptcy. She moves south to her brother-in-law's home after her husband's death because her own brother, the merchant Thomas Browne, is too stingy and cold-hearted to come to her aid. Browne lives with his wife and children, including his dissolute son, George, in an opulent city mansion. The third of the novel's families, the Grahames, are a trio of siblings—Robert, Richard, and Mary—whose late father, Edward Grahame, had been a pioneering American manufacturer. Mr. Grahame also died following a financial failure, and is succeeded by his college-educated son, Robert, who labors hard to repay his father's debts and to return the factory to a profitable state.

The three families become intertwined in numerous ways throughout the course of the novel. The novel's dramatic force comes from a journey the Montrose family makes to the North to meet Donald after his graduation from West Point. After some weeks of traveling, Donald falls in with a group of gamblers headed by George Browne and Richard Grahame. As with McIntosh's earlier novel, *Two Lives*, gambling serves as a parallel to speculation—engaged in for the same motives of greed and attraction to risk and resulting in the same consequences of physical illness, moral collapse, and financial ruin. Donald's seduction and fall is complete and catastrophic. After many nights unable to resist the "intense and dangerous excitement" and "intoxication" of the gaming tables, he finds himself in debt to Browne for five thousand dollars (126). Trying to recoup his losses, he loses to Grahame as well and, in an "act of murderous passion," attacks Browne and then falls ill with a brain fever and spends several months recuperating at the Grahame home, nursed by Mary Grahame (141, 145). In the meantime, the villainous Browne manipulates Donald's IOU notes to himself and Richard, taking advantage of Donald's carelessness and naiveté in leaving the amounts blank and adding usurious interest charges. By the end of the novel's first volume, a series of intricate financial maneuvers have left Donald in debt to George Browne's father for sixty-five thousand dollars, an amount that can only be raised by liquidating the entire Montrose estate and leaving his now-widowed mother and sister homeless and without support.

The second volume of *The Lofty and the Lowly* opens with multiple discussions and negotiations about how to pay Donald's gambling debts without having to either sacrifice Montrose Hall, the ancestral mansion, or sell any of the slaves. Eventually, Donald and his mother decide to mortgage the women's shares of the property, a move that fulfills the immediate obligation to Mr. Browne but leaves the Montroses in debt to the rapacious Northern (and implicitly Jewish) moneylender Uriah Goldwire and pins their hopes of paying off the new debt on future cotton profits. To ease the family's financial burden, Mrs. Charles Montrose and Alice return north to Massachusetts, where Alice takes on the typical panic fiction role of household and financial manager. First she learns to budget their meager income and does most of the household work herself; when the Panic of 1837 results in the suspension of banking operations, and thus leaves Alice and her mother without access to their funds, she earns money doing embroidery piece work, giving music lessons, and cultivating and selling flowers.

Both story lines conclude with rather melodramatic episodes and both feature the industrialist Robert Grahame as hero. In the spring of 1837, "the period of disaster and dismay, when men's hearts everywhere are failing them for fear," as McIntosh describes the panic, the collapse of the cotton market leaves the Montroses unable to sell their crop and therefore unable to meet the semiannual interest payment on the mortgage (2: 107). Goldwire forecloses on the estate and is about to take possession, but just as the three-day grace period for redemption is about to expire, Isabelle's suitor, Major Wharton, arrives dramatically on horseback from Florida, carrying a check for forty thousand dollars from Robert Grahame to pay off the mortgage and take over as a much more sympathetic and lenient creditor. The estate remains intact, Donald learns to become financially responsible, and eventually he marries Robert's sister Mary, his former nurse. Even more dramatically, Alice is abducted by her cousin George Browne and has to be rescued after an all-night chase by Robert Grahame and Major Wharton. Browne's crimes against Donald finally come to light, and Donald is recompensed with interest, while Alice and Robert fall in love and make plans to marry. As a final touch, Mr. Charles Montrose's supposedly bankrupt estate turns out to be worth thirty to forty thousand dollars, making complete the circle of financial restoration.

McIntosh's inclusion of both Northern and Southern characters and settings in the novel provides a fairly comprehensive view of regional economic conditions and the differing effects of panic on various parts of the country and people of diverse circumstances. The two characters who have died before the novel even begins, both of their illnesses compounded by the anxieties of failure, demonstrate not only the pervasiveness of economic loss but also the author's sophisticated understanding of its multiple causes. While we get very little detail about Charles Montrose's apparent bankruptcy, we do know that he was a Southerner of the planter class, a younger son with probably little opportunity for a successful career at home, who had gone north for business. His supposed failure and subsequent illness are attributed simply to "foolish speculations," suggesting the combined roles of investor folly and speculative volatility in causing failure (11). Edward Grahame's bankruptcy was of an entirely different nature. One of the earliest American textile manufacturers, McIntosh depicts him as having risked his capital in building his factories for the worthy goal of securing "the financial independence of his country" through industrial self-sufficiency. The wartime economy during the War of 1812 had promised profitable returns for manufacturing, but resumed trade with Britain following the war had raised cotton prices and dumped cheap English goods in American markets, destroying Grahame's business. His ruin, therefore, was not due to any moral failing or lack of prudence but to explainable economic and political causes beyond his control.

When the Panic of 1837 hits late in the novel, its effects on both the North and South are governed by the regional particularities of investment, assets, social status, and occupation. We witness a Northern perspective through the difficulties of Alice and her mother, transplanted to a Boston suburb and struggling to maintain a modest household. Their small legacy, the income of which provides the bulk of their living, is invested in bank stock. They are thus affected both by the suspension of the banks, which hinders their access to their funds, and also by the unprotected value of the stock itself. Mr. Browne warns Alice that they might lose the whole sum unless they take advantage of "desperate speculators who might, perhaps, give half its nominal value for your Bank stock" (76). The principal consequences for the two women are a tightened budget and the necessity for Alice to earn money, marking her—temporarily, at least—as working class. This perspective tallies well with historians' accounts of the effects of panic on Northern urban laborers and the lower-middle class. Robert Grahame's textile mill, interestingly, seems to suffer no ill effects from the panic at all, suggesting that McIntosh may have perceived some Northern industrial concerns as relatively immune to the panic, financially stable enough to be secure from market fluctuations.

The effects on Mrs. Montrose, Donald, and Isabelle on their Georgia plantation are the most dramatic, in part because Donald's gambling debts have already placed them in a precarious financial position. Since the Montrose wealth is tied up largely in land and slaves, their inability to meet the mortgage payment as a result of the panic's effect on the cotton market means that, in an indirect way, the panic threatens their entire way of life. They will lose Montrose Hall, which signifies not only their physical home but also their ancestral history; they will also lose the land and the slaves, which signify not only the family's means of subsistence but also their status and identity as planters and slave owners in a society where such status is critically important.[11]

Further reinforcing this sense of threat to elite Southern identity is the moneylender Goldwire's expressed desire to possess Isabelle, the quintessential Southern "belle" and thus a symbol of Southern planter culture. On his initial visit to appraise the Montrose estate and draw up mortgage papers, he is overheard saying of Isabelle, "I'd give a good many hundreds of dollars for such a beautiful ______" (2: 37), and as the foreclosure is unfolding Mrs. Montrose feels a "creeping terror" of Goldwire's intentions toward her daughter, specifically his potential power to extort a marriage from Isabelle in exchange for a more favorable settlement. Contained in this fear is not only an anti-Semitic repulsion toward the person of the moneylender himself but dismay at the thought of Isabelle's beauty being treated as something to be purchased. The sacrosanct image of Southern womanhood is violated not only by Goldwire's implicit sexual desire for Isabelle but also by the commerciality of his conceptions of how to acquire her. McIntosh suggests here, in rather inflammatory terms, the vulnerability of Southern planter culture as a whole to the effects of panic and to the contaminating and rapacious touch of Northern commerciality. Financial need has put the Montrose family into the position of not only having to engage in business with a man beneath their social status but also of having the most fundamental elements of their planter identity commercialized, assessed in the starkly monetary terms of the marketplace.

Goldwire is one of the most blatant examples of McIntosh's regional and ethnic stereotyping in the novel, but despite her claims of writing to dispel the false images that Northerners and Southerners hold of each other, in fact, many characters in *The Lofty and the Lowly* display stereotypical traits. For example, immediately after disparaging clichés of the Northerner as cheap and greedy and the Southerner as lazy, spendthrift, and uncivilized, McIntosh confirms some of these very traits, portraying the Boston merchant Thomas Browne as a man marked by his stinginess and Colonel Montrose as contemptuous of having to work for a living. Browne, not wanting to have to support his sister and her children, writes a letter recommending that they be trained to support themselves; Colonel Montrose, outraged that Browne is "arranging a life of toil" for their common relations, declares that young Charles and Alice "shall have no need to labor while I have a home to offer them" (17). This clearly deliberate use of stereotype suggests that McIntosh's real concern may not have been to promote greater understanding and appreciation between North and South but rather to combat what she perceived to be the economic weaknesses underlying regional stereotypes, particularly the economic weaknesses of the South. Colonel Montrose's dismay at the prospect of a "life of toil" underscores the Southern prejudice against remunerated labor that McIntosh so deplores in *Woman in America*, where she laments the South's failure to develop its industrial and commercial resources. She makes this point even more explicitly during the Montroses' visit to the North, where she makes Mrs. Montrose a mouthpiece for her own concerns in an exchange with George Browne. Attempting to flatter Mrs. Montrose by praising the aristocratic qualities of the South, Browne gushes about Southern "repose of manner," in contrast with Northern ostentation and what he calls the North's "laboriousness." Rather than accept the compliment or acknowledge Southern superiority, however, Mrs. Montrose responds surprisingly by defending the North: its display of wealth is justified by its having more wealth to display, she says, while the North's lack of "repose" is a positive sign of "enterprise and industry . . . [and marks a] healthier and happier system than that in which all is stagnant." She concludes by remarking that Southern repose has been "too dearly bought," presumably at the expense of the kind of commercial energy that drives Northern economic development (95). Neither Mrs. Montrose nor McIntosh herself is truly granting Northern superiority here. Mrs. Montrose goes on to qualify her approval of Northern enterprise by rejecting the "jostling and browbeating" that accompany energy not harnessed by cultivation, while McIntosh's portrayals of the calculating merchant

Thomas Browne and his villainous son George make clear her severest disapproval of an unchecked and self-serving drive for money that she associates with Northern commercial interests. The real point that McIntosh is making is that flaws in the Southern economy have contributed to the region's relative lack of economic progress and must share some portion of the blame for the economic distress resulting from panic.

We see this distribution of blame most clearly in Donald's gambling losses. Both Donald and the men who manipulate his losses are partially responsible for Donald's fall, each contributing in ways that represent what McIntosh apparently perceived as distinctive regional faults. Donald is too easily drawn into gambling because of traits that, McIntosh suggests, his Southern planter background has either permitted or actively instilled: a lack of discipline, no respect for labor, and a temperament that craves the excitement of gambling. Once hooked, Donald cannot stop nor does he prevent Browne from cheating him because his Southern pride has taught him to despise financial considerations; keeping track of his losses and gains seems petty and "trade-like" to him, so he signs notes without confirming their accuracy, a carelessness that allows Browne to alter the figures. But Donald's pride and lack of discipline are clearly outweighed by Browne's "Northern" faults of greed and exploitation. By taking advantage of Donald's weaknesses—deliberately enticing him to the gaming tables in order to win from him and then increasing the debt by fraudulent means—Browne displays a calculation, an intent to harm, that contrasts sharply with Donald's thoughtlessness and makes him far more culpable for the near loss of the Montrose estate. Although Browne's merchant father despises his lack of work ethic and illicit methods of gain, father and son actually share the trait that McIntosh is condemning in Northern businessmen: a desire for money that overshadows any humane considerations and thus allows cruelty, exploitation, and even fraud toward others in the pursuit of profit.

Translating Donald's misfortunes to a national scale, McIntosh is clearly suggesting that Southerners need to look at the role that their own lifestyles and ways of thinking have played in making their region's economy vulnerable to the effects of panic. Pride in the culture and wealth of elite planter society has hindered their economic development in commerce and industry, she implies. Even the agricultural sector has lagged because the upper classes do not deign to run their plantations themselves. Donald's contempt for the details of his gambling debts signals a broader negligence toward property that invites deterioration. In addition, the cultural acceptability of gambling encourages dangerous risk taking on the markets; the larger speculative conduct that Donald's gambling represents has weakened the fabric of the Southern economy, McIntosh suggests. But the panic itself, the triggering event that turns these vulnerabilities into actual losses, those McIntosh pins on the North. It is the outsider who takes advantage of Southern weakness—the New York banker who manipulates currency or the Boston merchant who controls cotton prices—who forces the failures of Southern businesses, just as George Browne's manipulations almost force the confiscation of Montrose Hall. Southern pride and neglect are so dangerous precisely because they leave the South open to the machinations of an economic infrastructure controlled by and for Northern interests.

McIntosh's analysis of the needs of a Southern economy in the 1850s extended to her depiction of financial recovery as well as of financial loss. As with her earlier novel *Two Lives*, *The Lofty and the Lowly* does not present this recovery as either an opportunity for women to exercise greater economic agency or as more effectively accomplished by women, as Northern panic fiction implicitly claimed. However, unlike the female characters of *Two Lives*, who are either passive and subservient in economic matters or clearly transgressive, the women in *The Lofty and the Lowly* are both more varied and more realistic in their levels of financial understanding, competence, and desire for control. At one end of the scale, the widowed Mrs. Charles Montrose is completely helpless to manage her own affairs after the death of her husband, passively allowing her brother and brother-in-law to negotiate terms of her future support without her participation. Early on, she characterizes herself as having devoted herself entirely to the sentimental, rather than practical, aspects of life, saying, "my life, for many years, has been a life purely of the affections. I have read little, thought little, and felt—oh how much!" (24). Later in the novel, living with her daughter Alice in Boston, she remains dependent on the younger woman for financial support. In contrast, her sister-in-law, Mrs. John Montrose, plays a very active role in resolving the family's financial difficulties and displays the kind of competence and moral integrity with relation to finances typically seen in Northern panic fiction heroines. It is she who raises the issue that Donald's debts endanger the security of their "people"—that is, slaves—by putting them into his creditor's power. Donald's sense of honor places his personal reputation above his fortune, and thus he is prepared to sacrifice his entire property to pay off his debts and retain his honor. The women, however, see the welfare of their human property as more important than reputation, and thus Mrs. Montrose proposes that she and Isabelle sacrifice their shares of the inheritance to settle Donald's debts without having to sell any slaves. Donald eventually acquiesces to his mother's plan to mortgage the women's shares and further allows himself to be schooled by her in a more economical management of the plantation, as she proves herself to be "a most excellent and unsparing economist" in retrenching the domestic budget (2: 64).

The younger generation of Montrose women similarly presents varied degrees of financial understanding and competence. Isabelle, while much less passive than her aunt, represents a position in which women contentedly relinquish economic agency to men. She plays virtually no role—other than object of desire to the moneylender Goldwire—in the discussions of how to pay off her brother's debts, and later she intentionally chooses economic dependence within marriage. Standing to inherit one-third of her father's estate after the financial crisis has been resolved, Isabelle is offered the opportunity to manage her own property. Her future husband—the gallant Major Wharton, who played a role in rescuing the Montrose estate from confiscation—is not a wealthy man and thus honor dictates that he demonstrate his lack of interest in her fortune by resigning what would ordinarily be his right to his wife's property. When he insists that Isabelle's fortune be placed entirely in her own control, however, Isabelle exercises that control by immediately returning the favor—proclaiming that she surrenders "the sole entire control over this income to Major Wharton during my life" (2: 216). Thus, Isabelle demonstrates a certain degree of assertiveness in financial matters but uses that assertiveness solely to restore masculine control of her own finances and thereby maintain the hierarchical social order of plantation society.

Her cousin Alice ends up in a similar position of dependence, but she takes a much different route. Forced to be financially independent by the family's money difficulties and her desire not to be a burden, Alice comes the closest of any of McIntosh's heroines to being an agent of economic recovery. As discussed earlier, she practices household economy and supports herself and her mother through a variety of typical female employments, including piece-work, music lessons, and selling flowers, earning upward of four dollars per week. We also see her entering the male world of finance when she ventures out to her landlord's counting-house in order to negotiate for leniency on the rent during the panic. When her brother Charles returns from a long absence in the navy and is appalled to find her working for money, Alice expresses pride in her earning power and mounts a spirited defense against his objections. Her dismissal of his warnings of societal disapproval, her reiteration of their need, and her assurance that work makes her stronger rather than diminishing her health all suggest that McIntosh was advocating some level of financial independence for women—at the very least, social acceptance of women's self-support when circumstances make that necessary.

But when Charles counters all of Alice's arguments with a claim of ownership, saying, "you must remember, my dear child, now that I am at home, you are no longer to make bargains and hire yourself out as if you were free; you belong to me now," Alice accepts her "slave" status with a measure of relief: "I like that a great deal better, but I am not sorry to know that I can help myself" (2: 186). McIntosh has also made clear that Alice's independence is neither her natural state nor a state for which she is fit. When she makes her "bold adventure" to the landlord's office, for example, she is hardly bold and finds herself in a place that contains numerous threats to her well-being: "Timidly and slowly, shrinking from every eye, Alice wound her way among bales, barrels, boxes—a noose now hanging threateningly above her, and now a cry of 'take care there,' causing her to spring aside just as a barrel came rolling across her path" (2: 82). Unlike the heroines of Northern panic fiction, Alice is conscious of being in a world where she does not belong and that holds danger for her from which she ought rightly to be protected. Her negotiations also illustrate her naiveté in business, as her proposal to the landlord of 100 percent interest on the rent in exchange for late payment offers such self-ruinous terms that he—fortunately a generous man—jokes about it to the other men. Alice's vulnerability apparently makes her very appealing, and the desire to take care of her is not confined to her brother but is also one of the reasons Robert Grahame wants to marry her.

Ultimately, we see that, regardless of how independent or dependent the female characters are, how financially competent or passive, their place in the patriarchal hierarchy of plantation society remains subordinate to that of white males. McIntosh acknowledges important roles that women can play in difficult economic times, such as Alice's self-support and Mrs. John Montrose's counsel of sacrifice and compassion for the slaves, but these roles are merely supporting ones and not finally responsible for the family's economic restoration. Alice is rescued from her subsistence-level existence, first by Charles and then by Robert, while it is Robert's assumption of the role of Donald's creditor that delivers the Montrose estate from imminent dissolution. In fact, the women must, as Isabelle so dramatically does, explicitly and willingly accept subordinate roles within their family and society in order to restore the proper social order. Charles's claim that Alice is not "free" and that she "belongs" to him—and her grateful acceptance of that relationship—signals the parallel dependence required of women and slaves in a slavery-based society and the importance of each member's contented acquiescence to that hierarchy.

McIntosh underscores the importance of having the social order restored by employing both sentimental and melodramatic elements to a far greater extent than Northern panic authors did. In narrating Alice Montrose's efforts at self-support, for example, instead of employing the same calm and matter-of-fact style that Lee used to accentuate her heroines' competence and inspire emulation in middle-class female readers, McIntosh makes Alice seem vulnerable and pathetic, an object for readers' pity and fear. Readers of the time may have admired her for braving the hazards of the warehouse and for stepping into unaccustomed roles for the sake of her mother, but repeated scenes of Alice's weary exertions and descriptions of her as, for example, "shrinking" from male eyes as she approaches the landlord's countinghouse, seem designed to prod readers into hoping for Alice to be rescued from the drudgery of self-support and the terrors of self-assertion that it requires. Reader sympathy is also stirred by the scenes in which Mrs. John Montrose proposes the sacrifice of her own property to prevent the necessity of selling the slaves. Here, McIntosh employs sentiment not to make readers feel sorry for Mrs. Montrose but to inspire a sympathetic tenderness by her evident love for her dependents and her noble willingness to suffer in order to prevent their suffering. In both cases, sentiment functions to validate a hierarchical social structure—by moving readers to see Alice as being in need of protection and by portraying the relationship between owner and slave as a truly loving bond that acts in beneficial ways for the slave.

Sentimentality is often paired with certain melodramatic elements, especially the employment of contrast between a helpless, suffering victim (often female) and a powerful hero (nearly always male) who rescues that victim with extraordinary feats of strength, skill, or courage.[12] The drama scholar Jeffrey Mason argues that nineteenth-century melodrama actually derived from a "sentimental vision of humanity," playing on an audience's belief in natural human innocence and its desire to see that innocence protected against the forces of evil (12). Melodrama thus enacts fantasies of threat and dramatic repulsion of that threat to restore the original state of innocence that sparks the audience's sympathy. According to Mason, "the absolute imperative of melodrama is the restoration of the moral, social, and domestic order—and, consequently, the reassurance of the audience—by subjecting its characters to a high degree of risk and uncertainty and then lifting them out of danger" (18).[13]

McIntosh follows this formula in creating sentimental feeling for her suffering characters, then restoring their original states through melodramatic scenes of danger and rescue. The fact that melodrama nearly always portrays strife against an external adversary, rather than internal conflict, fits well with the Southern panic fiction model of threat from outside, while its stress on the possibilities for human action to change circumstances also fits McIntosh's advocacy of direct economic action.[14] The two heroes of McIntosh's melodrama are the industrialist Robert Grahame and Isabelle's fiancé, Major Wharton. They first come to the aid of the Montrose plantation when Wharton rushes Robert's check to the scene just in time to prevent the final foreclosure. The check, sent from Europe to a military installation in Florida many weeks earlier, had been delayed by storms and a mistaken address. Once Wharton receives it, he realizes the need for haste but is repeatedly impeded on his journey by roads washed out by flooding. He arrives with only minutes to spare, rescuing the family from the clutches of the gloating adversary Goldwire. Later, Robert and Major Wharton race together against time to recover Alice from the hands of her kidnapper, George Browne, saving both her life and her virtue. Locating the rented room in which Alice is being held, Robert shouts "Stand back!" before throwing the door open "with a force that sent George Browne reeling to the other side of the room." As George reaches for a pistol, Robert grabs his arm and wrenches the weapon away. As more footsteps are heard on the stairs, George escapes out a window, Alice sinks upon a couch with a "glad but feeble cry," then nearly faints and is caught by Wharton as he enters the room (254–55). In both of these melodramatic set pieces, moral, social, and domestic order is restored in ways that serve McIntosh's agenda. The helplessness of the victims at the hands of "villains," combined with the dramatic heroism of the rescuers, reinforces a sense of unequal power and ability between members of society and prompts readers to acknowledge and approve a hierarchical society in which some are dependent upon others. The plantation, with its own trappings of hierarchy in the ancestral mansion and scores of slaves, is preserved, while Alice is returned from her self-sufficiency to a state of grateful dependence.

What is perhaps most unexpected about the way McIntosh constructs these rescues is that while both of the heroes are white males, neither is the ultimate Southern patriarch, the plantation owner. As we have seen, the plantation owners in *The Lofty and the Lowly* are equivocal figures—not wholly responsible for their financial losses, like many of the merchants in Northern panic novels, but sharing some of the blame through bad judgment or character flaws. Colonel Montrose is essentially blind to his proper duties as a landowner, playing the role of gentleman of leisure rather than attending to his property and then dying halfway through the novel, only dimly aware of the financial catastrophe that awaits his heirs. Donald, of course, helps to bring that catastrophe about through his gambling and becomes, for a time, one of the victims that Robert and Major Wharton have to save. It is not until the very end of the novel that a chastened Donald is finally transformed into a model Southern patriarch, managing his estate with confidence and taking benevolent responsibility for his myriad dependents.

In the meantime, Robert and Major Wharton serve as Donald's role models, non-planters who embody lessons that McIntosh apparently believed plantation owners needed to learn in order to strengthen and protect the Southern economy. They are the novel's true agents of financial recovery, in part through their heroics but even more so through the qualities they possess that have led to their own respective successes, and offer examples for Southerners like Donald Montrose to emulate.

Major Wharton, the lesser of the two figures, is a Southerner from Virginia and apparently from the planter class, but he is without an estate or an inheritance. He is a man of moderate means who has become an army officer as a way of making his own way in the world. He first befriends Donald at West Point and later in service in Florida, counseling him on the importance of staying out of debt, claiming, "I never bought anything till I had the money in hand to pay for it; and I kept a regular account of my receipts and expenditures, that I might never be betrayed into expenses beyond my means" (247). Although Wharton is not a slave owner himself, he voices an important caution to that segment of the Southern economy, angering Donald at one point by comparing a debtor to a slave, held in bondage to his creditors. He explains that "no true gentleman is willingly a debtor" because such a state removes his ability to act freely and without constraint (250). Through Major Wharton, McIntosh advocates a kind of fiscal prudence that was not part of the stereotypical Southern plantation mindset but that she suggests is a crucial attribute for plantation owners to develop in order to maintain the autonomy on which they pride themselves.[15]

The most important model of financial recovery is the Northerner Robert Grahame. In addition to his generous loan to the Montrose family that allows them to retain their estate, and also his personal example of financial rectitude (demonstrated in his dealings with his dissolute brother Richard), Robert has restored his own family's financial position from the losses incurred by his father following the War of 1812. Like many of the female protagonists of Northern panic fiction, Robert begins the process of recovery by paying off his father's debts. Unlike those heroines, however, who raise the money primarily through strict economizing measures, Robert manages to pay his creditors through "long and wearisome" hours of toil—presumably in the textile mills that he is resurrecting—as well as by improving productivity through mechanical innovations and by selling the patent rights to one of his own inventions. Thus, financial recovery is clearly depicted as a masculine endeavor, not achieved through the avenues available to women, such as reformed consumer practices, but through labor, invention, and active wealth production—all masculine prerogatives. In fact, McIntosh characterizes Robert's economic recovery as a means of achieving manhood; in paying off his father's creditors, he honors the paternal memory and inherits his father's legacy of vision and courage.

That Robert's entrepreneurship and management of his manufacturing enterprises are meant to be seen as models for Southern economic development is made explicit at the end of the novel, when Donald adopts Robert's factories as a pattern for how to run the Montrose plantation. Efficiency, productivity, respect for labor, innovation—all the aspects of Northern society that Mrs. Montrose found so admirable earlier in the novel—are qualities that Donald plans to apply to the raising of cotton. His sister Isabelle, carrying on the female tradition of looking to the needs of the slaves, looks forward to implementing on the plantation an educational plan that Mary Grahame has developed for the children of factory workers. Donald's marriage to Mary at the end of the novel further cements this prospect of importing Northern habits to the South, as she brings with her the mind-set and experience of the thrifty and energetic Northern housewife. While McIntosh does not, of course, go so far as to advocate the adoption of a free-labor system in the South—and, in fact, echoes much of Caroline Hentz's defense of slavery as a benevolent institution—she does suggest that aspects of Northern industrialism could be advantageously applied even to the agricultural sector of the Southern economy.

The North thus plays an interesting double role with regard to the Southern economy in McIntosh's telling. Its risk-taking mentality, overriding love of money, and outright fraud and manipulation—as represented by George Browne and his ruthless father—threaten the financial stability and, indeed, the very existence of Southern plantation society. At the same time, however, Northern industry and innovation, when accompanied by moral integrity and financial responsibility, offer not only a model that the South could benefit from emulating but also the possibility of intersectional cooperation and understanding.

The foregoing examples of McIntosh's fiction show an interesting progression in her representation of panic, loss, and the Southern economy. From *Woman an Enigma* to *Two Lives* to *The Lofty and the Lowly*, McIntosh moves both from a very abstract, distanced narration of loss to an immediate, concrete representation and also from the very personal to a more societal perspective. The eighteenth-century European setting of *Woman an Enigma* bears only a romanticized resemblance to the Southern predicament of the author's own day, allowing her to focus more on the heroine's individual plight—a near orphan, bereft of her inheritance, finding a way to survive with integrity. While *Two Lives* shifts the scene much closer to home, and links the protagonists' experiences of failure to the familiar social phenomenon of speculative loss, McIntosh still tells the story as a kind of fairy tale, an extended journey to the land of corruption finally concluded with a safe return home to an unspoiled South.

It is in *The Lofty and the Lowly* that McIntosh most clearly and directly addresses the realities of potential loss for plantation owners and the systemic problems that make that loss more likely. McIntosh's detailed descriptions of complicated financial transactions as well as of Northern and Southern domestic life ground the novel securely in its antebellum present and provide for readers a sense of the author's economic agenda. McIntosh's uniqueness as a panic author, especially in *The Lofty and the Lowly*, lies not only in the depth of her knowledge of finance but most importantly in her direct advocacy of capitalist economic development as a strategy for preventing or minimizing the effects of panic and financial failure. Unlike Caroline Hentz, McIntosh does not try to defend the plantation by redefining it in purely domestic, noneconomic terms, but rather she speaks out in favor of making the plantation *more* of a capitalistic enterprise—more efficient, more productive, more innovative. In some ways, her vision of thus bringing (some of) the values of the marketplace to a space that has previously been carefully shielded from those values coincides remarkably with that of Northern panic authors like Lee and Follen, with the plantation setting of *The Lofty and the Lowly* allowing for a fuller realization of that goal. Whereas industrialization had largely removed economic production from the domestic spaces depicted by Lee and Follen, the plantation remained a space where the economic and the domestic were merged. However, McIntosh's agenda was not to enhance the economic power of the domestic sphere but to enhance the economic power of the South's principal revenue-producing "industry." McIntosh's economic discourse is thus situated more centrally on actual wealth creation than any of the other female antebellum panic authors, and her approach to this masculine realm is facilitated by the still domestic character of the plantation, by her own unusual level of experience and knowledge, and by her perception of the South's need for a more vigorous economic development.

Over the Top: Eliza Dupuy's *The Planter's Daughter: A Tale of Louisiana*

Before leaving the subject of Southern panic fiction, a particularly melodramatic example of the genre merits some attention. Eliza Dupuy's *The Planter's Daughter: A Tale of Louisiana*, first published in the panic year of 1857, exhibits many of same elements as McIntosh's fiction but in the sensationalist style of the popular story papers of the time. Dupuy was a Virginia native whose father, a merchant and shipowner, suffered financial failures and died in the 1820s, leaving the family in poverty. In her teens at the time, Dupuy made her own living as a governess and began writing short stories and novels for publication. Over the next several decades, she became a prolific and very popular writer, producing numerous pieces of magazine fiction and perhaps dozens of novels, many of them serialized in Robert Bonner's *New York Ledger*, the same periodical that published E. D. E. N. Southworth's work.[16]

Dupuy's positioning as an author of mass-marketed fiction may account for the relative scarcity in *The Planter's Daughter* of specific Southern references or direct economic commentary of a sectional nature. For example, although Dupuy sets the novel on a Louisiana sugar plantation, the slaves who work that plantation are barely mentioned and there is virtually no sign of the concern to defend slavery that so marks the fiction of Hentz and McIntosh. Nor was Dupuy apparently interested in the question of Southern industrialization. As *American National Biography* explains, Dupuy's publisher advertised the novel as nonpartisan, as "a Southern novel that is neither Anti-Slavery nor Pro-Slavery" (136). Attempting to appeal to a broad audience, then, Dupuy produced a novel without much Southern flavor and with little of the politically charged economic analysis that drives Hentz's *The Planter's Northern Bride* or McIntosh's *The Lofty and the Lowly*. What *The Planter's Daughter* does contribute to the body of panic fiction is a melodramatic plot and style, characteristic of Dupuy's popular fiction, that captures the frenzied emotionality of panic perhaps better than any other panic novel, whether from the North or South.

The protagonist of *The Planter's Daughter* is a sugar plantation owner named Charles Harrington, who actually has two daughters, Adele and Pauline, as well as a gambling son, Victor. Mr. Harrington becomes involved with a mysterious speculator named Reginald Malcolm, who promises to make money for Harrington through a complex scheme that involves buying and selling an estate with an unclear title to ownership. Malcolm has his own agenda, however, that is better served by Harrington's loss than his gain. While ostensibly courting the gentle Pauline, Malcolm has actually become obsessed by the idea of possessing the ravishingly beautiful Adele and believes that Harrington's ruin will put Adele into his power, forcing her to marry him. When the money that Harrington obtains to carry out the speculation is stolen, he does indeed mortgage his property to Malcolm, but Adele refuses to capitulate. At the climax of the novel, Harrington and Pauline both become dangerously ill, Malcolm disappears, and the plantation is destroyed in an apparent hurricane. After Harrington's death, his daughters eventually live happily ever after, Adele marrying the man that she loves, and Malcolm returning to Pauline a reformed man. But the Harrington line comes to an end with Victor's death from a gunshot wound and the sale of the Harrington plantation to pay off debts.

The basic elements of the plot and Dupuy's anti-speculation sentiments echo the typical narrative arc and rhetoric of both Northern and Southern panic novels. Harrington's failure is set into motion by a combination of extravagant habits that he cannot afford and a desire to increase his wealth quickly through a risky venture rather than waiting for the more gradual returns of his plantation income. Like McIntosh's Southern protagonists, his weaknesses are exploited by an outsider, the speculator who is not of the community and whose agenda involves control and acquisition of Harrington's own property—in this case, his daughter. Dupuy underscores the risky and less than upright nature of Harrington's speculation with the parallel plot of Victor's gambling, as discussed in chapter 1. As in almost all panic novels, the male protagonist's speculation results in the loss of the family home and the daughters' need to adapt to changed circumstances.

The uniqueness of *The Planter's Daughter* lies in Dupuy's sensationalist exaggeration of each of these plot elements. Panic fiction's characterization of speculation as a form of fraud and as both arising from and producing extreme states of desire, for example, takes on exaggerated form in the novel's multiple layers of financial fraud and deception. The original speculation that Malcolm proposes to Harrington is to purchase an estate that is being sold cheaply because of a defective title, making the legitimate ownership uncertain; Malcolm claims to have inside information that will allow him to obtain a clear title and then resell the estate for Harrington at full value, yielding a threefold profit. Whether this venture is legal and ethical, and whether Malcolm truly intends to carry it out as planned, are unclear. Before the purchase can be made, Malcolm's agent, a Mr. Withers, steals the fifty thousand dollars that he has been authorized to withdraw for Harrington and stows it on board a ship he plans to take to Europe. But before Withers can depart with his loot, he is murdered by another man, Bondy, who knows about the money and wants to steal it for himself.

At each level of this nested series of thefts—or intended thefts or possibly intended thefts—the respective perpetrator is tormented (sometimes physically) by the temptation of easy wealth and the desire for some kind of triumph. Withers, for instance, feels "blood rushing with electric speed through his frame" while waiting for the broker to turn over the gold, signifying both his great desire and the thrill caused by the risk he is taking (85–86). Malcolm most fully illustrates the obsessive desire associated with speculation, though, as Dupuy depicts his growing obsession with possessing Adele. The desire for money is here translated into sexual desire, but the language is nearly identical: like Withers anticipating his gold, Malcolm's "blood seemed rushing in a burning torrent through his frame" as he thinks of Adele (128). That Malcolm's feelings for Adele are not love is repeatedly made clear by his disregard for her dislike of him; his increasing passion is all about pure possession and control, a desire to have what others value and to gain it through financial force. By transferring Malcolm's desire from the monetary to the sexual, Dupuy not only sensationalizes the story but also intensifies the reader's sense of speculative desire as nonrational, as beyond the control of the will, as a product of passion rather than a rational act of profit.

Speculation's threat to domestic space—the family home—is similarly exaggerated and sensationalized in *The Planter's Daughter*. Unlike Northern panic fiction, in which failed families simply move to smaller, more affordable dwellings, or even McIntosh's *The Lofty and the Lowly*, in which the Montrose estate is nearly foreclosed on, the climax of Dupuy's novel features the literal destruction of the Harringtons' home by a massive storm. First a tornado strikes, and as the family flees from one part of the house to another, the "floor of the room they had left was rent in twain in the centre, by the resistless force of the wind." In the next blast, "the roof was lifted from the house, and whirled into the yard, leaving the blinding torrent of rain to pour through the tottering walls" (319). Finally, the levee breaks and as the storm abates, "the whole surface of the earth was covered with the flood, and every tree and shrub that might have risen above its level seemed to have been torn away by the tornado. A wild waste of turbid water now occupied the place of the cane-fields, so lately flourishing with verdant beauty" (324–25). The metaphor of the storm, destroying and washing away everything Harrington had built up just as his speculations swept away his financial aspirations, conveys in almost biblical language the devastation wrought by bad choices, both emotional and financial.

One reason for Dupuy's use of exaggerated passions and melodramatic devices—the novel also contains numerous gambling scenes, grave robbing, murder, and Pauline's near death from a broken heart—is simply that these were draws to readers who, by 1857, had become used to the sensational fare of popular story papers. Dupuy wrote regularly for this market and would have known well the expected elements of a thrilling adventure tale. A story about speculation and bankruptcy, with their inherent elements of drama, offered a prime opportunity to depict extremes of emotion and behavior. Thus it is reasonable to imagine that Dupuy may have chosen "panic" as a subject, not to pursue a rhetorical agenda or to seize the opportunity to comment on current economic conditions but, as a number of male panic authors did, simply to tell an exciting story. If so, one should at least note that Dupuy's style lends itself well to expressing the emotionality of panic that so many panic authors deliberately suppressed in order to model female agency in recovery. Characters' feelings create the narrative texture for the novel—Harrington's nervous anxiousness, Malcolm's steely but barely controlled determination, Adele's troubled conscience, Pauline's quiet despair. The ups and downs of their emotions and the extremes of their behavior create an atmosphere in which the conventions of an ordered society no longer function, no longer regulate people's relationships or their fates. In the stormy climax, the wind and water produce terror, seeming to pursue the family throughout the house, illustrating very graphically a sense of helplessness, of being swamped by waves of ruin that the broken levees of security have not been able to hold back. While the completeness of the ruin almost certainly exaggerates the material effects of panic, it conveys very effectively the emotional fallout—the sense of fear and despair that must have accompanied many people's experiences of sudden loss.

But there are other aspects of *The Planter's Daughter* that suggest Dupuy was writing more than an exciting adventure tale and that her melodramatic style may have been employed to make some serious points about speculation, panic, and failure. One such aspect is the novel's previously noted multiple layers of deception and fraud. Bondy murders Withers for the money that Withers has just stolen from Harrington, while Harrington is simultaneously being (perhaps) conned by Malcolm. It makes for great drama and suspense, but it also depicts a commercial world in which greed, manipulation, and theft are the norm. Only the broker who turns the money over to Withers is an honest man, notably and conspicuously honest against the backdrop of financial corruption, where even the innocent Harrington is drawn into shady dealings out of desire for a quick profit. Dupuy's layered thefts communicate well a commercial world where nothing is as it seems and no one can be trusted.

More significant, though, is Dupuy's manner of linking the supposedly nonfinancial plot elements to the speculation plot through metaphorical or allusive language. Just as other panic authors used images such as vapor or gilding, or extended motifs such as theatricality in McIntosh's *Two Lives*, to signify the insubstantiality and inherent falseness of speculative wealth, Dupuy imbues some of the most sensational aspects of her novel with allusions to the characteristics of a speculative economy. Malcolm's uncanny power over Harrington, for example, is his power to make mere words seem like substance: "With rare command of language, Malcolm communicated his plans to his eager listener, and impressed him with the firm conviction that the speculations undertaken by him, must be successful. He revealed just enough of his proposed enterprises to arouse the desire for gain in the mind of Mr. Harrington, and impress him with a belief in his vast resources, both of intellect and means; and then left the poison to work its legitimate result" (20). Throughout the novel, Malcolm's power over other characters is centered in his use of language, seemingly able to conjure real effects from the intangible power of his voice. In the end, of course, the inflated value of his words proves as worthless as his speculative scheme.

Another example of Dupuy's interwoven financial metaphors is her substitution of Malcolm's sexual obsession with Adele for the speculator's more typical monetary obsession, which is actually part of a broader motif in which matters of love and marriage stand in for financial transactions. At one point, Adele discounts what Malcolm feels for her as mere admiration, "but admiration is not love, Pauline; and I am the last person to accept the counterfeit" (46). Here, the superficial, even false, nature of Malcolm's feelings for Adele signals the lack of value his financial schemes have for Adele's father as well. In both realms, it is suggested, he has committed himself to that which has no real value. The realm of love, or specifically marriage, can also embody the risk-taking aspect of speculation. In a lengthy subplot, Harrington's niece Louise Ruskin and her mother are constantly weighing different marriage options and what kind of future each is likely to provide for Louise. Victor, who truly loves Louise but has no fortune, is seen as a poor matrimonial choice. "Think how different your life would be," Mrs. Ruskin tells her daughter, "united to a self-sustained man like Malcolm. Already the possessor of wealth, which the future will surely increase, he could afford you an elegant home in a large city where you could become the centre of a brilliant circle" (125). Marriage, like investing, can be a matter of calculating the probable risks and benefits, both monetary and emotional, and both, Dupuy suggests, depend on elements that cannot always be anticipated. Toward the end of the novel, when Adele tries to tell her father about Malcolm's threats to her, he replies, "speak plainly, child. I am no seer, and can not foresee what is about to happen" (239). While this line speaks volumes about Harrington's blindness to his own imminent failure, it also sums up one of the main themes of the novel. People *are* blind when it comes to the future; they cannot judge risks and consequences very accurately, either in finances or in relationships, and that is the problem with speculation—it depends upon effects that are often unknowable. Dupuy's repeated parallels between matters of love and matters of finance have the effect of blurring the line usually drawn between love and money and thus questioning conventional notions of each. Love discussed in financial terms loses something of its sentimental luster, while financial affairs couched in the language of obsession and desire are stripped of their rational, objective façade.

Dupuy's persistent conflation of love and money, combined with her relative reticence about Southern plantation life and slavery during a period of such intense sectional tension right before the Civil War, suggests, perhaps, that in addition to aiming at a broader popular audience, Dupuy may have had a somewhat different agenda from that of other Southern writers. In particular, her repeated references to marriage as a kind of speculation and to the importance of rejecting counterfeit love may indicate that she was just as interested in the configuration of 1850s marriage as she was in the survival of Southern plantation society. Nevertheless, *The Planter's Daughter* does echo a number of elements of distinctly Southern panic fiction, including its use of the outsider who brings failure to the Southern plantation and its attention to the question of how financial crisis affects the plantation economy. Dupuy's answers to this question appear to be rather different from those proposed by McIntosh. Rather than picturing the plantation regenerated by shunning the negative influences of the North and embracing the positive, as McIntosh does, Dupuy depicts her characters leaving the ruined plantation behind and adapting to more modest lives in a changed South. Adele marries a college professor, who seems to represent the possibility of a renewed Southern intellectual life. Pauline and her aunt operate a school for girls, championing both female education and the propriety of Southern women earning their own livings. Slavery is dramatically scaled back, with only a few personal servants retained from the original plantation holdings. Ultimately, even the outsider is able to be assimilated into this new existence, as the scoundrel Malcolm returns some years later, reformed and repentant, to marry Pauline. Thus, despite the extreme melodrama of the novel, we do not see any heroes or any restoration of the original social order of the plantation. In fact, hierarchy is actually lessened, although not completely eliminated, resulting in a society organized more around individual effort and marital partnerships.

Overall, Southern panic fiction of the 1840s and 1850s is a somewhat more diffuse body of literature than the Northern panic fiction of the 1830s. Plot, style, rhetorical strategy, and even central focus vary widely among the novels discussed above, reflecting the fact that Southern authors interwove their concerns about financial loss with other political or social issues. Panic is rarely the sole concern in these novels and thus the economic analysis of cause, effect, and solution for financial crisis is influenced by the authors' respective stances on issues such as slavery, industrial development, and marriage. Nevertheless, recurring situations and motifs such as the plantation setting, the external agent of loss or potential loss, the masculinized process of recovery, and a tendency toward melodrama link these diverse texts and point to common sources of anxiety, as well as a distinctly regional socioeconomic vision. In particular, we can see that each of these novels is informed by an increasing sectional polarity on the issue of slavery, how it compares socially and economically with Northern free labor, and how the North and South are respectively affected by economic crisis as a result of their different economies. In the next chapter, we will look at how a "second generation" of Northern panic fiction, published in the late 1850s, responds to these same concerns with very different results.

five

Freedom and Order

Proposing Solutions to 1850s Labor Problems

Early on in her novel *Mabel Vaughan*, published in the panic year of 1857, popular author Maria Cummins gives her readers an education in the realities of urban poverty. A young maid is fired by her wealthy employer for suggesting that some of the poor have better manners than the rich, and has her wages for the whole month withheld. After trudging home in the dark on wet pavement in thin shoes, to her family's scantily furnished basement apartment, young Lydia Hope offers her last sum of money to her "weary, care-worn" mother, who "inwardly shrunk from appropriating the wages of Lydia's daily slavery" (88). We learn that Lydia has gone into domestic service to help support her invalid sister after Mrs. Hope's savings are depleted by having to pay a fine to keep her son Jack out of jail when he was involved in a street brawl. Although Mrs. Hope operates a small shop out of their home, she and her children do not earn enough to move out of their "dilapidated tenement" with its "mouldy wall of bricks" and backyard strewn with rubbish (177).

The novel's title character, Mabel, the sheltered eighteen-year-old daughter of a wealthy New York businessman, becomes aware of these circumstances and is moved to try to help the Hopes. It is her sister Louise who has fired Lydia, and Mabel—reared in the country following her mother's death and thus uninitiated to the self-centered ways of wealthy New York society—rectifies that injustice by paying Lydia out of her own pocket. A few chapters later, walking on Broadway with her nephews and a male companion, Mabel receives her own lesson about the lives of the poor, when her party witnesses a young boy, "ragged, dirty, and bending beneath the weight of an old basket filled with half-burnt coals" (128). When the boy accidentally spills his coal, Mabel's immediate charitable impulse is to give him money to buy more, but she has spent all she had with her, and her companion refuses his aid, cynically suggesting that the accident was a ruse to gain their sympathy. But Mabel cannot forget the boy, and has continuing "painful visions . . . of dreary garrets, where half-starved children and despairing mothers crouched beneath scanty coverings, and cried and shivered with the cold" (131).

In many respects, these scenes could have come from the pages of a novel by Hannah Farnham Sawyer Lee or Eliza Follen, reflecting as they do those earlier authors' concerns with the relationships between social classes and the empowerment of middle-class women. Cummins defines appropriate relations between those who hire domestic help and the women they employ, negatively contrasting Louise's selfishness and lack of compassion for the poor with Mabel's thoughtful sympathy. In particular, Mabel's act of compensating Lydia for service already performed echoes the economic agency within a nurturing domestic realm that marked so many of the heroines of 1830s panic fiction. Later in the novel, when Mabel's father has lost his fortune and the Vaughan family resettles on the Illinois frontier, Mabel exercises that agency in ways very similar to earlier characters like Elinor Fulton and Amy Weston.

But a closer reading of the two scenes reveals a number of distinctions between Cummins's late 1850s social vision and that of her forebears. Most apparent is the detail with which Cummins renders working-class poverty. Each scene set in the Hope family home, for example, is replete with descriptive phrases evoking gloom, deterioration, and unwholesomeness. Where earlier panic novels might have briefly sketched a scene of need in order to provide their middle-class heroines an opportunity to demonstrate their charitable competence, *Mabel Vaughan* immerses its readers in the lives of the Hope family, making sure we can feel the damp chill of those "cellar-like" rooms and the weariness in Lydia's body and soul as she makes her way home, jobless. We also see the tenuousness of support and security for the poor in these scenes: Lydia's employment is completely dependent on the whims of her capricious mistress, who not only can dismiss her at a moment's notice but also can withhold earned wages with impunity; similarly, the boy's spilled coal suggests a living so precarious that a single stumble can deprive a family of necessary warmth or perhaps food.

A second distinction is that although Mabel is able to rectify her sister's stinginess with the contents of her purse, she is powerless to aid the boy and can only replay the incident and its implications of poverty in her mind, exemplifying an appropriate sympathy but without the financial means to change the circumstances of the poor. In part, Mabel's empty purse signifies the same economic disempowerment of women that Anna Warner makes so powerfully evident in *Dollars and Cents*, as discussed in chapter 3. The fact that Mabel's male companion could have helped the boy and did not, despite Mabel's urging, points to a masculine dominance in financial matters that prevents the sympathetic—but also rational and truth-seeking—female from acting on her disposition toward justice and benevolence. But even if Mabel's purse had been full that day, Cummins implies that the depth and breadth of poverty figured in Mabel's recurring visions of starving children and freezing mothers is simply a problem too vast for the resources of one person, however financially competent and empowered she might be.

The combination of this focus on the intractable impoverishment of the working class and Mabel's helplessness to relieve it makes it clear that Cummins does not share the same agenda of 1830s panic novelists, who sought to assuage middle-class readers' anxiety about social fluidity. Although Mabel does sustain a "fall" in her social status midway through the novel when her father goes bankrupt, these earlier scenes indicate virtually no anxiety about the stability of her position or a necessity to shore up that position, rhetorically, by emphasizing differences between classes. On the contrary, there is a sense that barriers between classes have become the problem—that social inequality has actually rigidified to the point where those of different classes have little communication with or even knowledge of each other's lives, and personal benevolence has become futile. The wealthy live in a protective bubble of privilege, oblivious to the wretched lives of those who serve them without hope of advancing even to a modest competence, much less to the status of the Vaughans and their social milieu.

In place of the social anxiety expressed in 1830s panic novels, we see a whole host of new problems hinted at in *Mabel Vaughan*, specific to an urban world in which rapid economic growth and industrialization have created a highly stratified society. Foremost among these problems is that wealth and the achievement of such privileged status have deprived many middle- and upper-middle-class women of the domestic duties and moral high ground that promised them a degree of autonomy and authority. Without the financial need for their labor, and under pressure to display family wealth through fashion and elaborate entertaining, the daughters and wives of rich men are consigned to roles that Cummins depicts as unfulfilling and morally detrimental. At the other end of the socioeconomic spectrum, Cummins directs readers' attention to the problems faced by the poor and working class—in particular, the conditions of extreme deprivation in which they live, despite often working long hours at grueling jobs. Low pay and lack of control over working conditions mean that even those laborers who are fully employed, as Lydia was, cannot use their strength and talents to raise themselves or their families out of poverty. Social mobility is merely a fiction to those who are not paid enough to meet basic daily needs. One of the larger social consequences of such deprivation is that it almost inevitably erupts into some form of unrest or outright violence, a consequence that Cummins implies in her references to Jack Hope's participation in a street brawl and his companionship with other underemployed young toughs. While the novel views Jack's rebelliousness only from the perspective of his mother and sisters, who worry about his salvation and fear for his safety, the suggestion that there were gangs of young men out roaming the city's streets at night, looking for trouble, signifies Cummins's sense of a potential threat to society as a whole posed by working-class restlessness and rage.

Cummins also captures a deep sense of class-based antagonism within the realm of employment in her depiction of the hostility between Louise and Lydia—an antagonism largely absent from earlier panic novels. The comment for which Lydia is fired—"I only wish you could see such children as I am used to; there's some among 'em that might teach a lesson even to a lady"—suggests profound frustration with a class structure that grants superiority and economic power based on possession of money rather than true merit (68). Louise's immediate and harsh response, and her later wrath at Mabel for "pay[ing] people for putting on airs and getting up scenes," reflects a mindset that expects complete subordination of employees (73). Mrs. Hope's reference to Lydia's "daily slavery" in Louise's employ reinforces the idea that employees are treated as less than full citizens, that, in fact, their very humanity is being negated in a fashion similar to that experienced by enslaved Africans in the South. Cummins's use of the image of slavery to describe Lydia's exploitation at the hands of her employer not only expresses the author's outrage in the strongest terms, though. It also signals her participation in one of the most bitterly divisive debates of the late 1850s, that of the meaning of free labor in a society that reduces the working class to the status of servants and in a nation that permits slavery. In her choice of words, Cummins reflects negatively on both Northern and Southern systems of labor.

It would be an overstatement to say that Cummins's depiction of a deeply divided society suffering the social and economic effects of class stratification was "typical" of 1850s Northern panic fiction, as that decade simply did not produce panic fiction in the same quantity or distinctiveness that marked the period immediately following the Panic of 1837. Many female novelists did pursue economic themes, including panic and loss, in their fiction, but without the striking similarity of narrative style or cohesiveness of message that would constitute a distinct "genre." One possible reason for the relative scarcity of panic fiction in the 1850s is that attitudes toward panic and failure were changing in society as a whole, as the market economy became normalized and risk itself more accepted. Novels aimed at reassuring and instructing readers in the wake of new and frightening economic circumstances may have seemed increasingly unnecessary. Another reason for the decline of female-authored panic fiction was almost certainly the changing literary marketplace and its expanding opportunities for women. The enormous popularity of women's fiction in the 1850s opened the door to styles and genres not previously associated with female authors. Fanny Fern's 1854 novel *Ruth Hall*, for example, a tale of loss and recuperation that a couple of decades earlier might have been written as a panic narrative, is rendered instead as a masterpiece of satire. E. D. E. N. Southworth and Ann Stephens similarly wrote novels about fluctuating economic fortunes and women's relationships to the marketplace, but enveloped their economic discourse in rollicking adventure tales and lavish paeans to consumerism, respectively.[1]

Nevertheless, there are some striking examples of novels from the period surrounding the Panic of 1857 that do center on the issue of financial failure (or the possibility of failure), depicting it in ways that reveal anxieties particular to Northern cities during that decade. This chapter will focus on two novels—Cummins's *Mabel Vaughan* and Alice Haven's *The Coopers; or, Getting Under Way* (1858)—that use panic as a focal point through which to address problems as diffuse as working-class urban poverty, increasingly antagonistic relations between employers and employees, middle-class women's disempowerment in a money-driven society, and threats to national prosperity posed by Southern slavery.

Both of these novels envision a form of middle-class domestication as the way to achieve economic harmony and social order, while explicitly repudiating slavery as an economic and social system. Both also portray the interests of middle-class women as bound up with the needs of the urban working class. However, the form this domestication takes, as well as the relationship constructed between "home" and social class structure, differs radically. Cummins joined with Northern reformers and free labor advocates to promote westward migration as a solution to the poverty of the urban working class as well as to the ruined fortunes of failed speculators and the plight of middle-class women bound by consumerism. Her domesticated frontier permits a more egalitarian society, in which those made powerless by the current class structure—upper-middle-class women like Mabel, as well as the working class—have a chance to exercise agency. Haven, by contrast, keeps her novel within a Northern industrial milieu, offering a professionalized home as a model workplace that avoids both the overt antagonism of Northern industrial employment relations and the oppression of slavery, but also precludes egalitarianism. Rigidified class roles are reinforced by clear boundaries between employer and employee, advancing the middle-class female employer's interests at the expense of her working-class employees.

Panic also plays disparate roles in these two novels, highlighting very different attitudes toward the rapid growth of the 1850s. For Cummins, who was probably writing *Mabel Vaughan* during the feverish period of speculation leading up to the crash during the fall of 1857, panic and failure provide a welcome check to the speculative economic system that she depicts as disempowering to women and the poor. Mr. Vaughan's failure destroys the life of idleness and consumerism that Mabel feels trapped by and allows her to create a more purposeful life for herself. Thus panic is actually depicted as enabling genuine domesticity rather than destabilizing it. For Haven, who may have been writing in the aftermath of the panic, as *The Coopers* was not published until the following year, panic serves more as a test or trial for the title characters, Murray and Martha Cooper. The prospect of failure and loss makes them afraid, but ultimately they weather their time of financial difficulty without failing and come out stronger. Although these reactions are clearly very different, both signal a national economy that has grown beyond the wild instability of the 1830s. In Cummins's telling, economic practices have developed too powerfully along the wrong path, and are in need of a shake-up. In Haven's more optimistic view, the economy is healthy enough to survive both the labor conflicts of the 1850s and the periodic downswings of the market.

Free Labor and the Urban Working Class

In order to better understand the specific solutions that Cummins and Haven promote in their respective novels, it is important to have some grasp of both the actual conditions of the urban working class in the 1850s and the discourses regarding labor that were prevalent during that decade. Following the Panic of 1837, the emerging divide between "middle class" and "working class" that was discussed in chapter 2 continued to grow as production of goods became both more centralized and more mechanized during the 1840s and 1850s. The well-documented movement of manufacturing out of homes and small artisan-owned shops into factories and larger workshops produced an urban working class in northeastern American cities that was distinguished from earlier generations of laboring people both by crushing poverty and by an unprecedented permanence. Although historians are careful to note that the majority of American workers in the antebellum era were still agricultural and that even the growing urban working class was not truly industrial yet at that time—since most early factories were erected in rural areas—the conditions of antebellum urban laborers were markedly affected by industrialization. According to Bruce Laurie, for example, many craft workshops employed far greater numbers of workers in the 1850s than in the 1820s and were beginning to use machinery rather than "hand equipment," especially in trades such as printing, garment production (cutting, sewing, and trimming), shoemaking, cabinetmaking, and the building trades (38–42). The division of labor entailed by such mechanized production reduced the chances for laborers to advance to the status of master craftsmen and increased the possibilities for exploitation by employers. Even those occupations not directly affected by mechanization were beginning to be filled by what Eric Foner terms a "permanent working class"—that is, workers who would remain employees of someone else for their whole working lives, rather than serving as journeymen en route to becoming masters and owners of their own shops. By 1860, Foner notes, those who labored for wages outnumbered the self-employed by a substantial margin (32).

Not surprisingly, this reduction in workers' autonomy was accompanied by a declining standard of living. As the cost of living nearly doubled between 1820 and 1850, urban wages stagnated or, in some cases, even went down. Even with children working to contribute to family incomes, depressed wages and frequent periods of unemployment during economic downturns made it very difficult for urban workers to avoid poverty. And where their rural counterparts might supplement wages with small-scale farm production or boarding fees, lack of land and cramped living conditions ruled out these means of support.

One reason for workers' weakened position in the marketplace was that the burgeoning trade union movement of the 1820s and 1830s had been broken by the Panic of 1837. According to Sean Wilentz, those union workers who were not automatically thrown out of work by the immediate mass unemployment following the panic were often discharged anyway as the severe work shortage gave employers the power to rid themselves of workers they deemed troublemakers (294–95). While unions and labor activism revived partially and sporadically throughout the late 1840s and early 1850s as the economy recovered, the movement as a whole could not regain its earlier power, in part because of recurring panics in 1854 and 1857 and in part because an influx of immigrants divided the work force along ethnic and religious lines. Although, according to Laurie, German immigrants brought with them a strong tradition of union radicalism and often allied themselves with native-born workers to demand better working conditions, impoverished immigrants without such traditions and ethnic groups, such as the Irish, who were barred from unions by nativist prejudice, were often used by employers as cheap labor to drive down all wages (100–102). When unions did attempt to strike for higher wages or improved conditions, as members of the newly formed New York Industrial Congress did in 1850, their efforts were often quickly suppressed with the use of immigrant workers as strike breakers and the help of new professional police forces, which protected employers and harassed strikers. This involvement of police escalated the level of violence associated with labor conflicts and, according to Wilentz, greatly increased antagonism between employers and employees. In August of 1850, the first fatalities in an American labor conflict occurred during a tailor's strike in New York City, when a clash between workers and the police resulted in two killed and dozens wounded (Wilentz 379–80; Laurie 103). The Panic of 1857 brought further class-based public strife in the form of unprecedented demonstrations in the streets by thousands of unemployed seeking relief from some quarter. Such actions signaled that working-class poverty and class-based labor conflicts were becoming serious problems in American cities, but there was little consensus among the nation's leaders about how to resolve these problems.

Since at least the eighteenth century, American ideas about work and the status of the worker had been colored by an ideology of "free labor"—essentially a belief in and commitment to the idea that white male workers were free to control their own labor and, rather than being chained to the status or occupation of their birth, could take advantage of opportunities to improve their social and financial condition. But "free labor" was a contested and contingent term, meaning different things to different groups; its meanings also shifted over time as conditions of labor changed. In the late eighteenth century, for example, "free labor" was employed specifically to contrast the social and geographic mobility available to American workers with the still-feudal conditions of the European working class, bound to the status and fiefs of their ancestors. The original emphasis of "free labor" ideology was on the worker's autonomy and self-ownership. The ability to be a free citizen was seen as implicitly linked with economic independence, as an employer's economic power over his workers could extend to political influence, negating employees' political independence.[2] Thus, owning land or being self-employed in a trade (or both) were the hallmarks of both free labor and citizenship, while the relative abundance of cheap land, a shortage of workers, and an established pathway from apprentice to journeyman to master made these goals achievable for many men of talent and determination. Their labor was "free" in the sense that they were able to control the conditions of their own work and were not beholden to or dependent upon an employer.

The economic changes discussed earlier, however, made such autonomy and self-employment increasingly difficult, especially for workers in the urban Northeast. As the number and proportion of American workers employed in wage labor increased in relation to self-employed property owners, this original framing of "free labor" no longer accurately described the American working class. One response to this change was the promotion of westward migration as a way to preserve the ideal of free labor by providing land ownership for the previously landless. A major proponent of westward migration for the urban poor was George Henry Evans, whose National Reform Association pushed for the free distribution of federally owned land to any citizen willing to live and work on their 160-acre farm for at least five years (Laurie 67, 100). By 1860, Evans's proposals became the heart of the Republican Party's Homestead Act, which Republicans saw as a way to solve a variety of problems. Encouraging the urban working class to become western landowners would simultaneously relieve overcrowding and jobless rates in northeastern cities, increase wage rates for those who remained, create an army of workers to help settle and tame the new western territories, and offer those who moved opportunities for economic independence and prosperity.[3]

While land reformers and Republicans sought to preserve and extend traditional modes of free labor in the rural West, within the northeastern industrial milieu the very concept of "free labor" began to shift. Rather than being defined by the worker's autonomy, which had been drastically curtailed by the centralization and mechanization of production, "free labor" was increasingly used to refer to a worker's ability to freely enter into contracts—that is, to choose where to work, to negotiate wages, and to leave a job at will. As Edward Balleisen discusses, the widespread bankruptcies of the 1840s also led to rhetoric about the "independence" of salaried white-collar work, comparing its regular salary and the absence of debt favorably to the risks and headaches of business ownership (204). As a result, political independence and economic independence began to be seen as completely separate issues, as employers and workers alike maintained the compatibility of free citizenship with wage labor. The concept of "self-ownership," which in the eighteenth century connoted self-employment or the absence of any employer's authority over oneself, had shifted by the middle of the nineteenth century to mean the ownership of one's own labor or the ability to "sell" that labor for the highest available wage. Thus, as Leon Fink argues, by the end of the nineteenth century, the demands of free labor were "less explicitly oriented to the process and control of work itself than to the social distribution of work's economic rewards"—that is, to the increase of wages (134).

Whereas eighteenth-century rhetoric of "free labor" had focused on the contrast between American and European modes of work, by the 1850s the term and concept were employed in the Northern states in direct opposition to Southern slavery. Both abolitionists and Northern industrialists found the concept useful in combating or deflecting the criticisms of Northern society voiced by Southern proponents of slavery like George Fitzhugh (discussed in chapter 4). As Fitzhugh and others defended the enslavement of workers in the South in part by denouncing the exploitation of what they called Northern "wage slavery," antislavery activists and factory owners countered with arguments centered on the superiority of "free labor." For abolitionists, this superiority was primarily moral, with the worker's ability to choose his or her own employment and to leave it without penalty signifying the personal freedom essential to simple humanity. For many former slaves, such as Frederick Douglass, the very wages that some saw as marking a lesser status than self-employment became a symbol of freedom and autonomy. Being paid for one's labor served as an acknowledgment that that labor was owned by the worker him- or herself, thus granting the worker a measure of self-ownership.[4]

Northern economists and industrialists, for their parts, trumpeted "free labor" as a more efficient and productive labor system than slavery. Because wages were usually tied in some way to productivity, either through a piece-rate system in which workers were paid by the item produced or simply through employers' demands for long working hours as a condition of employment, the Northern system of wage labor, they claimed, provided greater incentives for workers to produce more than enslaved workers who did not benefit financially from their work. In addition, the possibility for free workers to improve their conditions by hard work, however unlikely that may have become for the majority of the working class, was often cited in the North as the very engine of societal progress, the fundamental motivation that drove Northern industrial productivity and innovation. As the decade of the 1850s advanced, Northern use of rhetoric about free labor increased, with much political discourse, especially among Republicans, centered on the threat that slavery—even if confined to one section of the nation—posed to free society as a whole. Free labor was held up as a vital and endangered national icon—vital because indicative of national ideals of independence and liberty; endangered because of competition from slavery and the corruption inherent in a slave system.

There was, of course, a significant divide between the idealized rhetoric of free labor and the realities of life for most members of the urban working class. Proclamations about the freedom of workers to sell their own labor at the greatest advantage tended to gloss over the power differentials between employers and employees that made contracting an unequal venture. Not being compelled to work against one's will was indeed a great benefit, but as Leon Fink points out, workers were still legally bound to the commands of their employers while on the job, and had little means by which to recover disputed wages if they quit (120). Workers themselves had an ambiguous relationship to the concept of free labor, proudly vaunting their ability to freely contract and sell their labor as a demonstration of their claim to equal citizenry, on the one hand, but also demonstrating vigorously against the evils of "wage slavery" (Foner xxiii). One of the biggest contradictions of the "free labor" ideology was that it extolled the value of manual labor while simultaneously treating it as a temporary stage in a man's economic progress. At a time when manual labor was beginning to be seen by many as the province of slaves and immigrants, its chief value, it seemed, was its potential for raising the laborer's status *out* of a life of labor.

These contradictions between the rhetoric and the reality of labor in the 1850s are vital to an understanding of Maria Cummins's *Mabel Vaughan* and Alice Haven's *The Coopers* because both novels exemplify competing rhetorical strategies of the time for reconciling "free labor" ideology with the realities of urban working-class life. By promoting the reform/Republican solution of westward migration for her working-class characters, Cummins allies herself with those clinging to a model of autonomous free labor, imagining therein a mechanism by which all citizens might unite productive labor with equal rights as citizens. Haven, by contrast, embraces the later contractual definition of free labor, envisioning an idealized employment relation that recognizes the workers' fundamental rights while organizing their labor to the benefit of the employer. While Cummins sympathizes with the working class to a far greater degree than Haven, and recognizes the extent to which American ideals of fairness and opportunity were being denied to many urban laborers in the 1850s, both authors display a deep commitment to promoting their respective versions of free labor as alternatives to the various forms of "unfree" labor prevalent in their time.

But Cummins's and Haven's respective discourses about free labor and their solutions for class conflict are embedded within their larger projects, which share with earlier Northern panic fiction the principal goals of empowering the middle-class domestic realm and demonstrating appropriate responses to panic and economic failure. For Cummins, the problems of working-class poverty, upper-middle-class women's lack of agency, and speculative instability are all integrally linked—they are all results of the more fundamental problem of a societal value system that places monetary gain above all else. The urban working class can only recover its "free labor" status, she suggests, by the same means that are necessary to restore the nation's economic stability and women's ability to live lives of purpose—that is, the replacement of a stratified, money-driven value system with middle-class domestication. Thus, the establishment of a domesticated West, outside the corrupted marketplace of northeastern cities, becomes Cummins's primary narrative focus.

In Haven's novel, where the problems of labor are seen through the lens of domestic employment, it is domestic harmony that is dependent upon adherence to the principles of free labor, rather than the other way around. Although the needs of the working class, represented as a series of domestic servants, take a back seat to the concerns of Haven's middle-class main characters—including their anxieties over potential business losses—it is only when the Coopers' middle-class home functions as a model workplace, with attention to contractual obligations, that proper domestic order and economic stability are realized.

A Domesticated West: Maria Cummins's *Mabel Vaughan*

Maria Cummins was born in 1827, more than a generation after Catharine Sedgwick, Hannah Farnham Sawyer Lee, Eliza Follen, and other earlier panic fiction authors, and was part of that generation of domestic authors who achieved massive popularity in the 1850s. Like Lee and Follen, Cummins was a product of Massachusetts, born in Salem and living most of her adult life in Dorchester, near Boston. Her father was a lawyer and judge, her mother from a family of physicians. Cummins attended the Young Ladies School run by Catharine Sedgwick's sister-in-law, where she undoubtedly met Sedgwick and other writers of the day. In 1854, Cummins published her first novel, *The Lamplighter*, which became an instant bestseller and remained one of the most popular novels of the nineteenth century, both in the United States and in Europe. It was also the novel to which Nathaniel Hawthorne was apparently referring when he made his famous complaint about the "d——d mob of scribbling women" and their popular sentimental fiction. Cummins's subsequent three novels, including *Mabel Vaughan*, were also widely read, but did not match the popularity of her first. Cummins never married and died in 1866 at the age of 39.[5]

A product of the economic boom years of the mid- to late 1850s, *Mabel Vaughan* depicts two very different New Yorks—one of wealth and one of poverty, both of which victimize their constituents, albeit in very different ways. The principal storyline details the detrimental effects of wealth upon its possessors. When Mabel returns from the country to her father's splendid city mansion at age eighteen, she is caught up against her inclination in the fashionable but morally and intellectually bankrupt world of her wealthy family. Mr. Vaughan is completely absorbed in his speculative business ventures, Mabel's brother Harry runs with a "fast" crowd and drinks too much, and her sister Louise lives the epitome of a frivolous, antidomestic life—residing in a hotel, spending her time shopping and socializing, and leaving the care of her two young sons to the exhausted and mistreated Lydia. After their father travels west with Louise's husband to look after some land speculations in Illinois, Mabel and Harry go to live with an aunt, where they are invited to parties and dances nearly every night and Harry's drinking gets worse. Mabel becomes increasingly disillusioned with the emptiness and frivolity of their life, and believes that she could help Harry if only she could provide him with a quiet and loving domestic environment. But her social obligations to her aunt and sister, as well as her lack of her own home, make that impossible.

Mabel's concerns about Harry's behavior and her sense of powerlessness about her own life are finally brought to a climax in a series of crises: Harry is severely injured in an accident one night and lies senseless in a fever for weeks; shortly thereafter, Louise's husband is killed in a train wreck, and Mr. Vaughan's speculations fail, causing him to lose his immense fortune. Louise responds to these crises—particularly the loss of wealth—by falling into a delirium and dying. Mabel, by contrast, rises to the occasion. Finding that her father's mansion has been sold, she arranges Louise's funeral and packs up her nephews and travels with them by train, steamer, and carriage all the way to Illinois, where she surprises her father by moving in and setting up housekeeping. Finally able to live the domestic life for which she has been longing, Mabel transforms the temporary frontier residence into an orderly home and inspires Harry—recovered from his accident and repentant of his ways—to farm the land. Together, through farming and home building, they create a domesticated frontier that not only replaces Mr. Vaughan's speculative model of western development but also contrasts favorably with the artificial and antidomestic life of the moneyed eastern society they have left behind.

Throughout the first half of the novel, Cummins interweaves the story of Mabel's discontent with a secondary narrative centering on Louise's maid, Lydia, and her poor, working-class family. Lydia's mother operates a small shop in a "dilapidated tenement" in a poor quarter of the city, while Lydia supplements the family income with her earnings as a maid. A brother, Jack, works as a street vendor and runs with a rough, trouble-making crowd, while the youngest child, Rose, is an invalid. Mabel first becomes involved with the Hope family when she pays Lydia her rightful wages out of her own spending money after discovering that Louise had fired Lydia without cause, as discussed at the beginning of this chapter. Later, a sleighing accident literally dumps Mabel and her nephews on the Hopes' doorstep, resulting in the development of a warm friendship and patronage on Mabel's part, motivated both by sympathy for the family's poverty and genuine attraction to the warmth of the Hopes' home life, so lacking in the Vaughan mansion.

When Mabel makes her journey to Illinois, she is aided by another member of the working class, a friend of the Hopes named Owen Dowst, who is also traveling west. Formerly a teamster, or carriage driver, in the city, Owen has sold his horses and plans to "seek his fortune" by investing the proceeds in western land. After their arrival in Illinois, Owen goes his own way and we see nothing more of him until several years have passed. Then one day Mabel is taken by a landowning friend to visit the friend's farm manager, and discovers that he is none other than Owen, now married to Lydia; the entire Hope family (minus Rose, who died in New York) has migrated to the West seeking new opportunities. Owen and Lydia have become farmers and landowners in their own right, while Jack is making good as the foreman of a farm machinery factory.

For both the Vaughans and the Hopes, western migration and settlement offer a clear solution to the problems created by economic panic. Mr. Vaughan's speculative losses force him to liquidate his estate to pay his debts, resulting not only in the sale of their New York home but also in the forfeiture of the family's social position. Moving to their one remaining piece of property in Illinois thus provides both a less expensive place to live and an opportunity to avoid the social humiliation of continued contact with their former friends and acquaintances. For the Hopes, a move west offers the chance to escape the crushing poverty of urban working-class life, made far worse by the massive unemployment that typically followed in the wake of panic.

But Cummins suggests that, for both the working class and for upper-middle-class women like Mabel, such a move offers a kind of rescue not only from the consequences of panic but also from much larger social and economic conditions of the time. In Mabel's case, even before her father's failure, the wealth-driven society of New York actually strips her of any power to conduct her life according to her own values or will. Thus, as in the panic fiction of the 1830s, *Mabel Vaughan* portrays Mr. Vaughan's financial failure as a "fortunate fall" for Mabel. Like the earlier panic heroines Elinor Fulton and Sophia Harcourt, sudden poverty empowers Mabel to make economic decisions and to establish a household operated according to domestic values. More so than the earlier fiction, however, *Mabel Vaughan* illustrates how little power women possess when their male relatives are wealthy and when wealth is the measure of all value. As Nina Baym has pointed out, the fashionable life depicted in the novel, although populated by women, gives women little role other than that of conspicuous consumer of their husbands' or fathers' wealth.[6]

In effect, Mabel is constrained by a double bind. On the one hand, her family's wealth and position make it virtually impossible for her to refuse to engage in the fashionable pursuits and extravagant spending that her aunt and sister promote. Although she disapproves of the expenditure on dress that fashion requires, she cannot truthfully plead poverty, the only acceptable excuse for challenging social expectations. Mabel's reluctant acquiescence to social demands further erodes her sense of agency, Cummins suggests, by undermining the moral power she might have possessed if she had been able to abstain from such activities. At the same time, Mabel has no real control over the money that is the basis for her position. It belongs to her father, who neither consults nor informs her about its investment. Mr. Vaughan's sale of the New York mansion without her knowledge particularly underscores her economic powerlessness. Having been living with her aunt, Mabel discovers that the house and all of the family's belongings have been sold at auction only when she attempts to arrange to have Louise's funeral there. Her request astonishes the funeral attendant, who exclaims, "Is it possible, Miss Vaughan, that you are ignorant of the sale which took place last week; your father's estate was put up at auction, and knocked off at considerably less than its value, I should judge" (325). Unaware up to that point of Mr. Vaughan's failure, Mabel is caught by surprise. Not only does she have no input into her father's economic decisions, she is not even apprised of them, even when they involve the supposedly female-run space of the family home. Domestic power cannot exist, Cummins suggests, in a world in which money is the utmost value.

Ultimately, therefore, Mr. Vaughan's failure and the failure of the financial system that gave him his power actually function to remove many of the constraints that made Mabel dependent, and enable her to make her own choices. In contrast to her earlier frustration and helplessness, she becomes decisive and self-reliant. She masks the shock she feels at discovering the family's financial situation and, without consulting anyone, resolves and carries out her move to Illinois. Replying to her aunt's objections, Mabel says that her father "does not, of course, know how I am situated . . . and I can not be sure what he would think best; so I am obliged to judge for myself" (328). We see her sudden ability to act thus as stemming in part from the fact that there is no one else to make decisions for her, or to stop her from doing so. Louise is dead; Harry and Mr. Vaughan are out west. But this very absence of authority figures is symbolic of Mabel's larger freedom from convention, a freedom paradoxically granted by her father's failure. Because she no longer has the economic ability to participate in the life of fashion, she is finally able to refuse such a life and thus to exercise a degree of economic and social self-determination.

Arriving in Illinois to find her father's household in chaos, Mabel takes on the role of domestic manager, that component of female economic agency so crucial in earlier panic fiction. Freed from the social constraints of her former life that forced her into an ornamental rather than useful role, Mabel now can exercise her domestic skills and thereby contribute to the family economy. Furthermore, hers is now a position of authority—rather than being subjected to the will of others, as she was in New York, Mabel is here able to direct the affairs of the household. The "order" and "harmony" that she creates within the house—words that Cummins repeats several times within a few pages—signify not only Mabel's ability to clean and to arrange objects pleasingly but also her capacity as a woman to apply rationality to the chaos produced by masculine economics. While Harry and Mr. Vaughan continue to cling for some time to their hopes that the Illinois land may yet pay off as a speculation, and thus make no attempts to provide for the family's welfare, Mabel comprehends the futility of their expectations. Harry eventually acknowledges that it is Mabel who has understood from the beginning the family's exact economic position—that they are ruined. She has "never been blinded," he says, "never been deceived by all the prophecies of better days"

(376). She can see through the false promises of speculation as the men cannot, and thus is best able to guide the family back to prosperity through the establishment of domestic values.

Through Mabel's domestic appropriation of her father's property, Cummins enacts a transformation of westward expansion from a masculine economic enterprise that excludes women to a female-led project of extending the domestic realm. Mr. Vaughan, as the novel's representative speculator, has envisioned his piece of Illinois land solely as an investment. Having purchased the property in expectation of a new railroad line, he hopes to sell it off at a large profit, and then move on to further investments. He does not see the land as a potential home: "That his residence there would be otherwise than temporary,—that Mabel would ever dream of joining him, and sharing his deprivations,—still less that his grandchildren would be brought thither for protection and shelter, had never once entered the old man's busy and overtasked brain; and yet, by a train of circumstances, at once natural and strange, the remnant of his diminished family were united under the humble roof, where they seemed destined for an indefinite period to constitute a common household" (363).

Mabel's vision of the land as a place to create a permanent home for her father, brother, nephews and herself—one that will unite these individuals who have never lived together under one roof into a real family—turns it into a domestic space. Her domestication of the land does not, however, remove its economic potential, but rather changes it from speculative to productive. Under her influence and the example of their young neighbor, Bayard Percival, Harry begins to farm the land, reaping real "golden harvests" while his father merely dreams of them (378). Cummins depicts Harry and Mabel as partners in the business of providing for the family—Harry producing food and surplus cash from his agricultural labors, Mabel supervising the use and expenditure of Harry's yield.

By thus portraying westward expansion through settlement and agriculture as superior—economically as well as philosophically—to expansion through economic adventurism, Cummins argues for an important role for women in fulfilling the nation's Manifest Destiny. Creating homes in the West requires women's presence and labor, while the mere purchase and resale of property does not. Cummins advocates seeing the work of expansion as a partnership between men and women. While men have labored with "vigor" and "unparalleled energy" to tame the West, she claims, "the success which has redeemed the waste land, and made the wilderness glad, is no less due to the cheerful sacrifices, the patient toil, and the sympathizing heart of woman" (363).[7]

As critics have noted, this image of "domesticating" the West served for authors like Cummins both as an implicit rebuke to masculine models of exploitive expansion and, somewhat paradoxically, as a more effective means of physically and culturally assimilating western lands into the nation. Annette Kolodny, for instance, remarks on the importance for female pioneers of planting gardens in the wilderness. Such women "claimed the frontiers as a potential sanctuary for an idealized domesticity," she notes, rather than fantasizing about "massive exploitation" as men did. Their dreams of forming new communities contrasted pointedly with masculine rhetoric of conquest (xiii).[8] In her frequently cited essay "Manifest Domesticity," however, Amy Kaplan has characterized such domestication as simply a more thorough avenue of imperialism. Placing the term "domestic" in opposition to "foreign" rather than to the economic or political realm, Kaplan sees domestic writers as complicit with a national project of empire building and domestic ideology itself as the "site from which the nation reaches beyond itself through the emanation of woman's moral influence" (586).

Read through Kaplan's lens, Mabel's success in converting her father's land from speculative investment to domestic space strengthens the Vaughans'—and the nation's—claim to the land and renders it fit for civilization. Reclaiming the West not only from its native inhabitants and its natural wildness but also from speculators and adventurers, domestication further ensures that an established middle class will maintain its dominance over an expanding nation. We see this played out in Cummins's novel. Mabel's domestication of her father's western property breaks down the patriarchal hierarchies of the first half of the novel, shifting the center of power from Mr. Vaughan's individualist money-making schemes to a more communal sense of shared responsibility anchored by Mabel's domestic management. Financial exploitation of the land is replaced by a more cooperative vision of the land as a site for productive labor. At the same time, the greater permanence of the Vaughans upon their Illinois land ensured by Harry's agricultural ventures suggests simply a different kind of conquest—one in which Mabel's domesticity has become the dominant paradigm.

The institution of middle-class domestic values in western territories takes on particular significance in light of Cummins's promotion of westward migration for working-class easterners looking for socioeconomic advancement. Despite popular rhetoric about the need to "redeem" and "subdue" the wilderness, many Americans saw the West itself as redemptive—as a symbol of freedom, equality and economic opportunity. Unfettered by the conventions of the more established parts of the country, the West was often seen as a blank slate upon which to create a renewed society. In *Mabel Vaughan*, Cummins imagines just such a society, one that, while not exactly classless, is able to accommodate both the formerly wealthy who have suffered loss and the poor who are seeking economic advancement, and to integrate them all into a more egalitarian social structure.

We see a number of scenes in which people whose lives would either never have intersected in New York, or whose relations would have been governed by strict class hierarchies, interact on a roughly equal basis. In one such scene, Mabel and her domestic employee, Melissa, sit next to each other at a political address in the community meeting hall. More significantly, the Vaughans and the Hope/Dowst clan attend the same church, sitting in neighboring pews, and can socialize freely without the social stigma attached to Mabel's visits to the Hopes in the city.

Part of the credit for this lessening of social boundaries goes simply to the partial leveling of their financial statuses. As the Vaughans have retreated to Illinois to live less expensively following their losses, the Hopes find in the West much wider opportunities for economic advancement. In New York, for example, Jack Hope appeared to have no options other than hawking his mother's wares from a basket on the street, leading to an attitude of resentment and rebellion that threatened to land him in prison. In the West, however, due to his new position as a factory foreman that makes use of his mechanical inclinations, the budding hooligan Jack is now "Mr. John Hope, one of the pillars of the church and the township" (470). The honorific and less childish name, as well as a "shining suit of broadcloth," signifies that Jack's position of responsibility has transformed him from a "shabby urchin" to a middle-class gentleman. Likewise, Owen's small fund of money can realize far greater gains invested in western land than in any urban business. Although both men are technically still employed by others, Jack's supervisory position and Owen's land ownership remove them from the dependency and servile status of their lives in New York and endow them with the autonomy originally associated with free labor. As such, they have equal political status, if not equal financial means, to men like Mr. Vaughan and Harry.

But Cummins also makes clear that the common ground on which the formerly rich and formerly poor can meet on the frontier is a distinctly middle-class, domesticated space. Just as the Vaughans had to be transformed from their nondomestic city life in order to thrive in Illinois, the novel's working-class representatives must undergo a process of domestication in order to be integrated into Cummins's middle-class West. Rather than depicting Owen and Jack as single working-class men making their fortunes on the frontier, Cummins shows how their economic opportunities permit them to unite their families and create the kind of domestic life denied them in the east. Whereas in New York, factors such as illness, crime, the need for women to labor outside the home, and the literal deterioration of their substandard housing kept the Hope family separated from each other and made domesticity difficult, in the West we see them together and thriving as a family in their "snug farmhouse." And it is precisely this domestic context that makes them assimilable into a middle-class society and allows social mixing. When Mabel first visits the Hope family on their Illinois farm, it is significant that her attention is drawn first to their house: "'And this is the farm house!' said Mabel, as they now came in sight of a comfortable two-story dwelling, surrounded by spacious and substantial barns and granaries. 'How neat and thrifty everything looks!'" (456). Once inside, Mabel notes the "perfect order" that marks Lydia's home as a counterpart to her own, and first realizes who the inhabitants are when she recognizes the simple furnishings—the "rush-bottomed arm-chair" and "leather-covered bible" that used to grace the Hopes' dingy rooms in the city. Later, when the family is all assembled—including Owen and Lydia's new baby and Lydia's mother—and a tearful reunion has ensued, Mabel explicitly claims the Hopes as peers, saying to Owen, "Such a home, and wife, and child, and good name, as you can call yours, are indeed something to be proud of; and I am proud, I assure you, to claim you as an old friend" (459). Worlds apart in New York, Mabel and Lydia are now on an equal footing, linked by their identical roles as housewives, as domestic managers of their families' small farms, and as the domestic adhesive that bonds disparate family members together. The domestic rituals of visiting and tea taking forge a social link between the families that promises to erase the disparities of their backgrounds. Owen and Lydia's baby, born in Illinois, further signifies the creation of something new—a symbol of a new generation, not mired in the divisions and hierarchies of its parents.

Cummins does not suggest that one must be middle class to acquire domestic values. Indeed, it was behind the crumbling façade of the Hopes' cellar apartment in the city that Mabel found the desire for family life that was missing in her father's luxurious mansion. And it was the dying Rosie's civilizing influence on Jack that inspired Mabel's efforts to similarly domesticate her own brother. But in New York, in the face of strong social and economic forces that keep the working class from advancing, these inner qualities were not enough to enable the working class to actually achieve the functioning domestic life necessary to bridge the chasm between classes and become full citizens in society. In fact, neither the wealthy nor the poor, are able, in Cummins's view, to completely realize the "free labor" ideals of autonomy and self-ownership within the stratified class structure that imprisons the wealthy in a world of false values and the poor under oppressive conditions of poverty. The West allows both classes to meet in the middle—that is, in a middle-class domestic life that keeps wealth tied to the actual productivity of the land or related industry and raises the cultural level of the poor through the social rituals of the home. By making an attainable middle-class domestic life the basic building block for western society, Cummins softens the rigid social categories of the Northeast that relegated both the working class and upper-middle-class women to positions of powerlessness. And by populating her utopian West with families who create homes on the land rather than with individual men seeking their fortunes, Cummins maintains middle-class cultural dominance while acquiescing to western blurring of class distinctions.

If such middle-class domestication of the West can, in Cummins's view, alleviate the problems of urban poverty and a speculative economy, however, she finds her ideal threatened by the specter of slavery. So prominent in the nation's collective mind in 1857, slavery looms large even on the liberating prairies and sheltering homesteads of Cummins's Illinois and, in fact, is shown to pose a particular threat to the free labor society so carefully constructed in the pages of the novel. Cummins introduces the issue of slavery through the moderately abolitionist sentiments of Bayard Percival. Percival recurs throughout the novel as a mysterious man of integrity who comes to Harry and Mabel's rescue on several occasions, and ultimately becomes Mabel's husband. Spurred by the debate over whether the Nebraska territory should be slave or free, Percival runs for Congress. In a lengthy political speech, "reported" in full in the novel's pages, he argues that slavery is a great moral wrong, and that Nebraska should therefore be constituted as a free territory.

Percival's argument against slavery touches on the wrongs done to the enslaved, but is actually far more concerned with the potential for slavery, if allowed to exist in the western territories, to destroy the ideals of freedom and equality so central to conceptions of (white) western society. Giving voice to the philosophical underpinnings of free labor ideology, Percival asks his western audience, "To what are you indebted for your own unexampled prosperity? Is it not to the equality of human rights, the dignity which attends free and honest labor, the universal education of your children and the spread of Gospel truth?"(426). If these essential elements of a free society are not available to all of that society's members, Percival (and Cummins) suggests, they are effectively denied to all. And without equal opportunity, education, and belief in the value of labor, the "unexampled prosperity" that blessed the members of such a free society would cease to exist.

Part of Cummins's vehement rejection of slavery in the western territories may have been motivated by racial prejudice. Although she does not mention race, her near-egalitarian western community is implicitly all white, and while she can imagine the assimilation of a white working class into her middle-class ideal, very few white Northern writers of the time depicted harmonious mixed-race societies. But slavery, as an inherently hierarchical system, is also fundamentally incompatible with the model of society that Cummins envisions in *Mabel Vaughan*, regardless of race. Slavery cannot be assimilated into the larger community without destroying the very character of that community, which depends on the ability of each individual to achieve self-ownership. Thus, left to themselves, and fully conscious of their true self-interest, Cummins implies, the people of the West would reject slavery and elect to retain their free and independent society.

But the novel suggests that preventing the spread of slavery to the western territories is neither as simple as trusting to the people of the West to act on their own interests, or a sufficient response to slavery's evils. While most of the societal problems that Cummins deals with in *Mabel Vaughan* can be resolved through the creation of a new society in isolation from the flawed systems and institutions of the urban Northeast, the self-sufficient western model of domesticity is not enough, she implies, to prevent the taint of slavery from potentially encroaching on that ideal or from contaminating the virtue of the nation as a whole. In Percival, Cummins represents the need to look outward from the ideal space of the home to national problems such as slavery that cannot be solved through domestication alone. Percival's election to Congress and subsequent move to Washington in order to work against slavery suggest that the problem of slavery requires a political solution rather than a social one and that the responsibility for public service supersedes even domesticity and honest industry in such times of national and moral crisis. By having Percival and Mabel decide to marry, and thus depicting Mabel moving to Washington as well, Cummins suggests, at least to some degree, that women also share this responsibility to serve the public welfare in times of crisis, although Mabel's precise role is left undefined.[9]

By ending the novel with Mabel and Percival's move into the public realm of politics, Cummins disrupts, but does not abandon, her vision of a domesticated West as the solution to class divisions and the problems wrought by financial panic. The rest of the Vaughans and the Hope/Dowst family remain in Illinois and eventually prosper after some years of hard work. Mabel and Percival themselves split their time between Washington and Illinois, spending their summers on the farm when Congress is not in session. But at a time when the nation was becoming increasingly torn apart by sectional divisions, Cummins recognizes a need for public action that takes priority over private domestic life, in order to protect the free labor society that itself protects citizens against the oppressions of a stratified society.

Alice Haven's *The Coopers*

Providing a very different perspective on the threats of panic, slavery, and class-based labor conflicts is Alice Haven's 1858 novel *The Coopers; or, Getting Under Way*. Haven was born Emily Bradley in Hudson, New York, in 1827, the same year as Cummins. Her father having died when she was a young child, she was adopted by an uncle and raised mostly in New Hampshire, where she began writing stories as a schoolgirl. Several of her stories were published during the 1840s—under the pseudonym "Alice Lee"—in a Philadelphia periodical named *Neal's Saturday Gazette and Lady's Literary Museum*. Haven married the editor, Joseph C. Neal, in 1846, and continued, at his request, to be known as Alice. When Joseph Neal died just seven months after their marriage, she helped to edit the *Gazette* for about six years, simultaneously writing and publishing several series of Sunday school materials and children's fiction. In 1853, she married Samuel L. Haven, a New York broker with whom she had five children. She continued to write despite ill health, dying of tuberculosis in 1863 at the age of 35.[10]

Judging by the criteria used to define panic fiction in the introduction to this study—in particular, the criterion of having a central narrative focus on panic and failure—one might not consider *The Coopers* a panic narrative at all. After all, the title characters, the newly married Murray and Martha Cooper, whose adventures as they start out in business and housekeeping form the narrative core of the novel, never actually experience financial failure. There is a scene toward the end of the novel in which Murray worries about failing and readers are set up to expect him to declare bankruptcy, but in the end failure is averted and Murray's business turns a profit. Nevertheless, the combination of *The Coopers*' pervasive attention to economic themes, its depiction of anxiety about failure, and its date of publication—just a few months after the Panic of 1857—suggest that the commercial anxieties of the recent panic were almost certainly on Haven's mind. Rather than condemning the economic practices that led to panic and providing a model for how middle-class women might survive and recover from resultant losses, though, Haven presents a model for how to thrive within a tumultuous marketplace. Thus, unlike most of the panic fiction discussed so far, for Haven, panic serves as neither a devastating event nor a "fortunate fall," but rather as a symbol for the risks that are necessary to take in order to be financially successful in the economy of the late 1850s.

From the beginning of the novel, Murray and Martha Cooper's home is established as a site of economic exchange and their relationship defined in economic terms. Murray, we learn, is from a prominent and formerly wealthy family, for whom "poverty" has meant continuing to live well while racking up debt. He enjoys brandy and cigars and is used to charging all his expenses and worrying later about how his modest salary as a clerk in the Marine Bank will pay the bills. Martha is the economist of the family, a former Smith, for whom poverty meant "self-denial, industry, and a great many 'wants reduced to must haves' before they were satisfied" (32). She would prefer to have a budget and a household allowance out of which she could pay for everything up front—in short, a cash rather than a credit system. The disparity in their economic philosophies is reinforced in an extended scene in which Murray fantasizes about how he and Martha would furnish and landscape a home of their own if they could afford to buy one—which they cannot. As Murray enthusiastically "spend[s] in advance," his wife is torn between the appeal of his plans for the future and the discouragement of her own realistic assessment of their present situation.

Both Murray's optimism and Martha's pragmatism are rewarded, in a way, when Murray's uncle dies, leaving them five thousand dollars and naming Martha first on the bequest because he is confident she will not squander the money. In something of role reversal, Murray wants to use the legacy to buy the house he has been fantasizing about, while Martha believes it would be better spent in setting Murray up in business. Marshaling a number of economic arguments in her favor, Martha wins out, and "business *versus* real estate carried the day" (91). Murray and a partner, Steve Henderson, open a storage, or warehousing, business. Meanwhile, the Coopers find a small house to rent in the country north of New York City and Martha goes to work furnishing the home and learning to manage the household affairs. As Murray's business fades to the background, Martha's takes center stage; most of the rest of the novel details her struggles to become a competent household manager.

Throughout the novel, Haven takes pains to portray Murray's business and Martha's housekeeping as parallel domains, both "getting under way" as the novel's subtitle puts it, and equally enmeshed in the marketplace as they struggle to emerge as successfully run enterprises. One way in which this equivalence is established is by emphasizing the economic nature of domesticity through Martha's purchase of furnishings. In an early chapter, we see Martha shopping at Stewart's, the famous New York department store, where bird's-eye linen, fleecy blankets, snowy damask, tea napkins in a snow-drop pattern, a patent coffee roaster, china and glassware, lamps, furniture, carpets, and curtains all catch her desiring eye and are lavishly described by the narrator. While earlier panic fiction revealed the home's economic dimensions by describing which household goods had to be sold or dispensed with in times of crisis, *The Coopers* makes the same point by anticipating the wealth of material goods Martha will be able to acquire as the couple's finances permit. In a chapter entitled "The Frugal Housewife," echoing Lydia Child's famous household manual from the 1830s, Haven revises Child's advice on how to run a household on very little money, showing Martha being instructed by her mentor how to economize by actually spending *more* to buy the best quality goods that will last the longest. While Haven is certainly not advocating extravagance in these scenes, her legitimation of Martha's economic desire and of the notion of responsible consumerism reflects a far greater acceptance of materialism and the moral compatibility of virtue and economic striving than in the post-1837 era.

Martha Cooper is far more than just a consumer, however. Despite her husband's ironic musing that "women know nothing about business," she displays an extensive knowledge of and competence in the practical matters of business, as well as a broader comprehension of general economic conditions (90). Her application of this aptitude to the household is demonstrated early on, when she requests and eventually receives a housekeeping allowance from Murray, despite his complaint that "[t]hese private purses make a wife altogether too independent" (34). She is also the one to calculate the costs of furnishing a rented house and budgets the couple's purchases. In their discussion of how to invest the five thousand dollar legacy, Martha reveals her understanding of mortgages, arguing against the purchase of a house by citing "interest, and taxes, and repairs" as hidden expenses that Murray has not considered. In addition, during the early stages of Murray's storage business, she also pays close attention to the fluctuating values of the commodities being stored and transported: "She could tell you the last quotations in flour and grain, knew something of pork before it found its way to Fulton Market, and that, when wool advanced, it was neither 'Berlin' nor yet 'Saxony,' which the papers alluded to" (93).

Interestingly, and seemingly at odds with her insistence on a cash economy for the household, it is Martha who is most willing to embrace the uncertainties of business, signifying her greater understanding of changing economic conditions. Murray worries, with good reason, that their capital of five thousand dollars will be insufficient to go into business and that hard work and determination are no longer enough to make one's way in a market driven by huge amounts of capital. Fearing to risk their small legacy under such conditions, he prefers the tangible investment of a house. Martha, on the other hand, encourages her husband to capitalize on his assets, reminding him that he had earlier said "the storage business did not require much capital, only business friends; and [he] made so many in the bank" (89). Thus she focuses on what *can* be done with more connections than cash, and steers him toward an occupation that is appropriately symbolic of the expanding commercial capacities of the mid-nineteenth century. Martha's resistance to putting the legacy money into a house also reflects her greater attunement to a shifting economic terrain. The narrator's proclamation that "business *versus* real estate carried the day" resonates with the nineteenth-century shift from an agrarian to a commercial society. On Martha's recommendation, the Coopers forego—temporarily—the tangible property that a home represents for the more abstract ownership of a business, materially represented only by a handsome sign with "blue and gilt lettering" and pasteboard business cards. More explicitly than any other panic fiction family to date, they join the burgeoning commercial middle class, staking their futures on types of labor and property that had only emerged in the previous few decades.

In the final chapter of the novel, after many pages detailing Martha's struggles in the household, Haven returns us to the storage business counting room, in a scene that reminds readers of the economic reality that market risk can lead to loss and failure. Murray and his partner Steve Henderson are poring over the balance sheet for their second year of operation with "grave and thoughtful faces" and Steve's "forehead [is] bent almost into furrows" (311). As they leave the office and Murray returns home looking haggard, his seeming dejection almost exactly replicates the tone of similar scenes of anxious reckoning in earlier panic novels, in which the husband or father grimly faces his family and confesses his ruin or announces the need for retrenchment. Readers are led to expect, as Martha does when she sees him, that "something had happened," most probably that the business has failed or is about to (312). Murray keeps Martha in suspense for some time, refraining from telling her his news. But just as she is prepared to console him for loss and to take the blame for urging him to go into business, the narrative changes radically. Instead of announcing loss, Murray triumphantly proclaims a profit of "two thousand three hundred and odd, to the credit of each" (317). The outlook for the future looks good as well: "Splendid prospects for next year, too. We never began to do the business we are doing now; and a year from this, old lady, somebody is going to have a place of her own" (318). Thus, instead of regretfully arranging the sale of domestic comforts, the Coopers are able to celebrate hopes of a new home, while Murray's partner, Steve Henderson, rejoices that he can finally afford to get married and set up a household of his own.

With this startling twist on the usual panic narrative, Haven depicts the willingness to take a commercial risk as having a beneficial outcome, strengthening rather than destabilizing the domestic sphere. While the final scene does recognize and validate the anxieties attendant upon capitalist ventures, the author manifests a new attitude toward business, one that accepts a moderate amount of risk and displays confidence that a properly run business can actually survive periodic economic crises and even thrive under conditions of uncertainty. Risk taking is portrayed here not as an evil to be avoided or a practice born of the fever of greed, but rather as an inherent element of commerce and even as a necessary step toward individual and societal progress.[11]

In her housekeeping endeavors, which occupy the largest portion of the novel and are clearly Haven's principal concern, Martha goes through a similar sequence of struggle, uncertainty, crisis, and successful resolution. In contrast to her business acumen, Martha has no experience in running a household; thus, her many mistakes lead to a period of household chaos and physical collapse from exhaustion before she acquires the necessary domestic management skills. While Murray's narrative provides Haven with a means to address issues of commercial risk and potential business failure, Martha's allows the author to address the equally pressing issue of relations between employers and employees. Most of Martha's difficulties in establishing a successfully run household are related to the employment of domestic servants; rather than seeing her learn how to *perform* household tasks, we observe her learning, by trial and much error, how to hire, train, and supervise the domestic employees who will perform these tasks.

Given Haven's positioning of the home as a parallel economic space to the marketplace, and the home's mistress as a legitimate economic agent, the novel's focus on domestic employment relations appears intended as an analogy and alternative for the industrial labor conflicts so prevalent at the time. Here again, the author displays considerable optimism and confidence that potential economic crises can be weathered and resolved. Through her depiction of Martha's eventual success on the home front, Haven offers a professionally run domestic sphere as a model for the successful resolution of labor conflicts. This model resembles a contractual understanding of "free labor," in which employees are free to accept and withdraw from jobs and have individual rights while still under obligation to the employer on the job, and in which appropriate roles and responsibilities of employers and employees are carefully defined and distinguished. But the particular conditions of domestic employment also offer a number of factors that mitigate the antagonism and harshness associated with industrial "wage slavery."

In order to demonstrate how *not* to manage employees, each servant who passes through the Cooper household represents a particular deficiency, not only on the servant's part, but on the part of Martha's behavior as an employer. For example, the first maidservant, an Irish girl named Julia, is lazy, careless in her work and appearance, and openly insolent to Martha when reprimanded for work improperly done. She spends most of her time in the kitchen, gossiping with the cook, and repeatedly has to be reminded to fill the water pitcher in Martha and Murray's room. When Murray complains to Martha about this dereliction of duty, we see Martha's shortcomings as a "mistress"—her timidity, lack of command, and tolerance for shoddy work. At first, Martha simply offers to fill the pitcher herself, but when Murray insists that she call in Julia and reprimand her, Martha trembles under the girl's impertinent stare and offers in a "quavering" voice, "don't let it happen again" (50). Martha's greatest fear, it appears, is that if Julia is offended, she will simply quit, leaving Martha herself with all the work of the household and the care of a fussy baby. Thus, Martha takes pains to humor Julia and ignore her deficiencies, only to have Julia give notice anyway, sauntering off to be married, right in the middle of "house-cleaning, pickling, and preserving" (53).

The lesson that Martha takes from this episode is to choose her next servant more carefully, finding a new girl, Lucy, who is "just as neat as Julia was careless" (54). And for a while, her judgment seems confirmed, as Lucy performs her work quickly and efficiently, and cares for little Johnny with energy, taking him for long walks every day. But Martha's judgment has been based only on appearances. Impressed by Lucy's impeccable dress and manners, Martha declines to check her references, feeling that that would be an "insult" (57). Murray's comment that "The bank had no such scruples when your respected husband was required to give a ten thousand dollar bond before he could get the tellership" not only conveys his disapproval, but reminds us again that the Cooper home is a place of employment, and employment relationships should be guided by contractual requirements, not by sentiment or blind trust. Not surprisingly, Martha's trust in Lucy soon proves unfounded, when Murray accidentally sees her with the baby in a "filthy alley" near the business district, when she was supposedly walking with him in the park. As it turns out, Lucy has not only been taking Johnny to "low places," but also keeping him quiet with candy. Martha is further dismayed to find Lucy had been discharged from her former position for stealing and that her tales of mistreatment at that position had been largely fabricated. Martha is repaid for having listened to Lucy's gossip by finding herself slandered in turn after Murray has promptly paid the girl's wages and discharged her.

Although the lesson learned from the Lucy fiasco would seem to be that domestic servants should be hired in a professional manner and based strictly on work qualifications, Martha's third and final hiring experience finds her choosing an inexperienced but appealing young laundress over a stern, "sharp-featured" woman who claims to have the cooking expertise that the Coopers need. Tiny's honesty in admitting that she does not know how to cook but is willing to learn, as well as her sweet nature, wins Martha over after her experience of Lucy's deceit and pride. But although Martha's decision eventually proves fortunate, and Tiny serves the family well, the combination of Tiny's ignorance and Martha's inexperience as a domestic manager produces household chaos until Mrs. Henderson (Murray's partner's mother) arrives for an extended visit and sets everything to rights. At the center of the novel, in a chapter entitled "The Crisis," a series of mishaps and illnesses produces a scene in which dinner time finds only dirty dishes and partially peeled vegetables heaped around the kitchen, while a pile of dirty laundry attracts flies and chickens are pecking at the scraps on the unswept floor. Both the cook and Johnny are sick in bed, and after the doctor has come and left remedies for whooping cough, Martha, utterly overwhelmed by exhaustion and disorder, collapses in hysterical sobbing.

In many ways, these scenes resemble the chapters in 1830s panic fiction devoted to "the servant question," such as in Lee's *Elinor Fulton* and Sedgwick's *Live and Let Live*, discussed in chapter 2. Like those novels, *The Coopers* focuses on the proper relationship between a middle-class employer and her domestic servants and uses domestic management as a way of demonstrating middle-class women's economic competence. While servants' deficiencies are described and condemned—and Haven lays considerably more blame on domestic employees than either Lee or Sedgwick had—readers' attention is again primarily directed toward the behavior of the employer. It is Martha that we principally observe—helplessly allowing Julia to slack off, foolishly gossiping with Lucy, and observing Tiny's kitchen chaos with dismay. In showing us Martha's inexperience, lack of confidence, and failure to monitor her domestics' work, Haven follows the pattern of her predecessors in stressing the importance of "mistresses" having thorough knowledge of household work and providing their employees with proper training and supervision.

But whereas the earlier novels depicted the ideal mistress-servant relationship as a kind of benevolent female paternalism, held together with mutual—if unequal—bonds of love, Haven does not echo Lee's and Sedgwick's language of familial relation or emotional connection. She does not depict domestic servants as dependents bound to the family by affection. Rather, Haven's emphasis on training and supervision suggests that while she does not altogether abandon earlier notions of middle-class responsibility for modeling domesticity for the poorer classes, she regards the relationship between mistress and domestic as primarily that of employer to employee.

The precise form that this employer-employee relationship ought to take is a question that Haven takes some pains to define, and here we see Haven taking on the predominant models of her time. In a chapter on "The Servant Question" late in the novel, Martha Cooper is joined by a number of women in discussing the appropriate treatment of domestic employees. One of her neighbors, a Mrs. Graves, takes a very harsh view—one that appears to combine elements of a slaveholding mentality with the most oppressive aspects of Northern industrial labor, or "wage slavery." At one point, decrying her servants' desire for recreation and companionship, she exemplifies slaveholders' views of their laborers as having no human needs or rights of their own, but existing only to serve her needs. "They have no business to go out," she exclaims. "Company ruins them" (263). She seems mystified that when she refuses her maids a day off or the right to receive visitors, they leave her service. A few pages later Mrs. Graves again verbally denies her servants' humanity, this time with a phrase reflecting industrial oppression, telling another neighbor, "I want to find out how to get at one of those perfect machines like your Jo!" (268).

The extreme nature of Mrs. Graves's attitude and the fact that she is unsuccessful in keeping servants in her employ very long make it clear that hers is not the appropriate model for domestic employment. Martha's mentor, Mrs. Henderson, and the employer of the aforementioned "perfect machine," a Mrs. Phillips, advocate far more humane treatment of their servants, including explicit recognition of their status as human beings, with needs for both personal time and relationships outside of the house. Mrs. Phillips also makes a point of recommending a consistent manner of professional kindness toward servants—what she calls "uniform friendliness"—in stark contrast to Mrs. Graves's confessed alternation between indulgence and harshness (274).

But Mrs. Phillips also notes that the "law of kindness [is] a very different code from the absence of all restraint," and this is key to Haven's delineation of ideal domestic employment. The "secrets" to Mrs. Henderson's and Mrs. Phillips's success with their servants are training and supervision. When Martha wants to know where faithful and accomplished domestics can be found, and Mrs. Graves declares that "it's the place of my servants to know their business, and do it thoroughly," they expose their inexperience; good servants are made, not found, they are told (272). Mrs. Phillips then explains how she cured her cook of untidiness and waste by drawing attention to her sloppy habits and making it clear that they would not be tolerated: "I used to go [to the kitchen] regularly every morning, while she was making up her own room, and set out every dish, that was not what it should be, on a table in the middle of the room. . . . Sauce-boats with two spoonfuls of gravy, bits of butter, slops of cold tea, unwashed saucepans! Oh, dear, such a state as those closets were in!" (269)

Responding to the younger women's expressions of discomfort with seeming to intrude on their servants' domains, Mrs. Phillips asks, "How are you going to correct them then? I always tell a new cook that once a day she may expect me to take a general survey of her regions; and I never spare commendations where they are deserved" (270). Haven thus signals that, while domestic employees must be accorded respect as human beings, they are not autonomous; that is, they should not be permitted to direct their own labor. Their employers must be responsible for determining what work needs to be done and how it should be done, and for making sure that it is accomplished as desired.

In laying out these guidelines for successful domestic employment, and in implicitly contrasting her ideal with both dehumanizing labor practices and more autonomous forms of labor, Haven appears to present domestic employment as a potential model for labor relations in the larger world of the 1850s. Her rejection of the employees' ability to learn their work on their own or to direct their own labor suggests that she does not see the autonomous model of the independent artisan as being any longer a viable model for workers of the day. But the system of supervised labor that she advocates seems designed to expose and reject particular aspects of the dominant labor systems of the time, specifically Southern slavery and Northern industrial labor. Like other panic authors before her, Haven promotes domestic service as "free labor," differentiated from slavery because undertaken without coercion and performed for fair wages.[12] She emphasizes that servants must never have wages withheld, must be allowed reasonable freedom to come and go, and permitted to leave their jobs at will. She also distances her model from the abuses attributed to industrial employment, condemning the treatment of employees as "machines" and stressing the employer's responsibility for those they hire.

For Haven, the middle-class home seems to provide the ideal setting for employment relations that avoid the oppression and antagonism of slavery and industrial wage labor. For one thing, domestic labor in a modest middle-class household like the Coopers' involves only one or two employees, thus avoiding the image of large-scale industrial work forces or slave gangs; relations between the mistress and her cook or nursemaid are therefore more personal, even if not familial in nature. They know each other's names and something about their lives and personalities, rather than being simply "machines" or distant embodiments of power to each other, respectively. In addition, the values of caring and comfort that mark the domestic realm set a tone for relations that are at least civil, rather than abusive or antagonistic. A further positive factor is the correlation between domestic servants' work and that of the mistress herself, both engaged, although in different ways, in the tasks of maintaining a pleasant and orderly home. This suggests a model of supervision based on mentoring and cooperation, rather than the impersonal commands of the slave driver or factory foreman.

Unlike Cummins's vision of domesticity that blurs the lines between socioeconomic classes, however, Haven's domestic labor model actually reinforces class distinctions, achieving harmony through the establishment of and respect for clearly understood expectations and boundaries. Martha Cooper advances toward the kind of domestic order and harmony that Mabel Vaughan creates in Illinois only when she is able to specify and maintain proper distinctions between her own duties and privileges and those of her domestics. With her first servant, Julia, she fails to see herself as having the right to command Julia's labor, and thus tolerates a situation in which the household work is determined by the employee's whims, and the family's needs go unmet. Anxious to retain the next girl, Martha almost literally exchanges roles with her, doing much of the domestic labor herself while Lucy parades around town in fancy clothes. Lucy's stylish dress, which Martha interprets as a sign of her gentility, serves as a warning flag to the more skeptical Murray (and to the reader) that she will not perform appropriately as a domestic servant. When Martha expresses her satisfaction with Lucy to Murray by explaining that "she was dressed as well as I am," he replies, "very unsuitably for her position, then, I should say," later advising his wife half-jokingly to stop wearing the hair ornaments that are like Lucy's, in order to maintain a visible distinction (55). In both of these cases, domestic disorder is a direct result of Martha's failure to assert herself as an authority figure, allowing herself rather to be intimidated by the one and treated familiarly by the other.

In the final case of Tiny, who has no such pretensions to equality with the Coopers, and who both speaks and behaves with appropriate deference, Martha's failure is in misunderstanding the most important function of the mistress of the household. Blinded by her concern for economy, she attempts to save money by performing household labor, such as the family sewing, which could be done by a hired seamstress. Martha's mentor, Mrs. Henderson, teaches her that for "people in moderate circumstances"—that is, the emerging middle class—"that is not true economy which wastes your best capital, health and cheerfulness" (213). That is, a woman who can afford to employ domestic help does not economize best by doing the household labor herself, but by supervising others in its performance and keeping as her own domain personal service to her husband and the role of example and guide to her children. Echoing common formulations of the time, Mrs. Henderson's advice delineates clear divisions between the "moral" domestic role of the middle-class wife and mother and the physical domestic labor to be performed by her employees. Martha Cooper is able to achieve domestic order and harmony only when she puts this advice into practice and fully understands and accepts her role as employer.

The relationship that Haven constructs between the middle-class employer and her domestic employees is thus a complicated one. Haven recognizes a link between the plight of urban workers and the desires of middle-class women for greater autonomy. To some degree, domestic labor offers a model, if not a solution, for improving the lot of each. Rejecting the oppressiveness and antagonism of industrial labor, the domestic model embodies a form of free labor that respects the worker's humanity and forges a personal link between employer and employee. At the same time, the authority conferred by being an employer raises the status of a middle-class woman like Martha Cooper to an implied equality of sorts with her businessman husband. The working class and middle-class women do not advance in parallel as we saw in *Mabel Vaughan*, however, as Martha's authority is gained at the expense of her employees' voluntary subordination and a class hierarchy is carefully maintained.

In many respects this again resembles the mistress-servant relationships portrayed in the earlier panic fiction of Lee and Sedgwick, where such reinforcement of class distinctions through domestic employment served to assuage middle-class anxiety about the potential loss of status in times of economic crisis. Where *The Coopers* differs from these earlier novels, however, is that Martha's class status does not ever seem to be in question, only her status as a successful employer, or household manager. The suspense over whether Murray's business has failed or succeeded comes only at the very end of the novel, and thus does not create the kind of anxiety about loss and its potential social consequences that pervades the whole narrative in many panic novels. The narrative trajectory of the novel is a gradual but steady rise for Martha and Murray, with occasional crises to show that success is not automatic nor achieved without some hardship.

At the same time, there is little social pressure from below, despite Julia's lack of deference and Lucy's pretensions to gentility. Unlike Sedgwick's *Live and Let Live*, which celebrates the eventual social advancement of a domestic employee to the ranks of the middle class, or Lee's *Elinor Fulton*, which at least depicts the servant Lucinda as a fully developed character with a range of thoughts and feelings, Haven's novel treats its domestic servants as mere illustrations of the various problems that mark employment relations. The characters of Julia, Lucy, and Tiny appear only fleetingly in the narrative and then only as viewed by the middle-class Martha. We never see them alone and are not privy to their thoughts, other than what is manifested in their speech to their employer. More than in the 1830s panic fiction, working-class characters are genuinely depicted as a *class*, rather than as individuals. As Martha and Murray Cooper struggle to advance themselves, their servants are presumed to remain static, without legitimate goals of their own.

Thus we can see that both Cummins's and Haven's novels reflect a mid-nineteenth-century urban society in which class divisions have become more rigid, less subject to the fluidity that had made panic a cause for such social anxiety just twenty years earlier. Both novels also reflect an increasing societal consciousness of the downsides of such class divisions, focusing on how to cope with effects such as extreme poverty and labor discontent. The fact that Cummins uses financial panic as an opportunity for those marginalized by a hierarchical society to create a new, more egalitarian one, while Haven simply classes both panic and labor problems as challenges for the commercial/industrial middle classes to master, illustrates yet again the ways in which antebellum panic authors employed panic to further particular political, economic, and social agendas.

The existence of fewer female-authored panic novels from the 1850s and different attitudes toward panic reflected in those that do exist suggest that the prospect of economic loss may have occasioned less urgency in the 1850s than the 1830s. Nevertheless, the event of panic remained a powerfully suggestive focal point for authors throughout the antebellum era. Within their fiction, "panic" is the locus of multiple anxieties—about financial loss, social instability, moral deterioration, domestic disempowerment, political and economic subjugation, and labor conflict, to name the most prevalent. But panic also represents a "fortunate fall," a disruption of dangerous financial practices, an opportunity to change economic direction, and a test of economic strength. Panic is not only a subject for economic discourse in itself but also a way to talk about other urgent issues of the antebellum era, such as emerging class identities, changing gender roles, slavery, organization of labor, and patterns of commercial and industrial development.

We have only to look at recent headlines to realize that, although the nation's economy has changed substantially since the 1850s, the ambitions and desires that fueled antebellum boom periods and the fears and warnings expressed by the authors of panic fiction remain current. The anxieties about potential loss expressed by panic authors, their warnings against irresponsible economic practices, and even their calls for an economy guided by moral and rational behavior have been echoed repeatedly through the intervening decades, as Americans struggle to balance material ambitions with ideals of national character. Although antebellum panic authors might not recognize many features of our current economic system, their expressions of anxiety and hopes for reform more than 150 years ago still speak to our often conflicting desires for both prosperity and stability.

Notes

Introduction

1. Cathy N. Davidson's *Revolution and the Word* and Jane Tompkins's *Sensational Designs* are foundational texts that demonstrate the engagement of sentimental and domestic fiction in political discourse, showing how both genres often embraced very specific political viewpoints and attempted to influence American readers to think, feel, and act according to those viewpoints. Other examples of critics who have argued for a "politics of sympathy" in sentimental novels are Shirley Samuels, Julia A. Stern, Elizabeth Barnes, and Michelle Burnham.

Nina Baym's groundbreaking study *Woman's Fiction* was among the first to take the domestic novel seriously, finding it to promote women's independence within the fulfillment of domestic duty. Extending Baym's analysis, critics such as Carroll Smith-Rosenberg, Joanne Dobson, and Susan K. Harris have either emphasized the positive aspects of the female domestic culture portrayed in nineteenth-century women's fiction or located the value of such novels in their subversive subtexts, resisting patriarchal authority beneath the surface. Looking more specifically at the political and cultural discourse of women's fiction, Barbara Bardes and Suzanne Gossett have argued that a number of nineteenth-century female authors used their fiction to take positions on issues such as individual rights versus community order, the legitimacy of women's public speaking, and women's property rights, as well as to argue overall for a greater political role for American women. Other examples of work on domestic writing include Lora Romero, Nicole Tonkovich, Amy Kaplan, and Laurie Ousley.

2. The term "panic fiction" has also been used by critics such as David Zimmerman and Maria Carla Sanchez, who demonstrate that narratives about economic panic have been produced by both men and women, in multiple time periods. Although I attempt to specify "female-authored" and "antebellum" as often as possible, sometimes for the sake of simplicity, I simply use "panic fiction" with the qualifying terms implicit in my usage. Also, while the word "panic" evokes multiple connotations, including that of a psychological or emotional state, I am using the term primarily in its economic sense—descriptive

of a particular economic phenomenon in which commodities lose value rapidly and individual and commercial failures are widespread. "Panic" was used virtually interchangeably in panic texts with terms such as "crisis," "pressures," and "distress."

3. Michael Warner has argued that the "public sphere"—Jurgen Habermas's concept of an arena in which citizens come together freely to confer on matters of public interest, to exchange informed opinions, and to shape public policy based on conceptions of the common good—was not only constituted by face-to-face debate between members of the public body but also by print culture. In fact, Warner contends that the simultaneous development of a large reading population and independent forms of print—newspapers, broadsides, magazines, essays, and fiction—created "new opportunities for individuals to make public use of their reason" (x–xi). Although Warner argues that even this print embodiment of the public sphere was implicitly a white male domain—and that the very existence of such public discourse in print depended on such an identification—the private and often anonymous nature of writing and publication made it possible for some educated women to express views on public matters in print in a way that they could not have done in a public meeting. Publishing their political, social, or economic views in the form of novels or stories allowed female authors to shape public opinion without violating implicit—and sometimes explicit—bans on women's public participation. See also Ryan, *Women in Public* and *Civic Wars*, Burgett, and Isenberg.

4. Richard H. Brodhead places the formation of a domestic culture of letters in the 1830s and 1840s, noting that during those decades the number of novels published in the United States increased tenfold, while popular periodicals first began to flourish. This same period saw a rapid increase in the number of newspapers.

5. *New York Herald*, November 7, 1835; May 8, 1837; May 9, 1837. *Morning Courier and New-York Enquirer*, November 2, 1836; April 7, 1837. *New Orleans Picayune*, April 11, 1837. *Democratic Free Press* (Detroit), October 26, 1836; April 28, 1837.

6. Notable exceptions to this include McGrane, Van Vleck, and Sobel. More recent studies include Calomiris and Schweikart, Rousseau, Sandage, and Lepler.

7. See, for instance, Male, Vernon, Michaels, and Godden. Walter F. Taylor does treat a number of female authors but still places the origins of economic fiction within the post–Civil War period—the Gilded Age. Claude Flory considers male and female authors throughout his designated period, but somehow misses the novels discussed in this study.

8. On the economic preoccupations of antebellum male writers, see, for instance, Gilmore, and Watts.

9. Brown argues that the very stability inherent in the domestic ideal facilitated the transition to a market-oriented society by providing a "domain of individuality"—a stable means of defining the (male) self outside of the unstable public world (3). Merish notes the intimate connection between domesticity and consumerism, contending that middle-class identity rested largely upon the possession and sentimental care of appropriate domestic consumer goods.

10. Catherine Gallagher argues, for instance, that all realist fiction tends to represent

social issues in individual or personal terms because "private problems . . . seem responsive to individual efforts of will, whereas public problems do not" (114).

11. See, in particular, Samuels and Stern. Fichtelberg, Zimmerman, and Anthony all find ample usage of sentiment and sensationalism in the particular genres of panic response that they study, including male-authored panic fiction, pulp novels, cartoons, and penny press newspapers. The emotional content of these panic responses seem designed to either model a new way to be under circumstances of economic instability and failure or to deflect some of the anxiety of financial crisis onto an Other.

12. See Cvetkovich for a discussion of the tension between the production and regulation of affect in nineteenth-century sensation fiction.

13. Along similar lines, Andrew Cayton writes about how the Panic of 1819 disrupted a narrative of organic community in Boston. Prior to 1819, he argues, Bostonians still clung to Federalist ideals of consensus politics and a community of unified interests, not yet embracing the legitimacy of conflict or the right of individuals to pursue self-interest. But the panic, whose effects fell more heavily on workers and those of middling status than on the city's wealthy elite, served to demonstrate that not all Bostonians shared the same interests, and thus opened the way to alternative conceptions of social structure (143–47).

Chapter 1

1. This definition of speculation comes in part from Kindleberger 13.

2. Maria Carla Sanchez offers a similar catalog of panic fiction's condemnation of speculation, writing that "as a practice, it flouts the ability of things to remain stable, constant, and true. It flirts with the unknown, depends upon uncertainty (that something worth little today *may* be worth much tomorrow), is unabashed about taking advantage of the unaware, and of course, it sports a discomforting likeness to gambling—a similarity admitted even by its defenders. Speculation places little value on traditional moral values, particularly those of industry and frugality associated with republican virtue" (62).

3. Another comprehensive account of the growth during these three periods can be found in North.

4. A number of recent articles on eighteenth-century capitalist discourse have noted the appeal of speculative economics, in particular its ability to create what did not exist before. Most notable are Sherman, "Promises, Promises," Ingrassia, and Mulcaire. Today, of course, speculative investment has become institutionalized in the New York Stock Exchange and other stock and commodities markets.

5. These figures come from Feller (39, 172) and from Stampp, *America in 1857*, 217.

6. See Balleisen, Temin, McGrane, and Van Vleck for the international angle; Balleisen and Temin, in particular, elucidate the role of Britain's fluctuating policies of investing and then withdrawing specie from American development projects. McGrane, Feller, and Stampp similarly cite interrelated domestic causes for panic, including Jackson's Bank War and the Specie Circular of 1836.

7. *Niles' Weekly Register*, April 22, 1837, 114.

8. By the time of the Panic of 1837, these competing views on monetary policy were roughly identified with the Democratic and Whig political parties, although there was some overlap. Andrew Jackson's Democrats, who largely embraced the laissez-faire philosophy of European economists such as Adam Smith and David Ricardo and who thus believed that no individual or economic sector should receive any advantage over another, were strongly contractionist. They voiced many citizens' distrust of speculation and paper money and viewed banking—and the Second Bank of the United States in particular—as a symbol of "elitist privilege and illicit power" (Feller 170). They blamed the panic on speculation and the manipulation of prices by greedy bankers. Jackson's Whig opponents, on the other hand, believed for the most part in the necessity of government intervention for overall national prosperity. Defending the legitimacy of properly regulated banks, Whigs blamed the panic on the monetary destabilization of the president's Bank War, which ironically unleashed the very excesses of credit and speculation that Jackson deplored.

9. Quoted from Defoe's *Review* 3:18 in both O'Brien 615, and Sherman, "Lady Credit No Lady" 187. The figure of Lady Credit is also discussed in Mulcaire and Ingrassia.

10. From the *New York Journal of Commerce*, April 3, 1837, quoted in *Niles' Weekly Register*, April 8, 1837.

11. The quotation is from Benjamin Rush, *Medical Inquiries and Observations Upon the Diseases of the Mind* (1812; New York: Hafner, 1962).

12. Hudson notes that church membership figures rose from approximately 40 percent of the population in 1800 to 75 percent in 1835. Although definitions of church membership differed from twentieth-century conceptions, he contends that the latter figure confirms "reports of contemporaries that by 1835 the churches had won a conspicuous place in the life of the new nation," including de Tocqueville's famous declaration that "there is no country in the world in which the Christian religion retains a greater influence over the souls of men than in America" (126).

13. Definitions and applications of "republicanism" constitute a highly contested terrain among historians. Daniel T. Rodgers argues that the historicity of republicanism has been diluted by loose definitions and broad application to nineteenth-century discourse about women, race, labor, and slavery (32). Daniel J. McInerney contends, however, that the widespread adoption and adaptation of republican values and language among nineteenth-century groups such as the abolition movement simply demonstrates the pervasiveness of a republican legacy in American society (5). Other recent contributors to this critical reassessment of republicanism include Kloppenberg, who discusses the interrelation of Christian, republican, and liberal "vocabularies of virtue" (19); and McCurry, who identifies a distinct southern republicanism that emphasized property ownership as the principal condition of political independence and equality. Although panic authors do occasionally link their economic recommendations to the more strictly political aspects of a republican vocabulary (for example, "freedom" from debt), they tend to focus primarily on individual virtues such as simplicity, industry, and self-restraint.

14. Typical examples of this kind of discourse can be found in Fisk 2, 4, 8; Gouge 9, 28; and Carey, *Principles* 19.

15. See, for example, Fabian, *Card Sharps* and Lears.

16. Further evidence of the prominent place of slave speculation in Southern economies can be found in the record of periodic state prohibitions of slave trading, put in place for economic rather than moral reasons. In some states (for example, Georgia and Tennessee), such restrictions resulted from the political power of well-established planters, who had sufficient slaves for their own needs, and thus sought to curb further importations in order to keep slave prices high, avoid overproduction of cotton that would result in price depression, and maintain a population balance between whites and blacks. In states that were importing more heavily, such as Alabama, Mississippi, and Louisiana, briefer bans on slave importation—usually just for a year or two—resulted partly from desires to prevent a hemorrhaging of money from the state in times of economic depression and partly from fears of slave insurrection. Mississippi's 1832 constitution included a provision banning importation, but it was not enforced until after the Panic of 1837, at which time the importation of slaves was halted to prevent the draining of funds from the state. As a result of sudden enforcement, many who had purchased slaves on credit during the intervening years repudiated their debts, "declaring that all notes arising from slave-trade purchases of 1833–37 were void" because constitutionally illegal (Tadman 84–87).

17. For more on early nineteenth-century resistance to economic individualism see, for instance, Watts, *The Republic Reborn*, and Matthews.

18. The most common figure representing the integration of financial value and use value in panic fiction is the farmer. At a time when land speculation was rampant throughout the western states and territories, authors such as Hannah Farnham Sawyer Lee, Caroline Kirkland, and Maria Cummins present those who settle and cultivate the land as the ones who understand and appreciate its true value. Cummins's stance on land use is treated at greater length in chapter 5.

19. Critics such as Michael T. Gilmore have also written about the ambivalence toward capitalist development manifested in the works and lives of canonical American authors such as Emerson, Thoreau, Hawthorne, and Melville—courting the literary marketplace, for instance, while expressing consternation at the processes of commodification and industrialization (8).

20. *New York Herald*, May 11, 1837; *Morning Courier and New-York Enquirer*, May 9, 1837.

21. Despite Lee's claim that the panic "made no distinction of persons," McGrane contends that, in fact, its effects varied widely according to region and economic status. Some areas suffered relatively little, such as New Hampshire, where banking practices were conservative and public improvement projects were conducted by private companies unaffected by the withdrawal of investments. Pennsylvania apparently weathered the 1837 panic but was hit hard when the U.S. Bank of Pennsylvania crashed in 1839. In the South, Mississippi and Alabama suffered the most, as sharply falling cotton prices devastated their one-crop, credit-dependent economies. The effects on western states was delayed, McGrane notes, because they were more diversified than the South but still more agriculturally oriented than the Northeast and thus less immediately affected by overtrad-

ing; nevertheless, scarcity of money eventually caused great hardship for western farmers (106–27). Similar variations occurred following the Panic of 1857, according to Huston, who contends that the South and the western agricultural states were hit hardest over the long run, while the eastern financial establishment recovered quickly and the far west (California) was virtually unaffected. Collapsed grain prices and the lack of a market made western farmers unable to pay their debts, which slowed recovery for the nation as a whole (Huston 30). Nearly all note that in the urban northeast, the poor and working class suffered the most, even if they did not lose the largest amount of money.

22. Banta primarily addresses psychological or spiritual, rather than financial, failure. She discusses authors' treatment of the ability to grasp America's meaning, to find one's true destiny, or to make one's destiny fit the times (203–4).

23. Charles Van Ravenswaay argues that the mid-1830s economic boom ended with the collapse of Herman Briggs & Co., a mercantile house dependent on the cotton trade, in New Orleans in March 1837. Whether or not Herman Briggs was the first concern to fail, clearly the bank suspension was in response to, as well as the cause of, massive business failures.

24. Temin and Sobel provide similar accounts of the bankruptcies and bank suspensions of 1837.

25. Stampp 222; Van Vleck 64–79. Also see Huston.

26. Lee's sequel to *Three Experiments*, for instance, titled *Elinor Fulton*, resumes the Fultons' story after the failure and traces the family's gradual moral and financial recovery. Follen's *Sketches of Married Life* (1838) begins with the failure of the protagonist's fiancé, setting the stage for a novel about her response to that and her father's later loss.

Chapter 2

1. This estimate of the number of copies is from Mott, who claims that *Three Experiments of Living* was one of only four bestsellers from 1837—along with Hawthorne's *Twice-Told Tales* and Dickens's *Pickwick Papers*—with sales equal to or greater than 125,000, or 1 percent of the national population during the 1830s (306).

2. Although a number of panic authors wrote out of financial need—some due to panic-related losses, others to widowhood or simply need for more income—their biographies suggest middle- or upper-middle-class backgrounds. Lee was the daughter of a physician and the widow of a naval officer, Oakes Smith the daughter of a ship captain, step-daughter of a merchant, and wife of the newspaper editor Seba Smith. Sedgwick's background was more privileged. Her father, Theodore Sedgwick, was a prominent statesman who served at different times in the Massachusetts legislature, the Massachusetts Supreme Court, the House of Representatives (where he was Speaker from 1799 to 1801), and the Senate; her mother, Pamela Dwight Sedgwick, was also from a socially prominent family. Sedgwick and Oakes Smith were also fairly well educated for women of that time, further suggesting at least middle-class status.

3. Wilentz 240–41; also Feller 129–31.

4. See, for instance, Stansell 95–100. Stansell discusses in particular the Bowery cul-

ture of New York City between 1830 and 1860. Young working men and women, termed Bowery "B'hoys" and "G'hals," frequented particular theaters, dressed in colorful and distinctive styles, and flouted genteel standards of speech and behavior.

5. Blumin 67–78; see also Feller 124.

6. William Charvat, for example, claims that many of the American romantics saw themselves as part of an intellectual elite and viewed the rising commercial middle class as a threat to their "status as arbiters of culture" (64). Michael Newbury reads this class-based anxiety rather differently, contending that authors such as Hawthorne and Melville were actively seeking to position authorship within "middle-class social space" as defined against less privileged models of labor such as industrial wage slavery (28–29). In both cases, these contemporaries of panic authors are characterized as attempting to defend class positions defined by education and culture against purely economic indicators of status.

7. My use of the term "middle class" in the rest of this chapter, while seeming perhaps to gloss over the complexities and divisions of middling status discussed above, is congruent with panic authors' attempts to define a stable class position for their characters and readers, if not precisely consistent with their terminology. I shall attempt, where appropriate, to indicate differences in authors' own definitions of what constitutes the genteel middle ground.

8. Biographical information from Kunitz and Haycraft 460 and Blain, Clements, and Grundy 642.

9. A particularly American model for such simultaneously economic and moral credit is found in Benjamin Franklin's *Autobiography*, where he describes his efforts to build his printing business through the establishment of a good reputation.

10. Markman Ellis similarly argues that British sentimental fiction represented commerce as an agent of civilization, "augmenting relations of trust and association, polishing social relations and refining the manners" (153).

11. This distinction between an admired wealthy elite and those who merely aspire to such status is often marked in panic fiction by a respective relinquishment or embrace of fashion and luxury, symbols that derive from a republican tradition that denounced luxury as incompatible with and dangerous to an independent republic.

12. While Americans from the Puritans onward certainly participated in this attitude, Christine Stansell argues that eighteenth-century tolerance for the poor hardened into blame during the first decades of the nineteenth century, when increasing numbers of poor and levels of poverty strained society's capacity for benevolence (34).

13. The basis for Sedgwick's acceptance and promotion of social mobility is the distinction she makes between equality of position and equality of personhood—a distinction that is in turn based on the author's gradually evolving support for a more egalitarian society (see Kelley, *The Power of Her Sympathy* 31). While she recognized that Americans occupied very disparate social and economic positions, she maintained that in "personhood"—a concept that encompasses rights as well as character—all members of the republic had equal standing. All were entitled to respect, to self-determination,

and to equal opportunities for advancement through their own abilities. Thus Lucy, even from the beginning of *Live and Let Live,* is seen as inferior to her various employers only in economic circumstances and in her lack of experience. Ultimately, she is able to join their ranks because in all else, including those qualities that domestic authors deemed essential—intelligence, morality, manners—she is already equal or has an equal capacity to develop.

14. Fabian, *Card Sharps* 126–27. Fabian provides a fascinating illustration of success and failure in acquiring class-appropriate identification in her comparison of two former slaves, Denmark Vesey and William Ellison. Vesey, who won the money to buy his freedom in a lottery, retained his identification with the slave community and ended up leading a slave revolt, while Ellison, who gradually saved the money to free himself through diligent labor, came to identify with the community of wealthy planters, to the extent of buying slaves himself.

15. Lee thus advocates a manner of social mobility that Nicole Tonkovich characterizes as "deferred and contingent" (101). Nineteenth-century domestic writers such as Catherine Beecher and Sarah Hale, Tonkovich contends, similarly maintained that the personal qualities necessary for middle-class status were entirely learnable but that the achievement of such status could not be immediate and was contingent upon a voluntary deference to those of higher status. Immigrants, in particular—a population that panic fiction uniformly depicts as socially non-mobile—needed to defer their dreams of social mobility to their children or even grandchildren.

16. See especially Wilentz 295.

17. Another western panic-era narrative, Caroline Kirkland's *A New Home, Who'll Follow?* (1839) demonstrates considerable ambivalence about the possibilities for social equality. While relating the relative classlessness of Michigan frontier society, Kirkland simultaneously remains attached to her own middle-class conceptions of status and property ownership. Similarly, she perpetuates class distinctions in her characterizations even while declaring that such distinctions do not exist.

18. The concept of "harmony of interests" was applied to a variety of contexts in nineteenth-century America. The idea, if not the term, may have originated in Adam Smith's contention in *Wealth of Nations* (1776) that the interests of the community would be best served by individuals pursuing their own true self-interests. The American economist Henry Carey employed the term in his 1851 book *The Harmony of Interests* to refer to competing sectors of the economy—manufacturing, agriculture, and trade. Many others, including panic authors, were concerned with demonstrating that the interests of different socioeconomic classes were interdependent and thus best served by harmony. Lang argues that as class divisions intensified in the 1840s and 1850s, "the doctrine of the harmony of interests was expounded not only as economic theory but as spiritual principle" (129).

Chapter 3

1. The National Union Catalog attributes *Living on Other People's Means, or the History of Simon Silver* to Lee herself, but evidence from the book's introduction, as well as a significant difference in tone from Lee's novels, suggests that the author was in fact male

and that the novel was intended as an imitation of Lee's. The introduction to Lee's *Elinor Fulton* refers to recent publications that had capitalized on the success of her *Three Experiments of Living* by imitating its title and subtitles as well as subject matter. This is supported by the following statement in *Living on Other People's Means*' introduction: "The title of the following story was suggested by the popular publication to which its name refers. . . . The writer has no particular individual in view. He has only attempted to embody in the history of one person, several of the incidents which have happened to many." A similar novel titled *Fourth Experiment of Living. Living Without Means* is also probably a male-authored imitation of Lee.

2. See, for instance, Norton, Kerber, Matthaei, and Kessler-Harris.

3. Norma Basch notes that the earliest statutes granting married women property rights were enacted largely to protect family property in the wake of panic-related bankruptcies. One of the first such laws, enacted in Mississippi in 1839, came right on the heels of the panic, while Michigan's 1844 law specifically "exempted the wife's property from the husband's debts, a measure that suggests links between marital property reform and the need to clarify debtor-creditor relations" (27).

4. For characterizations of the separate spheres ideology, see for example, Ryan, "Femininity and Capitalism in Antebellum America" and *The Empire of the Mother*, Baker, Baym, Bloch, and Matthews. Gillian Brown notes the prevalence of a home-marketplace dichotomy in nineteenth-century ideology and literature, but she argues that they were complementary rather than opposed, the stability of home actually enabling the risk and competition of marketplace economics.

5. Kessler-Harris 48; Goldin's figures are much higher—33 percent in 1850—but are only for women aged 10–29, most of whom were probably single. These figures, as far as I can determine, do not include enslaved women.

6. Although they differ markedly in their assessments of the power and effect of moral influence, Douglas, Baym, and Kelley (*Private Woman, Public Stage*) have all documented domestic fiction's role in helping to create a nineteenth-century ideology of separate spheres. Their interpretations remain influential despite more recent work by critics such as Brown, Coultrap-McQuin, Romero, and Merish, complicating the relationship between domestic authors and a noneconomic domestic ideology.

7. De Grave notes that confidence women tended to flourish in places of rigid social structure (for example, eastern cities) that limited women's abilities for legitimate role expansion and in times when roles for women were particularly circumscribed. The West and the later nineteenth century gave women more legitimate opportunities for individual achievement, and the numbers of confidence women diminished (De Grave 53–54).

8. Edward Copeland notes a similar economic empowerment of women through the control of domestic consumption in British women's fiction just a few decades earlier. He argues that the gothic novels of the 1790s, which symbolically depict women's lack of economic power and vulnerability to economic distress through images of confinement and terror, give way in the early 1800s to portrayal of women's "active economic engagement" through consumerism.

9. These examples are taken from revised editions of Child's and Beecher's texts: the

twenty-first edition of Child's *American Frugal Housewife*, published in 1838, and the second edition of Beecher's *Treatise*, published in 1842.

10. Julie Matthaei notes a connection between the "scientific homemaking" movement and the rise of capitalism in nineteenth-century America (157–86). Although the movement did not reach its peak until the early twentieth century, Matthaei traces it back to the domestic writings of Catherine Beecher, contending that emphases on efficiency, economizing, and the division of labor paralleled the rationalization of capitalist commodity production.

11. See, for instance, Matthaei, Baker, and Ryan, *Women in Public*.

12. Biographical information from James 638–39.

13. Early on in the novel, as Edward is leaving for China, Amy expresses her frustration at being barred from remunerated labor by her gender and class: "I shall expect you to think that money-making is very pleasant work, for my sake. I only wish I could help you, and do something myself; but, on the contrary, here I am doomed to uselessness, because my father is a rich man" (Follen 66).

14. Historians and literary critics have debated whether women's nineteenth-century charity and reform work was a genuine criticism of and alternative to male economic development that ignored (and created) human need or whether it actually allowed such development to proceed untrammeled. Ruth Bloch and Gillian Brown both argue that the relationship between reform and capitalism was as much complementary as oppositional.

15. Many nineteenth-century women authors wrote out of financial necessity, including Sarah J. Hale, Fanny Fern (Sara Willis Parton), E. D. E. N. Southworth, Hannah Farnham Sawyer Lee, and Louisa Tuthill, who began literary careers after widowhood or marital separation forced them to find a livelihood. Harriet Beecher Stowe, Lydia Maria Child, Eliza Follen, Ann Stephens, and Caroline Lee Hentz wrote in part to supplement their husbands' inadequate earnings. Others, like the Warner sisters, were directly affected by the Panic of 1837, including Augusta Jane Evans Wilson, who suffered poverty as a child from her father's losses; Elizabeth Oakes Smith, whose husband was bankrupted by land speculations; and Maria McIntosh, who had lived on an inheritance until her investments were wiped out by the panic. See Blain, Clements, and Grundy and Kelley, *Private Woman, Public Stage*.

16. Such naturalization of economic phenomena corresponds to a trend in the 1850s, noted by Ann Fabian, away from the religious and moral explanations for panic of the 1830s and toward a discourse of natural disaster that distanced economic cycles from moral, or even human, agency ("Speculation on Distress").

Chapter 4

1. Cardozo's economic views are summarized and discussed in Leiman. His unusually even-handed positions on the causes of and remedies for panics are outlined in the chapter on "Business Cycles."

2. Historians have long debated the questions of whether slave labor was profitable to plantation owners and whether traditional plantations should be considered capitalist

enterprises, with no very clear agreement. Mark M. Smith sums up the major work in this area, including studies by Robert Fogel and Stanley Engerman, Stanley Elkins, Kenneth Stampp, John F. Olson, and Eugene Genovese, among many others. Ashworth covers much of the same ground, even more comprehensively.

3. See in particular Huston and Stampp.

4. Historians arguing that the South had a considerable industrial base include Fred Bateman and Thomas Weiss, Robert Fogel and Stanley Engerman (see Mark M. Smith 74) and, to some degree, Kenneth Stampp, who notes a boom in railroad construction during the 1850s (215).

5. See Temin, in particular, for detailed examinations of banking practices in the 1830s and early 1840s.

6. Biographical information from Moss.

7. The two novels were later published together (in 1852) as *Recollections of a New England Bride and of a Southern Matron.*

8. Moss makes an even stronger claim for the contrast between Gilman's two novels, charging that Clarissa Packard's domestic woes epitomize the "inherent instability" of the domestic sphere in the North and the little power that middle-class women actually wielded in that sphere (66). I think this view ignores the humor of *Housekeeper* as well as Gilman's promotion of the domestic role through showing how difficult it is to master.

9. Although the plot of *The Planter's Northern Bride* does not center on financial loss and recovery, and therefore the novel falls outside the definition of "panic novel" that this study uses, its economic agenda and startling vision of ruin near the end make it, in my mind, a kind of panic novel in disguise. At the very least, it serves as a fictional counterpart to the economic rhetoric of George Fitzhugh and a foil to the more directly panic-oriented fiction of Maria McIntosh.

10. Biographical information taken from James.

11. Since historical records show that slaves were actually more likely to be sold during periods of economic prosperity than at times of planter indebtedness, McIntosh's focus on the potential sale of the slaves seems more likely to represent a prevalent fear among the planter class, or to function as a defense of the benevolent concerns of slaveholders for their property, than to reflect historical reality (see Tadman).

12. The *OED* defines melodrama as "a dramatic piece characterized by sensational incident and violent appeals to the emotions, but with a happy ending" (quoted in James L. Smith 5). Smith also quotes at length from Frank Rahill, *The World of Melodrama*, to the effect that it is drama intended for a popular audience, that it employs stock characters such as a suffering heroine or hero and persecuting villain, and that it rewards virtue and punishes vice (5).

13. Mason also comments on the prevalence of female victims and male heroes in typical melodrama, noting that "the effect was to deny Woman her right to act or choose and to confer both the privilege and the burden of initiative on Man" (20). He argues, however, that this gender stereotyping did not reflect actual belief in this distribution of character but rather "betrays its authors' anxieties"—that is, reveals a desire within melo-

drama to ward off the wielding of social power by nondominant groups by portraying an "idealized" vision of who does and should wield that power.

14. These points are made in James L. Smith and Gerould's introduction to *American Melodrama*.

15. Edward Balleisen discusses the use of rhetoric of "enslavement" by bankruptcy reform advocates (15). Thus this appears to have been a common trope in both the South and North.

16. Garraty and Carnes note that there is no complete or definitive bibliography of Dupuy's work, due to a combination of factors: use of pseudonyms, anonymously published work, novels reprinted under different names, and some work published in Britain (136).

Chapter 5

1. Southworth's 1857 novel *The Hidden Hand*, for example, an exciting adventure tale featuring a fearless and resourceful young heroine, has been read as an allegory of appropriate and inappropriate responses to the volatile economy of the 1850s. Elizabeth Morrow Nix contends that Capitola, whose very name suggests the personification of capitalism, exemplifies economic behavior that produces "stability within change" (93). Steering a middle course between characters who epitomize greed and those who remain dangerously aloof from financial transactions, Capitola, in Nix's reading, "understands the importance of possessions in her society, is savvy about the workings of the market, and refuses to be its victim" (96). Ann Stephens's *Fashion and Famine* (1854) conveys many of the same morals as panic novels—that wealth cannot buy happiness and that virtuous poverty will be rewarded with moderate prosperity—but does so in a context of such sensual description of luxury that it clearly invites readers to desire as well as denounce.

2. The contrast between American and European workers is discussed by Steinfeld. The idea of self-ownership and political independence as the markers of free labor is discussed by both Fink and Foner.

3. Westward migration remained a popular solution to eastern poverty and overcrowding for most of the nineteenth century. The association between land ownership and independence was articulated perhaps most famously in Frederick Jackson Turner's "frontier thesis" of 1893. The historian Eric Foner notes the irony, however, that western homesteading, at least in the antebellum period, primarily benefited eastern farmers who were being squeezed out rather than the industrial laborers whom it was originally designed to aid, who had less interest in land ownership and who often could not afford to set up as farmers even on free land (32).

4. We see this especially in connection with Douglass's comments about his resentment in having to surrender his wages to Mr. Auld (415). The association of wage labor with self-ownership has also been discussed at length by Lovell and Klein.

5. Biographical information taken from James.

6. Baym makes this point both in *Woman's Fiction* (170–72) and in her introduction to *The Lamplighter*, where she contrasts the two novels by Cummins (xxviii).

7. In keeping with mid-nineteenth-century conceptions of women as more spiritual

than men, Cummins also proposes that women's participation in the project of national expansion will somehow "sanctify" what would otherwise be a merely material endeavor. The noble and wise Mrs. Percival, whom Mabel encounters on her journey west, proclaims women's ability and duty to "exert that softening, elevating, purifying spirit, which . . . sheds abroad in the community a nobler ambition than that of building cities in the wilderness, and subduing the elements to human will" (Cummins, *Mabel Vaughan* 355).

8. Domestication versus exploitation as contrasting models of territorial conquest go back much further than Kolodny's account—to discussions of the earliest American colonies (English versus French) as well as of modes of nineteenth-century westward expansion. See for instance, St. John de Crèvecoeur.

9. The potential conflict for women between public responsibility and the private ideals of domestic life are enacted in a scene at the Percival house on election night. Just as the house is literally divided that evening between Percival's political allies offering their congratulations in one room and a private gathering of friends and family in another, Mabel's thoughts are divided between approval of his shouldering of public duty and a sudden realization of her love for him as an individual. By having Percival and Mabel decide to marry and go to Washington together, Cummins resolves this tension between public duty and private inclination. Mabel can fulfill her desires for home and family while still supporting Percival's fight against slavery. Significantly, this joining together of public and private, national and domestic, occurs on Thanksgiving, a holiday designed both to promote national unity and to celebrate the virtues of home and family.

10. Biographical information taken from James.

11. The combination of optimism and pragmatism necessary for success under such conditions is also underscored in both of the novel's romantic relationships. In addition to Murray's and Martha's complementary characteristics, as previously noted, the pragmatic Steve Henderson similarly marries a woman of the opposite disposition, her levity and bold forthrightness giving balance to his more sober virtues.

12. Anne Lewis Osler makes a similar argument about the mistress-servant relationships in the novels of 1830s Northern authors, seeing them as consciously contrasted to Southern slavery. Authors such as Lee and Sedgwick, she argues, construct a female version of the free-labor ideology, considering the domestic servant as a worker with rights.

Works Cited

American Monthly Magazine. Review of *Elinor Fulton* and *The Harcourts*, September 1837, 305–308.

———. Review of *Live and Let Live*, October 1837, 395–6.

———. Review of *The Poor Rich Man and the Rich Poor Man*, November 1836, 516–9.

American Quarterly Review. Review of *Live and Let Live*, September 1837, 254–256.

———. Review of *The Poor Rich Man and the Rich Poor Man*, March 1837, 18–28.

Anthony, David. *Paper Money Men: Commerce, Manhood, and the Sensational Public Sphere in Antebellum America*. Columbus: Ohio State University Press, 2009.

Armstrong, Nancy. *Desire and Domestic Fiction: A Political History of the Novel*. New York: Oxford University Press, 1987.

Arthur, Timothy Shay. *Debtor and Creditor; A Tale of the Times*. 1847. New York: J. M. Fairchild, 1857.

Ashworth, John. *Slavery, Capitalism, and Politics in the Antebellum Republic*. Cambridge: Cambridge University Press, 1995.

Baker, Paula. "The Domestication of Politics: Women and American Political Society, 1780–1920." *American Historical Review* 89 (June 1984): 620–47.

Balleisen, Edward J. *Navigating Failure: Bankruptcy and Commercial Society in Antebellum America*. Chapel Hill: University of North Carolina Press, 2001.

Banta, Martha. *Failure and Success in America: A Literary Debate*. Princeton: Princeton University Press, 1978.

Bardes, Barbara, and Suzanne Gossett. *Declarations of Independence: Women and Political Power in Nineteenth-Century American Fiction*. New Brunswick: Rutgers University Press, 1990.

Barnes, Elizabeth. *States of Sympathy: Seduction and Democracy in the American Novel*. New York: Columbia University Press, 1997.

Basch, Norma. *In the Eyes of the Law: Women, Marriage, and Property in Nineteenth-Century New York*. Ithaca: Cornell University Press, 1982.

Baym, Nina. *Woman's Fiction: A Guide to Novels by and about Women in America, 1820–1870*. Ithaca: Cornell University Press, 1984.

Beecher, Catharine. *A Treatise on Domestic Economy.* 1841. Rev. ed. Boston: T. H. Webb, 1842.

Blain, Virginia, Patricia Clements, and Isobel Grundy, eds. *Feminist Companion to Literature in English: Women Writers from the Middle Ages to the Present.* New Haven: Yale University Press, 1990.

Bloch, Ruth. "The Gendered Meanings of Virtue in Revolutionary America." *Signs: Journal of Women in Culture and Society* 13 (1987): 37–58.

Blumin, Stuart M. *The Emergence of the Middle Class: Social Experience in the American City, 1760–1900.* Cambridge: Cambridge University Press, 1989.

Boydston, Jeanne. "The Woman Who Wasn't There: Women's Market Labor and the Transition to Capitalism in the United States." In *Wages of Independence: Capitalism in the Early American Republic*, edited by Paul Gilje, 23–47. Madison: Madison House, 1997.

Briggs, Charles F. *The Adventures of Harry Franco: A Tale of the Great Panic.* New York: F. Saunders, 1839.

Brodhead, Richard H. *Cultures of Letters: Scenes of Reading and Writing in Nineteenth-Century America.* Chicago: University of Chicago Press, 1993.

Brown, Gillian. *Domestic Individualism: Imagining Self in Nineteenth-Century America.* Berkeley: University of California Press, 1990.

Burgett, Bruce. *Sentimental Bodies: Sex, Gender, and Citizenship in the Early Republic.* Princeton: Princeton University Press, 1998.

Burnham, Michelle. *Captivity and Sentiment: Cultural Exchange in American Literature, 1682–1861.* Hanover: University Press of New England, 1997.

Calomiris, Charles W., and Larry Schweikart. "The Panic of 1857: Origins, Transmission and Containment." *Journal of Economic History* 51 (1991): 807–34.

Carey, Henry C. *Essay on the Rates of Wages, with an Examination of the Causes of the Differences in the Condition of the Labouring Population throughout the World.* Philadelphia: Carey, Lea & Blanchard, 1835.

——. *The Harmony of Interests, Agricultural, Manufacturing and Commercial.* 2nd ed. New York: M. Finch, 1852.

——. *Principles of Political Economy; or, the Laws of the Production and Distribution of Wealth.* Philadelphia: Carey, Lea & Blanchard, 1837.

Carlin, Deborah. "'What Methods Have Brought Blessing': Discourses of Reform in Philanthropic Literature." *The (Other) American Traditions: Nineteenth-Century Women Writers.* Ed. Joyce W. Warren. New Brunswick: Rutgers University Press, 1993. 203–25.

Cayton, Andrew R. C. "The Fragmentation of a 'Great Family': The Panic of 1819 and the Rise of the Middling Interest in Boston, 1818–1822." *Journal of the Early Republic* 2 (1982): 143–67.

Charvat, William. *The Profession of Authorship in America 1800–1870.* New York: Columbia University Press, 1968.

Child, Lydia Maria. *The American Frugal Housewife.* 1831. 21st ed. New York: S. S. & W. Wood, 1838.

Conkin, Paul K. *Prophets of Prosperity: America's First Political Economists.* Bloomington: Indiana University Press, 1980.

Copeland, Edward. *Women Writing About Money: Women's Fiction in England, 1790–1820.* Cambridge: Cambridge University Press, 1995.

Coultrap-McQuin, Susan. *Doing Literary Business: American Women Writers in the Nineteenth Century.* Chapel Hill: University of North Carolina Press, 1990.

Cummins, Maria Susanna. *The Lamplighter.* 1854. Ed. Nina Baym. New Brunswick: Rutgers University Press, 1988.

———. *Mabel Vaughan.* Boston: John P. Jewett & Co., 1857.

Cvetkovich, Ann. *Mixed Feelings: Feminism, Mass Culture, and Victorian Sensationalism.* New Brunswick: Rutgers University Press, 1992.

Davidson, Cathy N. *Revolution and the Word: The Rise of the Novel in America.* New York: Oxford University Press, 1986.

Davis, Rebecca Harding. "Life in the Iron-Mills." *Atlantic Monthly* April 1861.

De Grave, Kathleen. *Swindler, Spy, Rebel: The Confidence Woman in Nineteenth-Century America.* Columbia: University of Missouri Press, 1995.

Dobson, Joanne. "The Hidden Hand: Subversion of Cultural Ideology in Three Mid-Nineteenth-Century American Women's Novels." *American Quarterly* 38 (Summer 1986): 223–42.

Douglas, Ann. *The Feminization of American Culture.* New York: Knopf, 1977.

Douglass, Frederick. *Narrative of the Life of Frederick Douglass, an American Slave.* 1845. *The Classic Slave Narratives.* Ed. Henry Louis Gates, Jr. New York: Signet Classic, 2002.

Dupuy, Eliza. *The Planter's Daughter: A Tale of Louisiana.* Philadelphia: T. B. Peterson and Brothers, 1858.

Ellis, Markman. *The Politics of Sensibility: Race, Gender and Commerce in the Sentimental Novel.* Cambridge: Cambridge University Press, 1996.

Elmer, Jonathan. *Reading at the Social Limit: Affect, Mass Culture, and Edgar Allan Poe.* Stanford: Stanford University Press, 1995.

Embury, Emma C. *Constance Latimer; or, The Blind Girl.* New York: Harper & Brothers, 1838.

Emerson, Ralph Waldo. *Selected Writings of Emerson.* Ed. Donald McQuade. New York: Modern Library, 1981.

Fabian, Ann. *Card Sharps, Dream Books, & Bucket Shops: Gambling in Nineteenth-Century America.* Ithaca: Cornell University Press, 1990.

———. "Speculation on Distress: The Popular Discourse of the Panics of 1837 and 1857." *Yale Journal of Criticism: Interpretation in the Humanities* 3 (1989): 127–42.

Feller, Daniel. *The Jacksonian Promise: America, 1815–1840.* Baltimore: Johns Hopkins University Press, 1995.

Fern, Fanny [Sara Payson Willis Parton]. *Ruth Hall and Other Writings.* 1854. Ed. Joyce W. Warren. New Brunswick: Rutgers University Press, 1986.

Fichtelberg, Joseph. *Critical Fictions: Sentiment and the American Market, 1780–1870.* Athens: University of Georgia Press, 2003.

Fink, Leon. “From Autonomy to Abundance: Changing Beliefs about the Free Labor System in Nineteenth-Century America.” *Terms of Labor: Slavery, Serfdom, and Free Labor.* Ed. Stanley L. Engerman. Stanford: Stanford University Press, 1999. 116–36.

Fisk, Theophilus. “Labor, the Only True Source of Wealth: or, the Rottenness of the Paper Money Banking System Exposed, its Sandy Foundations Shaken, its Crumbling Pillars Overthrown. An Oration Delivered at the Queen Street Theatre, in the City of Charleston, S.C. July 4, 1837.” Ann Arbor, Mich.: University Microfilms. American Culture Series. Reel 405.6.

Fitzhugh, George. *Cannibals All! Or, Slaves Without Masters* (1857). *Antebellum Writings of George Fitzhugh and Hinton Rowan Helper on Slavery.* Ed. Harvey Wish. New York: Capricorn Books, 1960.

———. *Sociology for the South* (1854). *Antebellum Writings of George Fitzhugh and Hinton Rowan Helper on Slavery.* Ed. Harvey Wish. New York: Capricorn Books, 1960.

Flory, Claude R. *Economic Criticism in American Fiction, 1792–1900.* New York: Russell and Russell, 1937.

Follen, Eliza Lee Cabot. *Sketches of Married Life.* 1838. Revised ed. Boston: William Crosby and H. P. Nichols, 1847.

Foner, Eric. *Free Soil, Free Labor, Free Men: The Ideology of the Republican Party before the Civil War.* 1970. Oxford: Oxford University Press, 1995.

Foster, Edward Halsey. *Susan and Anna Warner.* Boston: Twayne Publishers/G. K. Hall & Co., 1978.

Fourth Experiment of Living. Living Without Means. Boston: Otis, Broaders, & Company, 1837.

Franklin, Benjamin. *The Autobiography of Benjamin Franklin.* Ed. John Bigelow. Philadelphia: J. P. Lippincott Co., 1868.

Gallagher, Catherine. *The Industrial Reformation of English Fiction: Social Discourse and Narrative Form, 1832–1867.* Chicago: University of Chicago Press, 1985.

Garraty, John A., and Mark C. Carnes, eds. *American National Biography.* New York: Oxford University Press, 1999.

Gerould, Daniel C. *American Melodrama.* New York: Performing Arts Journal Publications, 1983.

Gilman, Caroline. *Recollections of a New England Bride and Housekeeper* (1834) and *Recollections of a Southern Matron* (1838). New York: G. P. Putnam & Co., 1852.

Gilmore, Michael T. *American Romanticism and the Marketplace.* Chicago: University of Chicago Press, 1985.

Ginzberg, Lori D. *Women and the Work of Benevolence: Morality, Politics, and Class in the Nineteenth-Century United States.* New Haven: Yale University Press, 1990.

Godden, Richard. *Fictions of Capital: The American Novel from James to Mailer.* Cambridge: Cambridge University Press, 1990.

Godey's Lady's Book. Review of *Dollars and Cents*, vol. 45 (August 1852), 197.

———. Review of *The Harcourts* and *Live and Let Live*, September 1837, 140.

———. Review of *Mabel Vaughan*, vol. 56 (February 1858), 182.

———. Review of *Three Experiments of Living*, March 1837, 144.

Goldin, Claudia. *Understanding the Gender Gap: An Economic History of American Women.* New York: Oxford University Press, 1990.

Goodrich, S. G. "Address Delivered before the Inhabitants of Jamaica Plain, July 4th, 1835." *American Ladies' Magazine* 8.8 (August 1835): 468–69.

Gouge, William M. *An Inquiry into the Expediency of Dispensing with Bank Agency and Bank Paper in the Fiscal Concerns of the United States.* Philadelphia: William Stavely, 1837.

Hale, Sarah Josepha. *Northwood; or, Life North and South.* 1827. New York: H. Long & Brother, 1852.

Halttunen, Karen. *Confidence Men and Painted Women: A Study of Middle-Class Culture in America, 1830–1870.* New Haven: Yale University Press, 1982.

Harris, Susan K. *19th-Century American Women's Novels: Interpretive Strategies.* Cambridge: Cambridge University Press, 1990.

Haven, Alice Bradley. *The Coopers; or, Getting Under Way.* New York: D. Appleton & Co., 1858.

———. *Loss and Gain; or, Margaret's Home.* New York: D. Appleton & Co., 1860.

Hentz, Caroline Lee. *Marcus Warland; or, The Long Moss Spring.* Philadelphia: A. Hart, 1852.

———. *The Planter's Northern Bride.* Philadelphia: Parry & M'Millan, 1854.

Hudson, Winthrop S. *Religion in America.* 4th ed. New York: Macmillan, 1987.

Hunt, Robert. "A Domesticated Slavery: Political Economy in Caroline Hentz's Fiction." *Southern Quarterly* 34.4 (1996): 25–35.

Huston, James L. *The Panic of 1857 and the Coming of the Civil War.* Baton Rouge: Louisiana State University Press, 1987.

Ingrassia, Catherine. "The Pleasure of Business and the Business of Pleasure: Gender, Credit, and the South Sea Bubble." *Studies in Eighteenth-Century Culture* 24 (1995): 191–210.

Isenberg, Nancy. *Sex and Citizenship in Antebellum America.* Chapel Hill: University of North Carolina Press, 1998.

James, Edward T., ed. *Notable American Women, 1607–1950: A Biographical Dictionary.* Cambridge, MA: Belknap Press of Harvard University Press, 1971.

Kaplan, Amy. "Manifest Domesticity." *American Literature* 70 (September 1998): 581–606.

Kelley, Mary, ed. *The Power of Her Sympathy: the Autobiography and Journal of Catharine Maria Sedgwick.* Boston: Massachusetts Historical Society, 1993.

———. *Private Woman, Public Stage: Literary Domesticity in Nineteenth-Century America.* New York: Oxford University Press, 1984.

Kerber, Linda K. *Women of the Republic: Intellect and Ideology in Revolutionary America.* Chapel Hill: University of North Carolina Press, 1980.

Kessler-Harris, Alice. *Out to Work: A History of Wage-Earning Women in the United States.* New York: Oxford University Press, 1982.

Kindleberger, Charles P. *Manias, Panics, and Crashes: A History of Financial Crises.* 3rd ed. New York: John Wiley & Sons, 1996.

Kirkland, Caroline. *A New Home, Who'll Follow? Or, Glimpses of Western Life*. 1839. Ed. Sandra Zagarell. New Brunswick: Rutgers University Press, 1990.

Klein, Rachel Naomi. "Harriet Beecher Stowe and the Domestication of Free Labor Ideology." *Legacy: A Journal of American Women Writers* 18.2 (2001): 135–52.

Kloppenberg, James T. "The Virtues of Liberalism: Christianity, Republicanism, and Ethics in Early American Political Discourse." *Journal of American History* 74 (June 1987): 9–33.

Knickerbocker. Review of *Constance Latimer*, July 1838, 86.

———. Review of *Live and Let Live*, July 1837, 86.

———. Review of *Three Experiments of Living*, March 1837, 308–10.

———. Review of *Three Experiments in Drinking*, May 1837, 530.

Kolodny, Annette. *The Land before Her: Fantasy and Experience of the American Frontiers, 1630–1860*. Chapel Hill: University of North Carolina Press, 1984.

Kunitz, Stanley J. and Howard Haycraft, eds. *American Authors, 1600–1900*. Wilson Authors Series. New York: H. W. Wilson Co., 1938.

Lang, Amy Schrager. "Class and the Strategies of Sympathy." Samuels 128–42.

Laurie, Bruce. *Artisans into Workers: Labor in Nineteenth-Century America*. New York: Hill and Wang, 1989.

Lears, Jackson. *Something for Nothing: Luck in America*. New York: Viking, 2003.

Lee, Hannah Farnham Sawyer. *The Contrast; or, Modes of Education*. 1837.

———. *Elinor Fulton*. Boston: Whipple & Damrell, 1837.

———. *The Harcourts*. 1837.

———. *The Log-Cabin, or the World before You*. Philadelphia, George S. Appleton, 1844.

———. *Rich Enough; A Tale of the Times*. 1837.

———. *Rosanna, or Scenes in Boston*. Cambridge: John Owen, 1839.

———. *Three Experiments of Living*. Boston: Wm. S. Damrell, 1837.

———. *Worth a Million*. New York: S. Colman, 1838.

Leiman, Melvin M. *Jacob N. Cardozo: Economic Thought in the Antebellum South*. New York: Columbia University Press, 1966.

Lepler, Jessica. "1837: Anatomy of a Panic." Diss. Brandeis University, 2007.

Living on Other People's Means, or the History of Simon Silver. Boston: Weeks, Jordan & Co., 1837.

Lovell, Thomas B. "By Dint of Labor and Economy: Harriet Jacobs, Harriet Wilson, and the Salutary View of Wage Labor." *Arizona Quarterly* 52.3 (1996): 1–32.

Male, Roy R., ed. *Money Talks: Language and Lucre in American Fiction*. Norman: University of Oklahoma Press, 1980.

Mason, Jeffrey D. *Melodrama and the Myth of America*. Bloomington: Indiana University Press, 1993.

Matthaei, Julie A. *An Economic History of Women in America: Women's Work, the Sexual Division of Labor, and the Development of Capitalism*. New York: Schocken Books, 1982.

Matthews, Glenna. *"Just a Housewife": The Rise and Fall of Domesticity in America.* New York: Oxford University Press, 1987.

Matthews, Jean V. *Toward a New Society: American Thought and Culture, 1800–1830.* Boston: Twayne-Hall, 1991.

McCurry, Stephanie. "The Two Faces of Republicanism: Gender and Proslavery Politics in Antebellum South Carolina." *Journal of American History* 78 (March 1992): 1245–64.

McGrane, Reginald Charles. *The Panic of 1837: Some Financial Problems of the Jacksonian Era.* Chicago: University of Chicago Press, 1924.

McInerney, Daniel J. *The Fortunate Heirs of Freedom: Abolition and Republican Thought.* Lincoln: University of Nebraska Press, 1994.

McIntosh, Maria. *The Lofty and the Lowly; or Good in All and None All-Good.* 2 vols. New York: D. Appleton, 1853.

———. *Two Lives; or, To Seem and to Be.* New York: D. Appleton, 1846.

———. *Woman an Enigma.* New York: Harper & Bros., 1843.

———. *Woman in America: Her Work and Her Reward.* New York: D. Appleton, 1850.

Merish, Lori. *Sentimental Materialism: Gender, Commodity Culture, and Nineteenth-Century American Literature.* Durham: Duke University Press, 2000.

Michaels, Walter Benn. *The Gold Standard and the Logic of Naturalism: American Literature at the Turn of the Century.* Berkeley: University of California Press, 1987.

Moss, Elizabeth. *Domestic Novelists in the Old South: Defenders of Southern Culture.* Baton Rouge: Louisiana State University Press, 1992.

Mott, Frank Luther. *Golden Multitudes: The Story of Best Sellers in the United States.* New York: MacMillan, 1947.

Mulcaire, Terry. "Public Credit; or, The Feminization of Virtue in the Marketplace," *PMLA* 114 (1999): 1029–42.

New York Review. Review of *Elinor Fulton, Rich Enough*, and *The Harcourts*, October 1837, 457–63.

———. Review of *Live and Let Live*, October 1837, 447–57.

———. Review of *Sketches of Married Life*, April 1839, 494.

———. Review of *Three Experiments of Living.* March 1837, 247–49.

Newbury, Michael. *Figuring Authorship in Antebellum America.* Stanford: Stanford University Press, 1997.

Newman, Samuel Phillips. *Elements of Political Economy.* New York: H. Griffin; and Andover, Mass.: Gould & Newman, 1835.

Nix, Elizabeth Morrow. "An Exuberant Flow of Spirits: Antebellum Adolescent Girls in the Writing of Southern Women." Diss. Boston University, 1996.

North, Douglass C. *The Economic Growth of the United States, 1790–1860.* Englewood Cliffs, NJ: Prentice-Hall, 1961.

North American Review. Review of *Dollars and Cents*, *Queechy*, and *The Wide, Wide World*, January 1853, 104–23.

——. Review of *Live and Let Live* and *The Poor Rich Man and the Rich Poor Man*, October 1837, 475–81.

——. Review of *Mabel Vaughan*, January 1858, 287.

——. Review of *Rich Enough*, October 1837, 509–10.

——. Review of *Rosanna, or Scenes in Boston*, July 1840, 232.

Norton, Mary Beth. *Liberty's Daughters: The Revolutionary Experience of American Women, 1750–1800*. Boston: Little, Brown, 1980.

O'Brien, John F. "The Character of Credit: Defoe's 'Lady Credit,' *The Fortunate Mistress*, and the Resources of Inconsistency in Early Eighteenth-Century Britain." *ELH* 63 (1996): 603–31.

Osler, Anne Lewis. "'That Damned Mob': Northern and Southern Women Writers and the Coming of the American Civil War." Diss. University of Wisconsin–Madison, 1995.

Ousley, Laurie. "The Business of Housekeeping: The Mistress, the Domestic, and the Construction of Class." *Legacy: A Journal of American Women Writers* 23.2 (2006): 132–47.

Pessen, Edward. *Jacksonian America: Society, Personality, and Politics*. Rev. ed. Urbana: University of Illinois Press, 1985.

Phelps, Elizabeth Stuart. *The Silent Partner*. 1871. New York: Feminist Press, 1983.

Rodgers, Daniel T. "Republicanism: The Career of a Concept." *Journal of American History* 79 (June 1992): 11–38.

Romero, Lora. *Home Fronts: Domesticity and Its Critics in the Antebellum United States*. Durham: Duke University Press, 1997.

Rousseau, Peter. "Jacksonian Monetary Policy, Specie Flows, and the Panic of 1837." *Journal of Economic History* 62.2 (June 2002): 457–88.

Rush, Rebecca. *Kelroy*. 1812. Oxford University Press, 1992.

Ryan, Mary P. *Civic Wars: Democracy and Public Life in the American City during the Nineteenth Century*. Berkeley: University of California Press, 1997.

——. *The Empire of the Mother: American Writing about Domesticity, 1830–1860*. 1982. New York: Harrington Park Press, 1985.

——. "Femininity and Capitalism in Antebellum America," *Capitalist Patriarchy and the Case for Socialist Feminism*. Ed. Zillah R. Eisenstein. New York: Monthly Review Press, 1979. 151–68.

——. *Women in Public: Between Banners and Ballots, 1825–1880*. Baltimore: Johns Hopkins University Press, 1990.

Samuels, Shirley, ed. *The Culture of Sentiment: Race, Gender, and Sentimentality in Nineteenth-Century America*. New York: Oxford University Press, 1992.

Sanchez, Maria Carla. *Reforming the World: Social Activism and the Problem of Fiction in Nineteenth-Century America*. Iowa City: University of Iowa Press, 2008.

Sandage, Scott A. *Born Losers: A History of Failure in America*. Cambridge, MA: Harvard University Press, 2005.

Sedgwick, Catharine Maria. *Live and Let Live; or, Domestic Service Illustrated*. 1837. New York: Harper & Bros., 1844.

——. *A New-England Tale.* 1822. Ed. Victoria Clements. New York: Oxford University Press, 1995.

——. *The Poor Rich Man, and the Rich Poor Man.* 1836.

Sherman, Sandra. "Lady Credit No Lady; or, The Case of Defoe's 'Coy Mistress,' Truly Stat'd." *Texas Studies in Literature and Language* 37.2 (Summer 1995): 185–214.

——. "Promises, Promises: Credit as Contested Metaphor in Early Capitalist Discourse." *Modern Philology* 94.3 (February 1997): 327–49.

Smith, Adam. *An Inquiry into the Nature and Causes of the Wealth of Nations.* 1776. Ed. Edwin Cannan. Chicago: University of Chicago Press, 1976.

Smith, Elizabeth Oakes. *Riches without Wings, or The Cleveland Family.* Boston: George W. Light, 1838.

Smith, James L. *Melodrama.* London: Methuen & Co., 1973.

Smith, Mark M. *Debating Slavery: Economy and Society in the Antebellum American South.* New Studies in Economic and Social History. Cambridge: Cambridge University Press, 1998.

Smith-Rosenberg, Carroll. "The Female World of Love and Ritual: Relations between Women in Nineteenth-Century America." *Signs: Journal of Women in Culture and Society* 1 (1975): 1–30.

Sobel, Robert. *Panic on Wall Street: A History of America's Financial Disasters.* New York: Macmillan, 1968.

Southern Literary Messenger. Review of *Dollars and Cents,* July 1852, 446.

——. Review of *Live and Let Live,* November 1837, 690–91.

——. Review of *The Poor Rich Man and the Rich Poor Man,* May 1837, 331–34.

——. Review of *Stories from Real Life,* December 1837, 742.

Southworth, E. D. E. N. *The Hidden Hand; or, Capitola the Madcap.* Serialized 1859. Ed. Joanne Dobson. New Brunswick: Rutgers University Press, 1988.

"The Spirit of Enterprise." *American Ladies' Magazine* 9.3 (March 1836): 132–33.

St. John de Crèvecoeur, Hector. *Letters from an American Farmer.* London: Thomas Davies, 1782.

Stampp, Kenneth M. *America in 1857: A Nation on the Brink.* New York: Oxford University Press, 1990.

——. *The Peculiar Institution: Slavery in the Ante-Bellum South.* New York: Knopf, 1956.

Stansell, Christine. *City of Women: Sex and Class in New York, 1789–1860.* Urbana: University of Illinois Press, 1987.

Steinfeld, Robert. *The Invention of Free Labor: The Employment Relation in English and American Law and Culture, 1350–1870.* Chapel Hill: University of North Carolina Press, 1991.

Stephens, Ann Sophia. *Fashion and Famine.* New York: Bunce & Brother, 1854.

Stern, Julia A. *The Plight of Feeling: Sympathy and Dissent in the Early American Novel.* Chicago: University of Chicago Press, 1997.

Stowe, Harriet Beecher. *Dred: A Tale of the Great Dismal Swamp.* Boston: Phillips, Sampson & Co., 1856.

Tadman, Michael. *Speculators and Slaves: Masters, Traders, and Slaves in the Old South*. Madison: University of Wisconsin Press, 1989.

Taylor, Walter Fuller. *The Economic Novel in America*. New York: Octagon Books, 1969.

Temin, Peter. *The Jacksonian Economy*. New York: W. W. Norton, 1969.

Tompkins, Jane. *Sensational Designs: The Cultural Work of American Fiction 1790–1860*. New York: Oxford University Press, 1985.

Tonkovich, Nicole. *Domesticity with a Difference: The Nonfiction of Catharine Beecher, Sarah J. Hale, Fanny Fern, and Margaret Fuller*. Jackson: University Press of Mississippi, 1997.

Turner, Frederick Jackson. *The Significance of the Frontier in American History*. Madison: State Historical Society of Wisconsin, 1894.

Tuthill, Louisa C. *The Young Lady's Home*. New Haven: S. Babcock, 1839.

Van Ravenswaay, Charles. "'No Elysium': Prosperity and Hard Times in 1830s St. Louis." *Gateway Heritage* (Fall 1991): 4–21.

Van Vleck, George W. *The Panic of 1857: An Analytical Study*. 1943. New York: AMS Press, 1967.

Vernon, John. *Money and Fiction: Literary Realism in the Nineteenth and Early Twentieth Centuries*. Ithaca: Cornell University Press, 1984.

"The Wants of the Age. Part II. Moral Culture." *Lady's Book* July 1837: 23.

Warner, Anna Bartlett. *Dollars and Cents*. New York: George P. Putnam, 1852.

Warner, Michael. *The Letters of the Republic: Publication and the Public Sphere in Eighteenth-Century America*. Cambridge, MA: Harvard University Press, 1990.

Watt, Ian. *The Rise of the Novel: Studies in Defoe, Richardson and Fielding*. Berkeley: University of California Press, 1964.

Watts, Steven. *The Republic Reborn: War and the Making of Liberal America, 1790–1820*. Baltimore: Johns Hopkins University Press, 1987.

———. *Romance of Real Life: Charles Brockden Brown and the Origins of American Culture*. Baltimore: Johns Hopkins University Press, 1994.

Weyler, Karen A. *Intricate Relations: Sexual and Economic Desire in American Fiction, 1789–1814*. Iowa City: University of Iowa Press, 2004.

———. "'A Speculating Spirit': Trade, Speculation, and Gambling in Early American Fiction." *Early American Literature* 31.3 (1996): 207–42.

Whalen, Terence. "Poe's 'Diddling' and the Depression: Notes on the Sources of Swindling." *Studies in American Fiction* 23 (1995): 195–201.

Wilentz, Sean. *Chants Democratic: New York City & the Rise of the American Working Class, 1788–1850*. New York: Oxford University Press, 1984.

Wood, Sally Sayward Barrell Keating. *Dorval; or the Speculator*. Portsmouth, NH: Nutting & Whitelock, 1801.

Zimmerman, David. *Panic! Markets, Crises and Crowds in American Fiction*. Chapel Hill, North Carolina Press, 2006.

Index